IRISH PANTRY

Traditional Breads, Preserves, and Goodies
to Feed the Ones You Love

NOEL McMEEL

with Lynn Marie Hulsman

RUNNING PRESS
PHILADELPHIA · LONDON

For
MY FAMILY

Books published by Running Press are available at special discounts for bulk purchases in the United States by corporations, institutions, and other organizations. For more information, please contact the Special Markets Department at the Perseus Books Group, 2300 Chestnut Street, Suite 200, Philadelphia, PA 19103, or call (800) 810-4145, ext. 5000, or e-mail special.markets@perseusbooks.com.

ISBN 978-0-7624-4575-2
Library of Congress Control Number: 2013943522

E-book ISBN 978-0-7624-5071-8

9   8   7   6   5   4   3   2   1
Digit on the right indicates the number of this printing

Designed by Frances J. Soo Ping Chow
Edited by Kristen Green Wiewora
Food Stylist: Mariana Velasquez
Food Stylist Assistant: Claudia Ficca
Prop Stylist: Marieellen Melker
Typography: Abraham Lincoln, Berthold Baskerville,
Caligula Dodgy, Janda Stylish, and Univers

Running Press Book Publishers
2300 Chestnut Street
Philadelphia, PA 19103-4371

Visit us on the web!
www.offthemenublog.com

CONTENTS

Acknowledgments

I want to thank my entire family
for the love and support that made this possible.

My beloved father didn't get to see this book but he would be so proud.

To my mother, there are no words to express my love and gratitude.

Deep thanks to all my siblings:
James and Sinead, and their children Owen, Anne, and Jimmy;
Conor and Celine, and their children Don, Conor Jr., and Gemma;
Owen and John; and my sister Ita,
whom we all miss every day of our lives.

The team at Running Press has been brilliant. To my visionary editor Kristen Green Wiewora, who had a plan from the first and has firmly and gently brought it to fruition. Thanks as well as my excellent photographer Steve Legato, to creative director and designer Frances Soo Ping Chow, to project editor Annie Lenth, to publicist Suzanne Wallace, and the entire marketing and sales group who have been so supportive.

Warmest thanks to my patient, unflagging, and fabulous writer,
Lynn Marie Hulsman. Lynn, you are MAGIC, and this book simply
would not have been possible without you.

Thanks to my agent, Sharon Bowers, who loves me like family
and always sounds happy to hear my voice on the phone,
no matter what I'm ringing about.

And finally, all my gratitude to Dessie Clements
for always being there.

Introduction
IS AN IRISH PANTRY DIFFERENT THAN ANY OTHER?

To me, the Irish pantry is a treasure trove of wholesome, tasty delights with some keeping properties, where on any day of the week you're sure to find such snacks and treats as pastries we call cutting cakes, or some lovely potted meat to spread onto a crispy, homemade cracker to enjoy with a cup of tea.

In the house where I grew up, nestled in the countryside of Toomebridge, Country Antrim, my mother's kitchen pantry featured a cooling marble slab and sighing shelves laden with traditional and delicious treats standing at the ready to sustain my large family, or to celebrate the vibrant stream of expected and unexpected guests we loved to welcome. Making the most of the bounty of the land, working hard with your own two hands to preserve it, and opening the home to share it—these were the core principles where I grew up. I'd go so far as to say it's the Irish way.

As a well-known chef and former farm boy, I place myself squarely shoulder to shoulder with my fellow Celts—sensible people who plan for every eventuality while thoroughly enjoying the gorgeous offerings provided by nature, year-round, never being caught short.

I learned the basics of what makes life worth living growing up in a thatched-roof house on our family farm in Ireland, the Land of the Saints and Scholars: Seek abundance enough to share, nourish the body, delight the senses, and surround yourself

with warm company. Food is life, and I keep the best food possible immediately at my fingertips, ready to enjoy and offer. It's a healthier, less expensive, more delicious way to live.

My old-fashioned methods and practical map for filling your larder have roots in the wisdom of my people, but reach easily into today's world. "When he's not fishing, he's mending his nets," goes the old Irish saying. Taking care in the planning of what you'll eat in a pinch on a cold rainy night or when an unexpected passel of loved ones turn up will allow you to relax and enjoy small moments, nurturing yourself, and to show love to those around you with a gesture, with no words needed.

My philosophy around food has roots in my homeland's ancient past with a modern twist, and it's every bit as Irish as I am: Find the very best locally grown seasonal ingredients. Support farms and grocers that respect the earth. Prepare meals that delight and excite the senses, but don't get seduced into overcomplicating. Above all else, let the natural flavor of good food shine through. This is the kind of food I keep at arm's reach to sustain and delight myself, and feed the guests who drop in and gather round my table.

While it's true that I no longer live in a humble, thatch-roofed farmhouse like Rock Cottage where I grew up, I still take pride and satisfaction in stocking my own Irish pantry. I'm pleased to share advice about preparing and serving earthy, homey slow food in hopes that your pantry will become the cornerstone of your kitchen.

SWEET TRADITION:
LOVELY IN, LOVELY OUT

In my family, we look forward to visits from friends and relatives for two reasons: good company, of course, and the delicious treats that are always laid out. I almost can't recall a visit from someone in my family when we didn't break out the tins of homemade shortbread. It's a staple in all of our kitchens, like eggs or milk. The recipe I use has been handed down for generations, and, at this point, no one in my family even needs to glance at it. We've all committed it to memory through the sheer repetition of baking these "bickies" countless times. I don't mind telling you . . . there's a bit of competition about which one of us executes it best. In my mum's house, we'd store it in old Victorian biscuit boxes, partially rusted inside from age but lined meticulously with paper.

When guests departed, we sent them along with care packages of whichever sweets, jams, or chutneys we had stored in the cupboard. Aunt Greta was a star participant in these exchanges. Famous for her boiled cake, she taught her daughter, Mary, to make it. Firm but moist, it was laden with delicious fruit. Between the two of them, they could hardly carry one in the door because it weighed a ton. Whatever she brought us was replaced on her way home: lovely stuff in, (different) lovely stuff out.

For a special occasion, such as a birthday, we might wrap our offerings in bits of brightly colored fabric, paper, and ribbon. More often than not, the same tins traveled back and forth, from house to house. It felt good to share, and was a treat to sample the handiwork of the other talented home cooks amongst our family and close friends.

CHAPTER ONE

JAMS, JELLIES, AND SPREADS

HOME CANNING
AND PRESERVATION

Thrifty Irish farmwives and experts in the culinary arts know that canning, or "putting by," food is an excellent way to use what's ripe and plentiful during seasonal harvest cycles. In my gran's day, before deep freezes and supermarkets, and, even in my mum's day, when food scarcity sometimes loomed, families depended on canned food for survival. Learning methods to keep food tasty and safe long term was essential.

To can is to process food in a sterile environment, then seal it in an airtight container. There's more than one way to keep food. Pasteurization, applying high heat, refrigerating, and freezing are among them. Any long-lived commercial jam, jelly, marmalade, preserve, or curd you'll find in a store has been treated to kill microorganisms and to deactivate food-spoiling enzymes. Once processed, food must be vacuum-sealed with meticulous care to keep the air, and microorganisms living in it, out.

Classes in home canning and food preservation are springing up the globe over, fueled by the new conscious food movement. Done the way my mum taught me, home canning is an economical, safe way to lay by foods for ages. With scrupulous sterilization practices, including starting with fresh food, boiling your equipment, and sealing at the right temperature under proper conditions, home canning poses almost zero danger. Done improperly, you'll run the risk of exposure to botulism, a nearly undetectable bacteria that grows even in low-oxygen conditions, such as in a poorly sterilized or wrongly sealed jar.

In this book, I'm suggesting in some cases that you rely on your refrigerator and freezer to help preserve. I'll be honest: In my own home I'm a little more loosey-goosey. I use a basic water-bath method of heating and sealing for many home-canned foods, but I've a basic knowledge about how edible chemicals interact. The water-bath canned recipes included in this book are only for the high-acid, fruit-based jams made with lots of sugar. Part of my casual approach in my own home stems from the fact that in Ireland kitchens are generally a good deal colder than they are elsewhere in the world. I wouldn't advise this for everyone, but I'll leave a turkey carcass out overnight on the marble slab in my pantry.

For the long term, I urge you to consult library books for expansive, step-by-step canning recommendations, to visit official government websites about food safety and preservation, and to beg your practical aunts to school you in fundamentals. You'll take a lot of pride in lining your cellar shelves with countless jars of long-lasting staples. Until you've the proper training, though, why not use your fridge? I've a good idea that because my recipes here are for small batches, none of these goodies will sit long before they're eaten.

SAFE AND STERILE:
GOOD PRACTICES FOR HOME CANNING

BOIL AND BOIL AGAIN

We all know that boiling water kills germs. So it stands to reason that we must sterilize jars and lids for canning. But why, then, must we make sure our jams are boiled? And for heaven's sake, you might ask, is it strictly necessary to then pop the sterile jars, filled with hot jam, into more boiling water? And if we plan to boil filled jars, why did we boil them when they sat empty in the first place?

The short answer is that each type of boiling serves a different purpose. The first boiling is to sterilize the container. Boiling the jam itself reduces and thickens the fruit pulp and allows the natural pectin to gel. The final boil—the water bath—kills any harmful airborne microbes introduced during the ladling step and forces a good seal.

All of this work is in the interest of risk reduction. As no method is 100 percent reliable, I think the extra assurance of safety is worth the time invested. Sugar is a preservative, and botulism has a hard time surviving in high-acid environments. You'll need to use your own judgment, but I'm comfortable recommending this method for such foods as apples, apricots, berries, cherries, cranberries, peaches, and pears. As with many cooking methods, home cooks who live in high altitudes will need to factor in the pressure change when canning.

STERILIZING JARS FOR CANNING

First off, jars should be made from glass and should be checked for any cracks or chips. They are pleasantly inexpensive at your local grocery or hardware store, and can be reused, so long as they maintain their integrity. Be sure to use jars with two-piece lids made from glass, plastic, or metal that feature a rubber seal to create a vacuum. The lids and seals should be washed carefully in hot, soapy water and air-dried. The following heat-sterilizing methods are for the glass jar only.

TIPS FOR EVERY METHOD

• Never fill a cold jar with hot preserves, or a hot jar with cold preserves, or the glass might break.
• Remove jars from sterilizing heat source only as needed, or they will cool too much.
• Leave a ½-inch (1.3-centimeter) headspace when filling jars.
• After filling each jar, wipe the rim with a clean tea towel.
• Don't overtighten the lid, as it could cause the seal to fail.
• Sterilize more jars than you think you'll need. In the worst case, you'll have extra clean jars. In the best case, you'll make your job easy should you find yourself in midstream with extra preserves on your hands.

BOILING METHOD

This is the traditional way, known to grannies across the globe. Place empty jars in a large, deep pot (a pasta pot will do nicely) and cover them with water. Boil the jars for 10 minutes, then carefully remove them, as needed, with a jar lifter or tongs, and take the jars out only as you need them, resting them on a heatproof trivet or pad. Fill the jars with hot jam or preserves, using the previous tips.

OVEN METHOD

My favorite way to sterilize jars is in the oven. It's nice and tidy, and it keeps the jars hot until you're ready to use them. Preheat your oven to 350°F / 180°C degrees—no hotter. You don't want the glass to break. Line each shelf (but not the bottom) with three or four layers of newspaper, then lay the jars on top in rows, taking care that they don't touch, and heat for 25 minutes. Use a jar lifter or tongs, if you have them, to remove the jars. If not, simply use sturdy oven mitts and take out the jars only as you need them, resting them on a heatproof trivet or pad. Fill the jars with hot jam or preserves, using the tips on page 17.

DISHWASHER METHOD

This method is sinfully easy. Fill your dishwasher with clean, cold jars and set the machine to rinse with a heated drying cycle. Try to time the end of the cycle to when your jam or preserve will be ready. Use the jars one at a time from the dishwasher, then fill with hot jam or preserves, using the tips on page 17.

MICROWAVE METHOD

To get started using this modern method, wash the jars by hand in hot, soapy water. Rinse, then leave them to sit in a basin of clean, hot water. When your jam or preserve is ready, microwave the damp jars one at a time, for 1 minute each, then fill with hot jam or preserves, using the tips on page 17.

RED RASPBERRY JAM

THE CONCENTRATED, INTENSE FLAVOR OF THIS JAM IS SUMMER IN A JAR, as far as I'm concerned, and an excellent way to enjoy the sunny bounty of this little red fruit's brief season even in the cold darkness of winter. This is a sweet jam. I love it for pouring over pound cake, and using it as a topping for really good-quality, full-fat, vanilla-flecked ice cream.

MAKES ABOUT
4 CUPS / 945 MILLILITERS JAM

---

4 cups / 800 grams granulated sugar

4 cups / 600 grams raspberries

Juice of 1 lemon

Preheat the oven to 225°F / 110°C. Pour the sugar into a shallow baking dish and heat it in the oven for 20 minutes. Put your raspberries and lemon juice into a deep, nonreactive saucepan (stainless steel or enamel will do nicely). Bring to a full boil over high heat, mashing the mixture with a potato masher. Boil for 1 minute, mashing constantly. Add the warm sugar, then return to a boil, stirring occasionally, and continue to boil for about 6 minutes, still stirring occasionally, until the mixture starts to form a gel.

Test using the Spoon Test (see page 20) or Wrinkle Test (see page 20) and boil until the mixture thickens. Ladle into hot, sterilized jars (see page 17), leaving a ½-inch / 1.3-centimeter headspace, and seal using the hot water bath (see page 43) for 15 minutes. This should keep for up to 1 year in a cool, dark place, if properly sealed.

TESTING FOR DONENESS

Irst-time jam makers can sometimes feel intimidated around guessing whether the preserves are done or not. I like to use these handy ways of checking for the "doneness" of jams, jellies, and preserves.

SPOON TEST

Start out by putting three or four metal spoons in your freezer for at least an hour. When your jam has cooked, lay one frozen tablespoon on the counter and drop in about a teaspoon of jam. Don't dip the frozen spoon into the boiling jam, though! Your goal is to cool the jam to room temperature. Leave it for a minute or two, then touch your finger to the bottom of the spoon. If it has cooled completely, pick up the spoon, holding the handle upright and bowl pointing downward. Eyeball the jam as it rolls off the spoon: Is it a singular ball or does it divide into streams? What you want is one glob that is the consistency of corn syrup or honey as it slides off your tablespoon, which lets you know it's at the setting point. It shouldn't be watery, nor should it separate. If this happens, cook your jam for another few minutes and try the spoon test again, with a fresh frozen spoon.

WRINKLE TEST

Alternatively, you can use the tried-and-true wrinkle test. Put three or four saucers into the freezer. When you think your jam is done, spoon a dollop of the boiling jam onto a cold saucer, let it cool on the countertop until the bottom of the plate is no longer warm, then give the jam a push with your finger. It should have about the consistency of corn syrup or honey. If the jam wrinkles as you gently push it with your finger, it has reached its setting point.

BLACKBERRY AND
LIME JAM

BLACKBERRIES GREW ALONG THE EDGES OF MY PARENTS' LAND AT ROCK COTTAGE, and my brothers, sister, and I competed to fill our pails so we could rush them home to our mother, who'd work her magic. She spun them into steamed puddings with custard and smashed them into a sauce to ladle over hot slabs of butter cake. When they were plentiful, she'd preserve them for the time when the canes on which they grew dropped their leaves to become bare, brown branches.

Good blackberries are plump and of a deep color, neither too firm nor too mushy. To know whether they're ripe and ready, you have only to smell them . . . the aroma is like sweet wine, and has me stretching out my tongue to taste the fruit before the berries ever reach a pail. I have blackberry brambles around the periphery of my own land, and I truly enjoy passing a late summer's or early autumn's afternoon by picking berries and stewing them into this sweet-tart jam. There's them that say, "He who has water and peat on his farm has the world his own way," and I have to agree. All is provided, and we've simply to receive it.

MAKES ABOUT
2 CUPS / 500 MILLILITERS JAM

---

2 limes

2 cups / 250 grams blackberries

2 cups / 400 grams granulated sugar

Cut the limes in half, then squeeze the juice into a small bowl. Using a spoon, dig the pulp out of the rinds and add it to the juice, then remove any seeds and discard them (see "Easy Juicing," page 167). Combine the lime juice and pulp with 2 tablespoons of water in a medium, heavy-bottomed, nonreactive saucepan, and cook for 20 minutes over low heat. Increase the heat to medium, add the berries and sugar, and continue to cook, stirring occasionally, for 30 minutes, or until thickened and set.

Test using the Spoon Test (see page 20) or Wrinkle Test (see page 20) and boil until the mixture thickens. Ladle into hot, sterilized jars (see page 17), leaving a ½-inch / 1.3-centimeter headspace, and seal using the hot water bath (see page 43) for 15 minutes. This should keep for up to 1 year in a cool, dark place, if properly sealed.

TRADITIONAL MARMALADE
WITH IRISH WHISKEY

DEEP WINTER'S THE TIME FOR SEVILLE ORANGES, also known as bitter oranges and marmalade oranges. I love to pass a cold and misty January afternoon by filling my kitchen with the perfume of the steeping, fragrant peels of these jewel-colored beauties. I make my preserves that much more grown-up with the warmth of Irish whiskey. Native to China, and brought to Spain via Africa, the Seville was Europe's only orange variety for 500 years after its twelfth-century arrival. Its unique flavor is at home alongside Asian-spiced bitter greens, saffron-scented rice, and yeasty wheat beer. This particular marmalade is gorgeous on a slice of toast served with a pre-bedtime hot whiskey or with strong, milky tea in the morning.

MAKES ABOUT
6 CUPS / 1⅓ LITERS MARMALADE

2¼ pounds / 1 kilogram Seville oranges

7 cups / 1½ kilograms granulated sugar

Juice of 2 lemons

6 tablespoons Jameson Irish whiskey

Cut the oranges in half, then squeeze the juice into a small bowl. Using a spoon, dig the pulp out of the rinds and add it to the juice, then remove any seeds and reserve them (see "Easy Juicing," page 167). Combine the orange juice and pulp with 2 tablespoons of water and set aside. Tie up the seeds in 2 layers of cheesecloth, using kitchen string.

Using a paring knife, remove most of the pith from the peel, then cut the peel into matchstick strips and place them in a medium bowl. Fill with cold water to cover and add the seed pouch. Cover and let soak on the countertop for at least 8 hours.

After soaking, simmer the peel, soaking water, and seed bag together in a large, heavy-bottomed saucepan for 4 hours or until the peel is soft, then remove and discard the seed pouch. Add the sugar, lemon juice, and reserved orange juice and pulp to the pan and cook over low heat, stirring constantly, until the sugar has completely dissolved. Bring to a boil and, stirring occasionally, cook for 15 or 20 minutes, until the marmalade is done.

Test for doneness using the Spoon Test (see page 20) or Wrinkle Test (see page 20). Once set, add the whiskey and stir until blended. As the marmalade begins to cool and become firm in the saucepan, stir from the bottom up to distribute the peel.

Ladle into hot, sterilized jars (see page 17), leaving a ½-inch / 1.3-centimeter headspace, and seal using the hot water bath (see page 43) for 15 minutes. This should keep for up to 1 year in a cool, dark place, if properly sealed.

RHUBARB AND GINGER
PRESERVE

MY MOTHER LOVES EVERYTHING ABOUT RHUBARB, from its willingness to grow almost anywhere, to its hearty resistance to cold and drought, to its persistence in coming back year after year with no effort on her part. It's such a gorgeous plant—all big green leaves and slender gem-pink stalks—that it seemed almost a shame to pluck it from the land around our cottage. Almost. Until my mum would spin this early-spring to late-summer plant into buttery rhubarb dumplings or flaky-crusted rhubarb tart. This is one of my favorite preserves, with its lovely pinky-red color and sweet tartness, along with the tingle it gets from the ginger. I serve this to guests in my home with fresh-from-the-oven soda bread and strong coffee as a late-winter pick-me-up.

MAKES ABOUT
4 CUPS / 950 MILLILITERS PRESERVE

2¼ pounds / 1 kilogram fresh rhubarb, chopped

2 cups / 400 grams granulated sugar

Zest and juice of 1 lemon

1 (2-inch / 5-centimeter) piece fresh ginger, finely grated

In a large glass bowl, combine the rhubarb, sugar, lemon zest and juice, and ginger, and toss lightly. Cover and let stand for 4 hours at room temperature.

Transfer the mixture to a large, heavy-bottomed saucepan, bring to a boil, then lower the heat and simmer for 45 minutes, stirring occasionally, until the mixture has thickened and the rhubarb has begun to break down. Remove the mixture from the heat and mash with a potato masher. Ladle into hot, sterilized jars (see page 17), leaving a ½-inch / 1.3-centimeter headspace, and seal using the hot water bath (see page 43) for 15 minutes. This should keep for up to 1 year in a cool, dark place, if properly sealed.

BRAMLEY AND
ROSEMARY JELLY

APPLES HAVE BEEN CULTIVATED IN IRELAND for over 3,000 years. Legend has it that Saint Patrick planted apple trees and famously did so at Ceangoba, an ancient community not far east of Armagh. Laws from that civilization, dating back to around 1000 BC, prescribed punishment for cutting them down. Ireland's oldest apple varietal, the Bramley, still enjoys the soil and climate around County Armagh, known as Orchard Country.

This recipe is one my mum made every September at apple harvest time. Bramleys contain a high level of natural pectin and a lovely tartness. If you can't lay your hands on these, Granny Smiths or another tart apple will do nicely. The infusion of rosemary deepens the apple-y flavor, making it lovely with roast pork.

Jam sugar, also called gelling sugar (not to be confused with preserving sugar, which contains no pectin and simply has a larger grain), contains the correct amount of natural pectin that is lacking in certain fruits. It's readily found in most supermarkets and at some greengrocers. It helps jellies, such as my Bramley and Rosemary, set quickly so they retain their fresh fruity flavor and natural color.

MAKES ABOUT
8 CUPS / 2 LITERS JELLY

---

5 large Bramley or other tart cooking apples, quartered
(no need to peel or core)

20 small sprigs rosemary,
plus 1 tablespoon rosemary leaves, divided

Cider vinegar, as needed

Granulated sugar, as needed

Jam sugar, as needed (see headnote)

In a large saucepan over high heat, combine the apples, rosemary, and 2½ cups / 595 milliliters of water in a large pan. Bring the mixture to a boil, then simmer it for an hour, stirring occasionally. After an hour, remove it from the heat and allow it to cool.

Set a large, clean basin or mixing bowl on the floor and place a jelly bag, if you have one, or a bag fashioned out of a single layer of cheesecloth, open inside it. Pour the cooked mixture into the jelly bag or into the middle of the cloth. Tie the jelly bag, or gather the ends of the cheesecloth together using kitchen twine, and suspend it with strong string over the basin from a long, wooden spoon propped across the backs of two chairs, allowing the juice to drip through overnight. Do not press the bag to release more liquid; it will make the jelly cloudy.

The next day, discard the contents of the jelly bag and measure the amount of juice (I had 7½ cups / 1.75 liters). For every 2½ cups / 595 milliliters of juice, add 2 tablespoons of the vinegar, 1¼ cups / 225 grams of the granulated sugar, and 1¼ cups / 225 grams of the jam sugar. (I added 6 tablespoons of vinegar, 3¾ cups / 870 grams of granulated sugar, and 3¾ cups / 870 grams of jam sugar.)

Combine the juice mixture in a large saucepan over high heat and add ½ tablespoon of the rosemary leaves, chopped. Heat to a boil and keep at a rolling boil, stirring occasionally, for about 15 minutes, or until the jelly begins to set.

Remove the jelly from the heat. Using a slotted spoon, scrape off any scum that has formed on the surface and discard. Gently stir in the remaining rosemary leaves. Test using the Spoon Test (see page 20) or Wrinkle Test (see page 20) and boil until the mixture thickens. Ladle into hot, sterilized jars (see page 17), leaving a ½-inch / 1.3-centimeter headspace, and seal using the hot water bath (see page 43) for 15 minutes. This should keep for up to 1 year in a cool, dark place, if properly sealed.

NOEL'S WAY

- Spread on a wheel of mild cheese, such as Fivemiletown Creamery's smoked Brie, and serve with water crackers.
- Serve as a condiment with succulent, garlicky roast pork or lamb.
- Stir a tablespoon into gravy to heighten the flavor.

JAM, JELLY, PRESERVES, OR MARMALADE?

A question for the ages, it seems, one might ask, "Is this spread jam, jelly, preserves, or marmalade?" when presented with a lovely sweet or savory topping to spoon out onto a hot and yeasty slice of toast. Food writer and home cook May Byron tells us, "After long and careful investigation, I find it impossible to differentiate between jams and marmalades." She attempts to put us at our ease by declaring in her 1917 *May Byron's Jam Book* that she thinks it's wisest not to discriminate. "If any recipe calls a thing jam, marmalade, or preserve, I shall follow suit." By that or any other name, "'twill taste as sweet."

ROSE HIP SYRUP

TO ME, ROSE HIPS ARE A GIFT FROM GOD: They just show up and present themselves to you, no work required: more evidence that living off the fat of the land is a brilliant way to conduct life. In my home, we scoop the ashes from our coal-burning fireplace and sprinkle them on the rose bushes to help them grow strong. We're regifted with not only a feast for the eyes but a nourishing and delicious treat as well. I wait until after autumn's first frost to gather mine, when they're more pliant and tender, then I set to work preparing them for vitamin C–rich teas and cooking syrup to stave off winter colds.

Don't expect this syrup to taste like rose water. It leans more toward sharp and tangy, like hibiscus. In general, I like to rely on fruits themselves for natural pectin. In this case, I add packaged pectin because rose hips have just a trace amount naturally. Another quirk of the rose hips is the tannic acid in the seeds. If cooked into jams, jellies, or syrups, they'll leave a chalky aftertaste. Best to slit the pods and scrape out the seeds with the tip of a paring knife, to remove them.

I like to drizzle this delicately hued, shimmering nectar over a warm wheel of Brie to serve with a crusty baguette, or to spoon it onto wheaten bread with butter, or onto waffles made with a whiff of cinnamon in the batter.

MAKES ABOUT
2½ CUPS / 600 MILLILITERS JELLY

---

4 cups dried rosehips, split open and seeds removed

2 cups / 235 milliliters white wine

1 level tablespoon powdered pectin

Pinch of salt

1¾ cups / 350 grams granulated sugar

In a large saucepan over medium heat, bring the rosehips, wine, and 3 cups / 700 milliliters of water to a rolling boil. Lower the heat to a simmer, cover loosely, and cook for 1 hour. Mash the softened rosehips to make a coarse purée in the liquid.

Transfer the purée to a very fine mesh strainer or to four layers of cheesecloth (tie into a bag), strain out all the liquid into a clean saucepan, and let it sit overnight. Do not squeeze out the remaining juice, as this will turn the syrup cloudy.

The following day, add the pectin, a big pinch of salt, and the sugar, and cook this mixture for 20 to 45 minutes, stirring constantly. Boil until the mixture thickens to the consistency of pancake syrup, and pour into hot, sterilized jars (see page 17), leaving a ½-inch / 1.3-centimeter headspace, and seal using the hot water bath (see page 43) for 15 minutes. This should keep for up to 1 year in a cool, dark place, if properly sealed.

PERFECT LEMON CURD

NOTHING CHEERS UP A COLD AND CLOUDY MORNING LIKE THE TART, vibrant flavor of lemon curd spread across a warm scone or a bit of toast. This one suits my sweet tooth to a T. Use the best butter you can get your hands on to ensure dairy-rich creaminess to balance the sugar.

I've heard some beginning cooks say they shy away from whipping up a batch owing to tales of curdling, and the necessity to strain out bits of cooked egg white. Egg whites cook at a lower temperature than yolks do, and without lots of stirring on the part of the cook, white lumps can form in the pot, ruining the lovely, silky texture you want in a curd. With this recipe, you can rest easy, because the blending of the eggs happens in the beginning, before the mixture sits over heat. It's as easy to make as a simple cake, and turns out lusciously smooth, every batch!

MAKES ABOUT
2 CUPS / 470 MILLILITERS LEMON CURD

6 tablespoons / 85 grams unsalted butter

1 cup / 200 grams granulated sugar

2 large eggs

2 large egg yolks

$\frac{2}{3}$ cup / 160 milliliters freshly squeezed lemon juice

Zest of 1 lemon

$\frac{1}{2}$ teaspoon salt

In a large bowl, beat the butter and sugar together with an electric mixer until smooth. In a separate bowl, beat the whole eggs and yolks with a fork until fully blended. Then, a little at a time, add the beaten eggs to the creamed butter mixture, until smooth. Once smooth, mix in the lemon juice and beat for 1 minute on high speed. The mixture will look curdled in the mixing bowl because of the flecks of butter. It will turn satiny as it cooks.

Pour the mixture into a medium, heavy, nonreactive saucepan and cook over medium heat for 10 to 15 minutes, stirring constantly, until the curd thickens, never letting it boil. Test for set by coating the back of a wooden spoon and dragging your finger through it. If a distinct track remains, it's done. Remove from the heat and stir in the lemon zest, and salt. Ladle into hot, sterilized jars (see page 17) and store in the refrigerator for up to 3 weeks.

Throughout Ireland and Britain, there's a long-standing tradition of carving lanterns from such vegetables as potatoes, gourds, rutabagas, beets, and particularly turnips, which is what my sister and brothers and I used at Halloween for our jack-o'-lanterns to honor the tale of Stingy Jack.

As the legend goes, the sinful and worthless Jack—also known as Jack the Smith, Drunk Jack, and Jack O' the Lantern—trapped the devil himself by luring him up an apple tree and keeping him there by circling the trunk with crosses. He let him down on the condition he'd not take Jack's soul when he died. But when he died, his soul wasn't pure enough to enter heaven, and he was scared to wander alone in the darkness between there and the underworld. Jack asked to enter Hell. The resentful demon couldn't take his soul because of the bargain he'd made. He tossed Jack a perpetually burning ember to light his way on his ascent out, forever marking him as a denizen of the underworld. He carried it in a hollowed-out vegetable, fashioned into a lantern. When the Irish brought this tradition to the United States, they soon discovered that pumpkins were bigger and easier to hollow out, and a new custom was born.

For your best chance at raising carve-worthy pumpkins, you'll want to look at the variety. The egg-yolk yellow, midsize Dependable is a good choice, as the name might lead you to believe. Atlantic Giants also do quite well, if you're willing to temper your expectations. They'll thrive in Irish soil, but they won't live up to their names as they might in a warmer, sunnier climate.

If you're looking for the best cooking pumpkins, look to the following varieties: the Long Pie or Nantucket Pie, which is elongated rather than round, and has smooth and stringless flesh; the Small Sugar or New England Pie, which is particularly sweet, with a dense and smooth flesh; the Long Island Cheese pumpkin, so named for its shape's resembling a cheese wheel, featuring very sweet flesh; or the Winter Luxury, one of the sweetest varieties of all.

Of course, canned pumpkin has become easier to find in Ireland, and it'll do, but I prefer what's grown in my own backyard for optimal flavor, and freshness.

PUMPKIN BUTTER

AS FOR THIS DELICIOUS PUMPKIN BUTTER, don't confuse it with apple butter. It cannot be safely canned by using the traditional water-bath method and must be stored in your fridge. Pumpkin flesh makes for a dense liquid, rendering it nearly impenetrable to the heat needed to kill botulism spores. On top of that, pumpkin is a very low-acid food. So, while I don't recommend traditional canning, the good news for fans of this spread is this: It freezes very well.

MAKES ABOUT
3 CUPS / 715 MILLILITERS PUMPKIN BUTTER

---

4 pounds / 1.8 kilograms whole pie pumpkin

Olive or rapeseed oil for brushing

¼ cup / 60 milliliters apple cider

1 cup / 175 grams light brown sugar, packed

3 to 4 tablespoons pure maple syrup, to taste

1 tablespoon ground cinnamon

½ teaspoon freshly grated nutmeg

1 teaspoon vanilla extract

1 teaspoon freshly squeezed lemon juice

Pinch of salt

Preheat the oven to 350°F / 175°C and line a baking sheet with foil.

Wash the pumpkins and carefully slice the stem off the top with a very sharp knife. Cut the pumpkins in half from stem to tail, scoop out the seeds and guts with a sharp, metal spoon, and reserve the seeds to roast and eat later, if you like.

Brush the inside of each half with oil and place them face down on the prepared baking sheet. Roast for 45 minutes to 1 hour, depending on the size of your pumpkins, or until the skin and flesh are pierced easily with a fork. The pumpkins should roughly have the texture of a baked potato. Allow the pumpkins to cool for 30 minutes on your baking sheet, then separate the skin from the flesh with a large, sharp metal spoon.

Place the cooked pumpkin in a blender and blend until smooth. You should have about 4 cups / 950 milliliters of purée. Reserve any excess for another use.

Blend in the cider, brown sugar, maple syrup, cinnamon, and nutmeg until fully mixed.

Recipe continues

Spoon the mixture into a medium saucepan. Cover with a lid and prop the lid ajar with a wooden spoon. Over medium-high heat, bring the mixture to a low boil. Lower the heat and cook for about 10 minutes, stirring occasionally, allowing the mixture to thicken to a spreadable consistency. Once it's thickened, remove the pumpkin from the heat and stir in the vanilla.

Let cool completely, stir in the lemon juice and a pinch of salt, ladle into clean, sterilized jars (see page 17), and store in the refrigerator for up to 2 weeks.

APPLE AND SULTANA PURÉE

Dead easy to make, this simple fruit compote heightens any simple pastry to the level of memorable. I like serving this with hot pancakes, centering a pancake on a serving plate, then spreading it with the apple purée and topping it with another pancake. Repeat the process, using three pancakes in all. Drench the third pancake with apple purée, then add a spoonful of clotted cream and a drizzle of maple syrup.

MAKES
4 TO 6 SERVINGS

3 large apples, peeled, cored, and diced

1 vanilla bean, split lengthwise and scraped

4 tablespoons (½ stick) / 60 grams unsalted butter at room temperature

Pinch of sugar

3.5 ounces / 100 grams sultanas

In a large, heavy-bottomed saucepan, combine the apples, vanilla bean and seeds, butter, and sugar, add a splash of water, and cook the mixture over medium heat, stirring often, until the apples fall apart and are mashable with a fork. Mix in the sultanas and heat through, stirring firmly to break up the apples. Remove the vanilla pod before serving. Serve warm, or pour the mixture into a clean jar and store in the refrigerator for up to 1 week.

MULLED WINE AND
APPLE BUTTER

IN SEPTEMBER, I TAKE GREAT PLEASURE in walking my land with my huge, lumbering, rescued Golden Retriever, Ralph, and enjoying the season's first crisp chill in the air. The smell of coal-fire smoke, together with the turning of the leaves, takes me back to the days when I'd walk my family's land in Toomebridge, County Antrim, with my beloved dog, Nip. Early autumn begins the harvest season for Northern Ireland's Armagh Bramley apples, so outstanding that the European Union has conferred them with a special geographical indication status with the likes of such culinary miracles as Lough Neagh eels, Champagne from that eponymous region, and Parma ham. Returning home from those brisk childhood walks, I'd often be greeted with a tall, winter-spiced, apple tart that my mother made in her special deep earthenware dish.

This heady apple butter reminds me of what it was like to come home: warm, replenishing, and wrapped in comfort.

MAKES ABOUT
3 CUPS / 700 MILLILITERS APPLE BUTTER

---

3 pounds / 1.4 kilograms firm, tart apples (such as Armagh Bramleys or Granny Smiths), peeled, cored, and coarsely chopped

1 cup / 240 milliliters red wine

½ cup / 120 milliliters apple cider or apple juice

½ cup / 100 grams granulated sugar

¼ teaspoon ground cloves

¼ teaspoon freshly grated nutmeg

1 teaspoon ground cinnamon

Preheat the oven to 450°F / 230°C. Place the apples in a large roasting pan, and pour the wine, apple juice, and ½ cup / 120 milliliters of water over them. Bake for 20 to 30 minutes, or until the apples are soft enough to smash with a fork. Once they are soft, remove the pan from the oven and sprinkle the sugar and spices over them. With a potato masher, mash the mixture in the roasting pan, then return it to the oven, lowering the temperature to 350°F / 175°C, and bake for another 1 to 2 hours, stirring occasionally, until the apple butter is very thick and deep brown in color.

Ladle into hot, sterilized jars (see page 17), leaving a ¼-inch / 6-millimeter headspace, and seal using the hot water bath (see page 43) for 15 minutes. This should keep for up to 1 year in a cool, dark place, if properly sealed.

HONEYED
WHISKEY BUTTER

WE'VE A SAYING IN IRELAND THAT GOES, "What whiskey and butter won't cure, there's no cure for." I happen to think that's true, if a little sweetness is thrown in for good measure. Just a dab of this simple but rich topping will turn a simple dish into a celebration. Poured or spread onto already festive dishes, such as The McMeel Family Irish Christmas Cake (page 305) or plum pudding, Honeyed Whiskey Butter becomes the crowning glory.

It's a natural complement to Irish soda bread, served with a strong cup of tea. And melted atop a stack of fluffy pancakes, this decadent spread will kick-start your day, Irish-style.

MAKES ABOUT
3¾ CUPS / 170 GRAMS WHISKEY BUTTER

---

8 tablespoons (1 stick) / 113 grams unsalted butter,
at room temperature

2 tablespoons honey

2 tablespoons whiskey

Beat the butter with a mixer or a wooden spoon until smooth and creamy. Beat in the honey, then slowly beat in the whiskey, a little at a time, until the mixture is just mixed. Spoon into a small container and seal tightly. Stir before serving. Keeps for 3 days at room temperature. (If you refrigerate it, the whiskey will leach out of the mixture and sit on the surface.)

MAPLE-BUTTER SAUCE

OF COURSE YOU CAN SIMPLY SPREAD BUTTER on a thing, then douse it with maple syrup. You'd hear no complaints about it from me. But melt those two magic ingredients together with buttermilk, and you've a whole new definition of the phrase *velvety smooth*.

MAKES ABOUT
2 CUPS / 480 MILLILITERS SAUCE

1 cup / 480 milliliters pure maple syrup

1 cup / 480 milliliters buttermilk

8 tablespoons (1 stick) / 113 grams unsalted butter

In a medium, heavy-bottomed saucepan over low heat, combine the maple syrup, buttermilk, and butter. Stirring constantly, warm the mixture until the butter melts. Serve warm, or pour into clean, sterilized jars (see page 17) and store in the refrigerator for up to 1 week. This freezes well in tightly lidded plastic containers and will keep for up to 6 months. Thaw by heating in a saucepan before serving.

NOEL'S WAY

• Use it to top breakfast delights, such as flapjacks, porridge, and waffles.

• Stuff a crêpe with banana slices and toasted walnuts, and top with it.

• Contrast with savory foods, such as blackened asparagus
or spicy pecan-crusted salmon, by using it as a sauce.

RICH CHOCOLATE SPREAD

IF SOMETHING'S ALREADY GOOD IN ITS NATURAL ESSENCE, you don't want to doctor it up too much. To me, chocolate ranks high on that list, which is why I prefer this simple, homemade version of Nutella, using as few ingredients as possible and without the hazelnut flavor to complicate it. If you want your guests to swoon and moan with pleasure, I suggest using the highest-grade cocoa powder and bar chocolate you can lay your hands on.

MAKES ABOUT
1½ CUPS / 350 MILLILITERS CHOCOLATE SPREAD

½ cup / 100 grams granulated sugar

1 tablespoon unsweetened cocoa powder

¼ teaspoon salt

1½ teaspoons vanilla extract

4 ounces / 125 grams bittersweet chocolate, finely chopped
(I recommend 70% cacao, such as Scharffen Berger, if you can find it)

10 tablespoons / 150 grams unsalted butter

In a medium, heavy-bottomed saucepan, combine the sugar, cocoa powder, salt, and ¼ cup / 60 milliliters of water. Place the pan over medium heat and stir until the sugar and cocoa powder dissolve and the mixture reaches a simmer.

Remove the pan from the heat and add the vanilla, chocolate, and butter. Whisk until the chocolate and butter melt and the texture is smooth and free from lumps. Spoon the spread into a tightly lidded jar or tub, and store in the refrigerator for up to a month. Allow the spread to come to room temperature before serving.

BUTTERY SALTED CARAMEL SAUCE

THERE HAVE BEEN LOTS OF ARGUMENTS as to why Irish butter is superior. Some say it's because the cream is cultured before churning, as in the case of Kerrygold. Some say it's the grass eaten by the cows, fueling them to produce lovely milk with a high fat content. Some say it's the saltiness that offsets the sweet, creamy taste. Regardless of why, it calls me to slice off pats and pop them into my mouth straight. My policy is to use the highest-quality butter I can lay my hands on. From restaurateurs to home cooks and foodies, people the world over have a keen interest in locally sourced and artisanal food, and with good reason. Food found close to home usually means fresh and unprocessed food. Depending on where you live, be it Vermont or Wisconsin, or any-place near a family farm with a creamery, you might want to go the extra mile to get some high-quality butter. Use it in my recipe for Salted Caramel Sauce, and you'll know what it's like to drink gold.

MAKES ABOUT
2 CUPS / 480 MILLILITERS SAUCE

---

1 cup / 200 grams granulated sugar

¼ cup / 60 milliliters whole milk

½ cup / 120 milliliters heavy whipping cream

4 tablespoons (½ stick) / 60 grams unsalted butter, cut into chunks

1 teaspoon kosher salt, or ½ teaspoon sea salt

In a medium, heavy-bottomed saucepan, combine the sugar with ¼ cup / 60 milliliters of water over low heat and gently stir until the sugar dissolves. Increase the heat to high and bring the syrup to a boil without stirring. If crystals cling to the side of the saucepan, gently scrape them down into the boiling mixture with a wooden spoon dipped in water. Boil for 5 minutes, or until the syrup is amber in color.

Remove the syrup from the heat and whisk in the milk and cream, taking care not to burn yourself, as the mixture will sputter and bubble. Stir in the butter until completely melted and blended, then gently stir in the salt. Ladle into hot, sterilized jars (see page 17) and store in the refrigerator for up to 3 weeks.

NOEL'S WAY

• Serve as a dip with slices of tangy apple or soft, ripe pear.

• Swirl it in your iced coffee: To a tall glass of ice, add equal quantities of whole milk and cool coffee, plus a tablespoon of caramel sauce.

• Warm the sauce in the microwave or on the stove top before serving, and drizzle over slices of apple pie.

RED ONION AND GUINNESS MARMALADE

A NOSTALGIC STAPLE FROM FRENCH BISTRO CUISINE, onion marmalade is a standout condiment: Sugary, salty, savory, tangy, and fragrant, it offers something to everyone. It's so hearty and flavorful, it could almost double as a side dish. Good as it is on its own, it becomes a poem to Irish daily life when Guinness graces the jar. For me, the wholesome earthiness of the star ingredient, onions, along with the pubby flavor from the Guinness and the malt vinegar blend, call to mind memories of simple Irish meals, such as beef stew with thick slices of soda bread, and ploughman's lunches—food that'll warm and sustain you on a sleepy, rainy afternoon.

MAKES ABOUT
2 CUPS / 475 MILLILITERS MARMALADE

Canola or olive oil as needed

6 large red onions, sliced into thin rings

1¼ cups / 250 grams granulated sugar

1 teaspoon salt

1 (12-ounce / 360-milliliter) can Guinness

¾ cup / 180 milliliters malt vinegar

Pour enough oil into a large, heavy-bottomed saucepan to cover the bottom and heat over medium-low heat. Add the onions, cover, and let them sweat for 20 to 30 minutes, stirring occasionally, until the volume reduces by about half and they are golden brown and transparent.

Add the sugar and salt, mixing thoroughly, lower the heat, and cook for about 10 minutes, or until all the ingredients are fully combined.

Add the Guinness and vinegar, increase the heat, and bring the mixture to a boil. Boil hard for 5 minutes to simmer off some of the liquid, then lower the heat to low and cook without stirring until the mixture thickens to a jamlike texture.

Ladle into hot, sterilized jars (see page 17), leaving a ¼-inch / 6-millimeter headspace, and seal using the hot water bath (see page 43) for 5 minutes. This should keep for up to 6 months in a cool, dark place, if properly sealed.

PEACH AND APRICOT CHUTNEY

SWEET AND SAVORY, this chutney is a natural to pair with lighter meats, such as crown roast of pork, glazed duck, or grilled chicken. The tang of the orange-fleshed fruit, married with the exotic spices, elevates simply cooked standard home fare to the realm of "I can't believe you made this yourself!" It's proven to be so popular with guests at my table that I've often sent them home with one of the jars from my pantry. You may want to think about cooking up a double batch, right out of the gate!

MAKES ABOUT
2 CUPS / 475 MILLILITERS CHUTNEY

4 ounces / 120 grams chopped dried apricots

2 ripe, fresh peaches, peeled, pitted, and diced

2 medium-size ripe tomatoes, peeled, seeded, and diced

1 medium-size yellow onion, diced

¼ cup / 60 milliliters rice vinegar

1 tablespoon minced jalapeño pepper

1 piece fresh ginger, about the size of half your thumb,
peeled and grated

¼ teaspoon ground cloves

¼ teaspoon turmeric

¼ teaspoon ground cayenne pepper

3 tablespoons chopped fresh cilantro

In a small bowl, cover the apricots with warm, but not hot, water and soak for 20 minutes. Drain through a colander and transfer them to a nonreactive saucepan. Add the peaches, tomatoes, onion, vinegar, jalapeño, ginger, cloves, turmeric, and cayenne. Bring the mixture to a boil, then lower the heat and simmer, covered, for 20 minutes.

Remove the saucepan from the heat and stir in the cilantro, then ladle the mixture into hot, sterilized jars (see page 17), leaving a ¼-inch / 6-millimeter headspace, and seal using the hot water bath (see page 43) for 15 minutes. This should keep for up to 6 months in a cool, dark place, if properly sealed.

SPICED PEAR CHUTNEY WITH GINGER AND LIME

THERE'S LITTLE ELSE AS LUSCIOUS AS A SPOONABLE, perfectly ripe pear. Fragrant, sweet, and yielding, it's one of the only whole fruits I'll endorse as a dessert all on its own. If you're lucky enough to have a tree on your land, you know that pears only ripen once they've fallen to the ground. What to do with such a bounty handed over by Mother Nature all at once? Wash and eat as many as you can, then spin the rest into this warm and spicy condiment that sits as easily alongside a roast loin of pork as it does spooned onto a stack of flapjacks flanked by crispy bacon.

MAKES ABOUT
2 CUPS / 475 MILLILITERS CHUTNEY

---

4 large Anjou pears, peeled, cored, and cubed

1 small chile pepper (I suggest an Anaheim), seeded and minced

1 (1-inch / 2.5-centimeter) piece fresh ginger,
peeled and chopped

½ cup / 100 grams granulated sugar

2 tablespoons red wine vinegar

¼ teaspoon ground cinnamon

4.5 ounces / 130 grams sultanas

Zest and juice of ½ lime

In a medium, heavy-bottomed, nonreactive saucepan over medium-low heat, place the pears, chile pepper, ginger, sugar, and vinegar.

Stir well and cook, uncovered, over medium-low heat for 20 minutes. Add the cinnamon and sultanas and cook for another 5 minutes.

Remove from the heat and stir in the lime zest and juice, then ladle into hot, sterilized jars (see page 17), leaving a ¼-inch / 6-millimeter headspace, and seal using the hot water bath (see page 43) for 15 minutes. This should keep for up to 1 year in a cool, dark place, if properly sealed.

THE HOT WATER BATH

Some homemade delights should be kept refrigerated, and eaten within a few days or weeks. For others, canning with the water-bath method will keep them safe and shelf-stable. Individual recipes include boiling times and headspace allowances, but here's the basic gist:

Once your delectable comestibles have been chopped, spiced, cooked, and ladled into your sterilized jars, the jar rims have been wiped clean, and clean lids have been screwed firmly atop, it's time for the final step: the hot water bath.

Before sealing your jars, remove air bubbles, using a plastic spatula or long utensil like a chopstick. Never use metal lest it scratch the glass, which could weaken the jar and cause breakage during processing. Gently poke the utensil into the jar, and allow the air to escape around it.

Wipe the jar rims with a clean, damp tea towel. Center the lid onto the jar and lightly screw the metal band into place. Do not screw any tighter than you can comfortably do with your fingertips, or air won't be able to escape during the water bath process. This could mean buckled lids and cans that don't properly seal.

Place your filled jars carefully in the boiling water bath of the canning kettle or large pasta pot with a rack in the bottom to keep the jars from sitting directly on the bottom of the pot, and, therefore, the heating element. Take care that the water level is 1 inch / 2.5 centimeters above the top of the tallest jars. Cover your pot, and bring to a full rolling boil, then start the timer to boil for 15 to 25 minutes, or as indicated in your recipe. Then carefully lift out each jar with canning tongs or a jar lifter, if you have it (you can cover the ends of your regular tongs with rubber bands to make a homemade one). Set the jars on clean, dry towels and the sealing will happen as the jars cool. The jars are sealed when the metal lid vacuum-seals and you can lift a whole jar by holding onto the metal lid (remove the bands first).

If you have any doubt that a jar has sealed properly, don't despair. Simply refrigerate your treat and use it quickly. For high-sugar, high-acid foods, think weeks. For foods containing animal products, think days. Use your senses to help guide you. If it looks, smells, or tastes off, throw it out.

ORANGE-ONION CONFIT

WHEN MOST PEOPLE HEAR THE WORD *CONFIT*, they think of savory foods and duck. In fact, confit is simply any food cooked slowly over a long period of time as a form of preservation, making confit a natural pantry staple. The word *confit* comes from the French word *confire,* which means "to preserve." Sweet confits, such as jams and preserves, are cooked with sugar. Tomato confits might be cooked in vinegar. Meats, which are harder to preserve, are generally cooked in fats and oils, such as in the case of duck confit in goose fat. I love this particular recipe for the intense orange flavor that can hold its own in any sandwich, tempered by the sweetness of the long-cooked onion.

MAKES ABOUT
4 CUPS / 950 MILLILITERS CONFIT

6 large yellow onions

4 to 6 tablespoons olive oil, divided

½ cup / 100 grams granulated sugar

2 cups / 475 milliliters orange juice

½ teaspoon salt

Slice the onions from tip to tail into thin slices, not crosswise in rings. In a large, heavy-bottomed sauté pan or Dutch oven, heat 2 to 3 tablespoons of the olive oil, then add the onions and cook thoroughly for 45 minutes, stirring occasionally, over medium-low heat, until the onions are tender and golden brown. If they seem to be steaming, add more oil to the pan.

When the onions have reduced their water content and are browned but not burning, add the sugar. Lowering the heat to medium-low and stirring constantly, cook for about 10 minutes, until the onions are soft and caramelized. Add the orange juice, raise the heat to high, and cook for another 15 or 20 minutes, until the juice has cooked off almost completely. When the mixture has a jamlike consistency, remove the pan from the heat, and add the remaining 2 to 3 tablespoons of olive oil and the salt.

Ladle into hot, sterilized jars (see page 17), leaving a ¼-inch / 6-millimeter headspace, and seal using the hot water bath (see page 43) for 15 minutes. This should keep for up to 6 months in a cool, dark place, if properly sealed.

NOEL'S WAY

• Add ½ cup (120 milliliters) of red wine vinegar for a pleasant, mouth-puckering twist.

• Add ½ cup (120 milliliters) of cassis for an exotic aroma and a slight kick.

• Serve as a sauce for long-roasted meats, such as pork roast,
sprinkled liberally with cracked black pepper.

GARLIC AND BACON CONFIT

TOGETHER WITH SALT-OF-THE-EARTH FOLK, fields of green grass, heartbreaking music, and fine whiskey, pork is one of Ireland's sweetest and most bountiful resources. The focal point of many traditional dishes such as a breakfast fry-up; a bacon bap; or a bacon, cabbage, and potato supper, pork refuses to go unnoticed in Irish cuisine. On any given day and twice on Sunday, you might even find a meal of pork, with a side of pork. Me, I love the sweet, salty, and rich flavor it imparts to anything it touches. I could eat this confit straight from the jar with a spoon, but I like to save it to smash onto warm yeasty rolls before layering on slices of strong cheese, or stirring into pots of beans for seasoning.

MAKES ABOUT
1½ CUPS / 350 MILLILITERS CONFIT

3 whole garlic heads, broken into cloves

1 cup / 236 milliliters extra-virgin olive oil,
plus a little more as needed

1 teaspoon sea salt

2 strips streaky bacon

To peel the garlic, fill a large bowl with ice water and place it near the stove top on a level countertop. Half-fill a medium saucepan with water and bring it to a rolling boil. Drop the garlic cloves into the boiling water for 20 seconds.

Drain the garlic and plunge the cloves into the ice water. Drain again, dump them onto a clean tea towel, and pat them dry. Transfer them to a cutting board, cut off the roots, and slide the skins off with your hands. The cloves should peel easily.

Place the peeled garlic cloves in a medium, heavy-bottomed saucepan over medium heat and cover with the 1 cup / 236 milliliters of olive oil, adding a bit more if the cloves aren't fully covered. Add the salt. As soon as the oil begins to bubble, lower the heat to the lowest setting and cook for about 45 minutes, stirring occasionally.

While the garlic cloves are simmering, fry the strips of bacon until they are very crisp, then set them aside, allowing them to drain in a single layer on top of sheets of brown paper (draining on a paper towel will make it soggy). Reserve the bacon grease in the pan.

Once cool, crumble them into a dish and set aside. With a spatula, carefully scrape any bacon fat left in the skillet into the pan with the simmering garlic cloves.

After about 45 minutes, when the garlic cloves are pale gold and fork-tender, remove the pan from the heat and gently stir in the bacon crumbles. Refrigerate immediately, and store for no longer than 2 days. For longer-term storage, freeze it for up to 6 months.

NOEL'S WAY

• Spread the confit onto a pizza crust, dot with tomato slices and fresh mozzarella chunks, and top with shredded basil leaves before baking.

• For a simple supper, stir a heaping spoonful of the confit into a pot of warm pasta, then sprinkle liberally with freshly grated Parmesan and black pepper before serving.

• Smear the garlic cloves onto slices of pumpernickel bread, layer on freshly sliced red onion rings, top with thick slices of sharp Cheddar cheese, and broil until bubbly. Serve with English mustard.

SPICY LEMON CONFIT

TO MY EAR, THE PHRASE *lemon confit* sounds beautifully intricate and sophisticated, evoking images of sultans from faraway lands sitting at low tables, eating from silver trays. In fact, this lovely-to-have-on-hand condiment is remarkably simple and homespun. One trip to the local market yields everything you need to whip up this fragrant accompaniment to fish, chicken, or strong cheeses with olives.

MAKES ABOUT
2 CUPS / 450 GRAMS CONFIT

---

3 large lemons

¼ cup / 50 grams kosher salt

1 sprig fresh rosemary

4 leaves fresh basil

1 sprig fresh oregano

1 small mild chile pepper
(such as a banana pepper or an Anaheim)

1 teaspoon black peppercorns

1 teaspoon paprika

1 teaspoon granulated sugar

Rapeseed or canola oil

Half-fill a medium saucepan with water and bring it to a rolling boil. Place the lemons in a metal colander and submerge them in the saucepan, then run them under cold water, to blanch them. Repeat this 3 times to reduce the bitterness of the peel. Slice the lemons, peel and all, into ⅛-inch / 3-centimeter-thick rounds. Layer the lemon slices and the kosher salt in a nonreactive bowl, cover, and leave at room temperature overnight.

The next day, chop the rosemary, basil, oregano, and the chile pepper finely and place them in a large mixing bowl. Add the peppercorns, paprika, and sugar, and toss until mixed. In clean, prepared jars, layer the salted lemon with spoons full of the spice mixture, leaving a ½-inch / 1.3-centimeter headspace at the top of the jars. Store in the refrigerator for up to 1 month, keeping the lemons covered completely in oil. For longer-term storage, freeze for up to 6 months.

NOEL'S WAY

• Warm a tablespoon of lemon confit with 3 tablespoons of butter,
and serve on the side as a sauce for broiled fish.

• Spread the confit on sliced rounds of baguette, top with goat cheese and fresh thyme,
and broil. Served the croutons atop fresh spinach salad with bacon.

• Toss chickpeas and pitted olives together with olive oil,
red wine vinegar, and a pinch of sea salt. Stir in a liberal spoonful of
the lemon confit, and serve with warm pita bread.

TOMATO-CHILE JAM

AT MY HOUSE, WE GROW TOMATOES OF EVERY SHAPE and hue, and we grow them anywhere they'll take root: in the greenhouse, in pots on the deck, and on tall plants staked firmly by the fence. There's nothing like the acidy-sweet, vegetal aroma of a perfectly ripe tomato warmed by the sun and pulled directly from the vine. There's no other way to say it: They just smell so *alive*, like the rain that falls on them and the dirt they spring from.

In Ireland, there's a glut that happens in late August after the hot summer sun—interrupted by liberal rain—has provided good growing conditions for tomatoes. That's the season when everyone is harvesting them by the armload, and they're as hard to gift to your neighbors as litters of kittens. Don't tell on me, but I've been known to leave paper bags full anonymously on the doorsteps of houses, shops, and churches rather than see them go to waste! This hot, sweet, and über-fresh tasting savory jam is one of my favorite condiments, and I serve it with everything from cheese and cracker platters to hamburgers to roast joints of beef. When they're handy, I like to use a mixture of yellow, red, and black tomatoes to give the chutney a nice deep color.

MAKES ABOUT
2 CUPS / 475 MILLILITERS JAM

6 medium-size mild chile peppers
(such as Anaheim or banana peppers)

3 medium-size fresh ripe tomatoes, cored and chopped

1 green bell pepper, seeded and chopped

2 garlic cloves, crushed

1 (1-inch / 2.5-centimeter) piece fresh ginger,
peeled and grated

⅔ cup / 60 grams granulated sugar

⅓ cup / 80 milliliters red wine vinegar

In a large, heavy-bottomed saucepan, combine all the ingredients. Bring to a boil and simmer, uncovered, for 30 to 40 minutes, stirring occasionally.

When thickened, ladle into hot, sterilized jars (see page 17), leaving a ½-inch / 1.3-centimeter headspace, and seal using the hot water bath (see page 43) for 15 minutes. This should keep for up to 6 months in a cool, dark place, if properly sealed.

SAVORY WHISKEY BUTTER
WITH SHALLOTS AND KOSHER SALT

ANYONE WHO KNOWS ME KNOWS I LIKE THINGS SIMPLE. Although I've enjoyed my world travels—beginning with my tours as an Irish step dancer as a youth and continuing with my culinary training—and have a deep appreciation for innovative cuisine, at heart I really am a meat-and-potatoes man. Give me a fresh, grass-fed beef steak, cooked perfectly, with a fragrant, crispy-jacketed baked potato on the side and I'm on cloud nine. Top my tender steak with a dollop of this seasoned Irish butter redolent of earthy onion and tangy mustard, and I'm sent straight to heaven.

Of course it's fun to thrill guests at my table with surprising and exotic dishes I learn from the blue-ribbon chefs around the world whom I'm privileged to call my friends, but it's been my experience that when handed a glass of stout and sat before an Irish steak dinner after stepping out of the chill night, my guests look at me as if I've shown them the Holy Grail.

MAKES ABOUT
½ CUP / 125 GRAMS WHISKEY BUTTER

---

2 small shallots, minced

2 tablespoons Irish whiskey

8 tablespoons (1 stick) / 113 grams unsalted butter,
at room temperature

½ teaspoon Dijon mustard

½ teaspoon Worcestershire sauce

1 teaspoon chopped fresh parsley

In a small bowl, combine the shallots and whiskey and let stand for up to 4 hours.

In a medium bowl, beat the butter until it's creamy and smooth. Beat in the shallot mixture, mustard, Worcestershire, and parsley, stirring lightly just until the ingredients are mixed.

Pack into a small bowl or ramekin, cover loosely, and store at room temperature for up to 2 days. (If you refrigerate, the ingredients will separate.)

HOSPITALITY AND
THAT HOMEY FEELING

I s there anything as basic and lovely as bread? The simple aroma of it floating out of the oven immediately puts one at ease and touches something deep within a person, offering the assurance that all is well. I suppose that goes for anything baked at your own hearth: fragrant cinnamon rolls, risen sweet breads, nutty banana loaf. In Ireland, we have a tradition of offering *céad mile fáilte* (pronounced "kad meel-a fall-sha") or "a hundred thousand welcomes." My mother trained my brothers, sister, and me to open the door to guests and look after them with hospitality once they were through the door.

When we were wee children, our granny lived in the house with us, and she and my mum got along famously, sharing the kitchen and baking right alongside each other. Frugal and sensible, the women saved biscuit tins and packed them full of home-baked treats to send home with my aunts and cousins. The best part was that the tins would make their way back to us, eventually, packed with the visitor's signature goodies! My favorite was my Aunt Mary's hedgehog cake. Such a treat; it must have been as thick as a chair cushion.

Never one to waste an opportunity to use what's to hand, my granny would flip the lids of her tins upside down to use them as molds for candies, such as cherry chews, currant squares, and caramels. She'd even scoop in raw batter and slide the tins right into the oven, for featherlight Madeira cakes and spicy coffee sponges with roasted, flaked almonds on top.

BARM BRACK

With a name transliterated from the Old English word *beorma,* for a fermented, yeasty liquor, and the Irish word *brac,* meaning "speckled," today's Barm Brack is either a sweet bread or a yeasty cake.

Neither fish nor fowl, the humble baked goodie falls somewhere between a healthful, workaday meal staple you could serve with butter alongside an evening meal of meat and gravy, and a dessert treat or afternoon sweet to be enjoyed with a hot drink and maybe a spoonful of jam.

Delicious and popular variations on the theme include Tea Brack, which uses baking powder as a raising agent instead of yeast, and Cider Brack in which the fruit is soaked in cider as opposed to tea, resulting in a juicier and lighter loaf.

Legend has it that in Ireland's wanting and frugal years gone by, the yeast to raise the bread dough for Barm Brack was skimmed from the top of vats of fermenting beer and recycled in preparation for the Halloween celebration that began as Oíche Samhain, or Samhain Night, which signaled the end of harvest and the time to settle in for the winter. This "feast of the dead" featured Barm Brack, a calorie-dense and fortifying food, perfectly designed for chill winter's evenings. Also served is colcannon, a dish of cabbage or kale and floury potatoes, and jellied eels. This menu is favored because, religiously speaking, this was a night of abstinence on which the consumption of meat was prohibited.

It's Irish custom to bake trinkets into the bread dough to divine the fortunes of the celebrants in the year ahead. The charms determine whether luck will be good or bad, and, while the specific charms vary from house to house, region to region, the two classics are the coin and the ring. If a coin is found, good fortune and wealth can be anticipated, and, if the finder gets the ring, an imminent marriage is predicted. Also popular are a small stick, indicating an unhappy marriage; a piece of cloth, which predicts poverty; and a pea or thimble, foretelling that the finder will not marry. Some families put in a medallion of the Blessed Virgin, which marks the finder for entrance into the priesthood or nunnery.

THE FAMILY BARM BRACK
(BAIRIN BREAC)

MY MOTHER KNOWS A THING OR TWO ABOUT MAKING BASIC BREAD. Barm Brack was a sustaining staple of the McMeel family table. Mum used to make bread over the coal fire, before we got a modern range. You could taste the earthiness of the turf fuel and wooden kindling sticks in the bread baked hanging in a pot over the fire. My mother likes to remind me that it was the only heat in the house. "You'd a choice," she says, "burn your shins or burn your back."

It's easy to make and gorgeous in its plainness. Hers is the recipe I learned on, and still use to this day.

MAKES
1 LARGE LOAF

---

9 ounces / 225 grams dried fruit (raisins, sultanas, currants, and/or chopped, candied citrus peel)

2 cups / 475 milliliters strongly brewed black tea

1 (¼-ounce / 7-gram) package active dry yeast

¼ cup / 60 milliliters whole milk, slightly warmed over low heat, plus more as needed

¼ cup / 50 grams plus 2 teaspoons granulated sugar, divided

1 large egg

2 cups / 240 grams all-purpose flour, plus more as needed

½ teaspoon ground cinnamon

½ teaspoon ground cloves

¼ teaspoon freshly grated nutmeg

5½ tablespoons / 80 grams unsalted butter, melted, plus more for buttering bowl and pan

1 teaspoon salt

In a large glass bowl, soak the dried fruit in the tea overnight.

The next day, mix the yeast, warmed milk, and 2 teaspoons of the sugar together in a small bowl and set aside for 5 to 10 minutes to allow the yeast to activate. In a separate small bowl, beat the egg. In a large mixing bowl, sift together the flour, remaining ¼ cup / 50 grams of sugar, cinnamon, cloves, and nutmeg. Make a well in the center of the dry mixture and add the yeast mixture, beaten egg, butter, and salt. Stir with a wooden spoon to mix the ingredients and bring the dough together. Add a pinch more flour if the dough is too wet, or a splash more milk if it's too dry.

Turn the dough out onto a floured work surface and knead for 5 to 10 minutes, or until the dough is smooth but still a wee bit sticky. Drain the dried fruit and knead a little of it at a time into the dough, until all the fruit has been incorporated. Place the dough into a large, lightly buttered bowl, cover it with a clean towel or plastic wrap, and set it in a warm corner for 1 to 2 hours, or until it doubles in size. Turn out the dough onto a lightly floured work surface and punch it down to deflate it, then knead it lightly for 2 to 3 minutes. Form the dough into a ball and place it in a buttered 7- to 8-inch / 18- to 20-centimeter round cake pan. Cover it with a clean towel or plastic wrap, and let rise again for 30 minutes to an hour, or until it doubles in size.

Preheat the oven to 400°F / 205°C. Bake the bread for 35 to 45 minutes, or until the top is brown and it sounds hollow when lightly tapped. Allow the bread to cool before slicing. Store in a breadbox or airtight tin for up to 3 days.

TRADITIONAL IRISH TEA CAKE

I'VE OFTEN HAD PEOPLE ASK ME how I keep a smile on my face all the time, and what's the secret of my happiness. The honest answer is that I value what's pure and good, and I've made it my life's work to surround myself with just that: the strength of my family, work that I love, a solid roof over my head, and habits that keep my body healthy.

I draw a lot of inspiration from my two brothers, John and Owen, twins who have been mentally and physically handicapped from infancy. It was said that they'd never walk and that they'd never live past childhood. I revel in the fact that they defied both predictions and have made it past their fortieth birthday, happy and cared for by the family they love. They take each day as a new blessing and always see the good in what's in front of them. For that reason, I delight in baking lovely treats that offer them distilled moments of pure pleasure, such as this simple cake that can only be described the way I describe my brothers: pure goodness and a gift from God above.

MAKES
ONE 9-INCH / 23-CENTIMETER ROUND CAKE

---

8 tablespoons (1 stick) / 113 grams unsalted butter,
at room temperature, plus more for buttering pan

1 cup / 200 grams granulated sugar

2 large eggs

1½ teaspoons vanilla extract

1¾ cups / 200 grams all-purpose flour

2 teaspoons baking powder

½ teaspoon salt

½ cup / 120 milliliters whole milk

¼ cup / 60 milliliters confectioners' sugar for dusting

Preheat the oven to 350°F / 175°C. Butter and flour a 9-inch / 23-centimeter round pan.

In a medium bowl, cream together the butter and sugar with an electric mixer on high speed until it's light and fluffy. Beat in the eggs, one at a time, then stir in the vanilla. Sift together the flour, baking powder, and salt and stir into the batter by hand, then stir in the milk.

Using a rubber spatula, spread the batter evenly into the prepared cake pan. Bake for 30 to 40 minutes, until it's golden brown on top or a toothpick inserted into the center comes out clean. Let cool on a cooling rack, then turn out the cake onto a serving plate and dust it with confectioners' sugar. Serve immediately, or store in an airtight tin or plastic cake keeper for up to 5 days.

THE HISTORY OF
IRISH SODA BREAD

When people think of Irish food the world over, soda bread is one of the first things that pops to mind. It's easy to make, dependable, and delicious. But there's more to the story than that. The climate and economics of the Emerald Isle helped place these loaves and farls into the kitchens of the Irish masses.

In the nineteenth century, ovens were common only in wealthy households, so the introduction of baking soda to home cooks and housewives allowed them to bake light, fluffy, risen loaves on the griddle or in a flat pot hung above a coal fire.

In the lean centuries past, there may have been shortages of many things, but sprawling fields of green grass was never one of them. Dairy has featured prominently as a backbone of Irish cooking, making buttermilk abundant and affordable. Add that key ingredient, along with the baking soda, to the soft flour produced by the wheat grown in Ireland's cool, wet climate, and you'll hit the jackpot. Previously, farm wives used yeast, which was expensive and ineffective at helping dough rise when used with the low-gluten, low-protein flour produced in Ireland.

Traditional, workaday Irish soda bread features only four ingredients: flour, baking soda, salt, and buttermilk, and it's cooked in a round skillet. Today, you'll find many variations on the shape and flavor for soda bread, and newer and more modern baking methods. Wheaten, gluten-free, sweetened with sugar and fruit (known as Spotted Dog), herbed with cheese or tomatoes, or baked in a bread machine, it all springs from the basic recipe, and it's as Irish as St. Patrick, misty weather, and Waterford crystal.

BOILED CAKE

IT'S A TRUE NORTHERN IRISH TWIST to call this cake "boiled" when it's not. To make a boiled cake, you boil the ingredients, but bake the cake.

When I was a teenager, my sister and I often took over the cooking for the household. She made the most unbelievable boiled cake, fashioned after my Aunt Greta's. Although our family lost my dear sister, Ita, more years ago than I care to count, I can still to this day taste it. Ita bossed me around the kitchen and chided me for being messy while I cooked. Somehow, it was always me standing at the dishpan clearing up after the both of us!

My boiled cake is very good, if I do say so. But so many dishes handed down by our mums, aunties, grannies, and sisters live only in memory. No matter how carefully we follow the recipe, the dishes will always be missing one special ingredient—them.

MAKES
ONE 8-INCH / 20-CENTIMETER CAKE

---

5 ounces / 150 grams sultanas

3 ounces / 75 grams dried currants

¾ cup / 175 grams dark brown sugar, packed

8 tablespoons (1 stick) / 113 grams unsalted butter
at room temperature, plus more for buttering pan

½ cup / 120 milliliters strongly brewed black tea

1 tablespoon vanilla extract

1 cup / 125 grams whole wheat flour

1 cup / 125 grams all-purpose flour

1½ teaspoons baking powder

Pinch of salt

1½ teaspoons ground cinnamon

3 tablespoons sherry

In a medium saucepan, combine the sultanas, currants, brown sugar, butter, ½ cup / 120 milliliters of brewed tea, and vanilla. Bring to a boil over medium heat, stirring occasionally. Cook for 20 minutes, then remove from the heat and set aside to cool.

Preheat the oven to 350°F / 180°C. Butter an 8-inch / 20-centimeter round cake pan.

In a medium bowl, stir together the whole wheat flour, all-purpose flour, baking powder, salt, and cinnamon. Add the dry mixture, along with the sherry, to the fruit mixture and mix well.

Pour the mixture into the prepared pan. Bake for 45 minutes, then lower the oven temperature to 325°F / 160°C and bake for 15 more minutes, or until a skewer inserted into the center comes out clean. Turn out the cake onto a cooling rack and allow it to cool before slicing and serving. Store in an airtight tin or plastic cake keeper for up to 7 days.

LIFT IT UP

Before the 1700s, housewives relied largely on yeast—often gathered from beer or other fermented beverages—as a leavening agent for cakes and breads. Baking soda and baking powder didn't come into play until the industrial revolution. Around the eighteenth century, the technique of beating as much air as possible into warmed eggs came into use, along with the idea of using forms and rings to shape cakes. Butter and shortening were withheld and these new applications of chemistry, along with better ovens with more easily regulated temperatures, gave rise to pastries that threatened to float away into thin air.

TRADITIONAL BUTTER POUND CAKE

I LOVE POUND CAKE BECAUSE IT'S A STURDY, COUNTRY FOOD made with ingredients that any farm wife would have readily on hand. Some of the moistest, tastiest pound cakes I've ever had came out of the kitchens of my family's neighbors, and I still think the reason is Irish butter. I've said it before, and I'll say it again: Use the highest-quality butter you can get your hands on. That's especially true for this cake that takes most of its flavor from that golden dairy delight.

Pound cakes originally got their name because they contained a pound each of flour, butter, sugar, and eggs. My mother still makes hers in this 1:1:1:1 ratio, weighing out 6 to 8 eggs in the shell and then weighing the butter, flour, and sugar. It works beautifully. It's a foolproof recipe in your back pocket that you'll be able to execute time and again. But if you prefer a slightly more straightforward approach, the measurements below will make you a fabulous cake without all that weighing.

Of course this rich cake is delicious on its own, but I also like to toast slices and spread it with Rich Chocolate Spread (page 36) or sandwich custard and fresh peaches between slabs and top it with whipped cream or vanilla ice cream.

MAKES
TWO 8 x 4-INCH / 20 x 10-CENTIMETER LOAVES

2 cups / 480 grams salted butter, at room temperature,
plus more for buttering pans

2½ cups / 500 grams granulated sugar

7 large eggs, at room temperature

4 cups / 480 grams all-purpose flour

2 teaspoons vanilla extract

Preheat the oven to 275°F / 135°C. Butter two 8 x 4-inch / 20 x 10-centimeter loaf pans and set them aside.

In a large mixing bowl, beat the butter for 1 to 2 minutes until it lightens in color, using an electric mixer set on medium speed. A little at a time, add the sugar to the butter, until it's all incorporated, then beat for 5 minutes, or until fluffy and very light in color.

In a small bowl, whisk the eggs. With the mixer set on a low speed, alternately add the eggs and flour, stopping to scrape the sides of the bowl occasionally. Add the vanilla and beat until blended.

Divide the batter between the prepared pans, smoothing the tops with a rubber spatula dipped in water. Space the pans evenly apart in the middle of the oven.

After 30 minutes, increase the oven temperature to 350°F / 175°C and bake for 30 minutes, then rotate the pans. Bake for another 15 to 20 minutes, until a skewer or thick fork inserted into the center of each cake comes out mostly clean, but with a crumb or two attached. If the cakes are browning too quickly, cover loosely with a sheet of foil.

Let the cakes cool in the pans on cooling racks for 30 minutes, then tip them out onto the rack and allow them to cool for another hour before slicing and serving. Store in an airtight tin or plastic cake keeper for up to 1 week.

SEEDY CAKE

I WAS ALWAYS AMAZED AT WHAT MY MOTHER had in that pantry of hers: It was like magic to see what appeared when our priest from Moneyglass Chapel, or the neighbor up the road dropped in for a visit without warning. Suddenly, there'd be a piping hot pot of tea under a cozy, and three or four selections of bread or cake, flanked by home-canned jam. And pure butter. Always butter. For some reason, this moist and distinctively flavored cake was always a darling of the old folks. I've no interest in aging myself, but I don't mind telling you I like a wee slice with a cup of tea in the afternoon, so I can see their point.

MAKES
ONE 8 X 4-INCH / 20 X 10-CENTIMETER LOAF

½ cup / 120 grams unsalted butter, at room temperature,
plus more for buttering pan

2 cups / 240 grams all-purpose flour, plus more for flouring pan

½ cup / 100 grams granulated sugar

3 large eggs

2 teaspoons baking powder

½ teaspoon kosher salt

2 teaspoons caraway seeds

½ cup / 120 milliliters milk

Preheat the oven to 350°F / 175°C. Butter and flour the bottom and sides of an 8 x 4-inch / 20 x 10-centimeter loaf pan, and set it aside.

In a large mixing bowl, using an electric mixer on high speed, cream the butter and sugar together until the mixture is fluffy and pale yellow in color, about 5 minutes. In a small bowl, beat the eggs with a fork, then add them a little at a time to the wet mixture, beating at low speed.

Sift the flour, baking powder, and salt together into a medium mixing bowl, then add the caraway seeds, mixing lightly with a fork. Add the dry mixture to the butter mixture, alternating with the milk, mixing on low speed, until the batter is very thick and firm. Spread the mixture into the prepared loaf pan and smooth the top with a rubber spatula dipped in water.

Bake for about 45 minutes, or until the top is lightly browned and a skewer inserted into the center comes out clean. Let cool in the pan on a cooling rack for about 15 minutes, then tip out the cake onto the rack and allow to cool for an hour before serving. Store in an airtight tin or plastic cake keeper for up to 1 week.

MADEIRA CAKE

OUR WEALTHY EIGHTEENTH-CENTURY FOREBEARS certainly knew how to luxuriate. I agree with one upper-crust tradition of theirs: A relaxing glass of something medicinal, along with this sweet and delicate sponge is an ideal way to while away the hours between midmorning and lunch. That said, abstainers and designated drivers don't seem to mind modifying the usual pairing by substituting a strong cup of Irish tea alongside a hefty slice of this comforting treat.

One might assume that Madeira cake features the eponymous ingredient, when, in fact, there's not a drop to be found in it. Instead, it's a deceptively simple sponge cake with a sophisticated appeal, meant to be served with a glass of sweet wine or Madeira, a tradition dating back to the nobility of nineteenth-century England.

Firm and light in texture, like a heavier, moister sponge, Madeira cake resembles pound cake, minus the substantial heft. The practice of sprinkling on superfine sugar before baking gives it an unusual crunchy-sweet crust.

MAKES
ONE 8 X 4-INCH / 20 X 10-CENTIMETER LOAF

8 ounces / 225 grams high-quality unsalted butter,
at room temperature, plus more for buttering pan

1 cup / 200 grams granulated sugar

1 teaspoon vanilla extract

½ cup / 120 milliliters milk

2 medium-size eggs

1½ cups / 225 grams all-purpose flour

¼ teaspoon lemon zest

Superfine sugar, for sprinkling

Preheat the oven to 325°F / 160°C. Butter and flour an 8 x 4-inch / 20 x 10-centimeter loaf pan.

Using an electric mixer on high speed, cream together the butter and sugar, and add the vanilla and the milk. Add the eggs one at a time, adding a tablespoon of the flour for each. Then mix in the rest of the flour a little at a time, on low speed. Once mixed, add the lemon zest and beat briskly for 10 minutes.

Smooth the batter into the prepared pan, sprinkle the top of the cake with the superfine sugar, and bake for 1 hour, or until a skewer inserted into the middle comes out clean. Let cool completely in the pan on a cooling rack before slicing and serving. Store in an airtight tin or in a plastic cake keeper for up to 3 days.

BASIC VICTORIA SPONGE CAKE

THIS MAY BE THE SIMPLEST CAKE YOU CAN MAKE from scratch; embellished, it delivers a substantial "wow factor." I recommend this as a first-try pastry if you're new to the kitchen, or to help your household's youngest bakers cut their teeth on.

The cake can be eaten as is, or with any fillings you like, but tradition says to spread one layer with whipped cream, one layer with strawberry jam, and dust lightly with confectioners' sugar.

Purported to be a favorite of Queen Victoria, who was said to enjoy a slice with her tea, this delicious, golden sponge goes down as a treat with everyone from the babies to the old folks.

MAKES
ONE 8-INCH / 20-CENTIMETER CAKE

---

4 medium-size eggs

Unsalted butter, at room temperature,
plus more for buttering pan

Granulated sugar

Self-rising flour

Strawberry jam

Heavy whipping cream, whipped

Confectioners' sugar for dusting

Preheat the oven to 325°F / 160°C. Butter two 8-inch / 20-centimeter cake pans and line their bottoms with baking parchment, then set aside.

Weigh the eggs in their shells. Weigh out the same amount each in unsalted butter and granulated sugar. Using an electric mixer on high speed, cream the butter and sugar together until the mixture is fluffy and very pale yellow in color, about 5 minutes.

In a separate small bowl, beat the eggs, using a fork, then gradually mix them into the butter mixture until incorporated. Weigh out the same amount of self-rising flour, and sift into the mixture. Using a metal spoon, fold it in gently until it's fully incorporated.

Divide the batter evenly between the two pans and bake for about 25 minutes, or until the cakes spring back after being gently pressed with your fingers. Turn out the cakes onto cooling racks and allow to cool completely. Once cool, spread one cake layer with whipped cream, one cake layer with strawberry jam, sandwich them together, and dust lightly with confectioners' sugar. Serve immediately, or store in an airtight tin for up to 2 days.

COFFEE SPONGE CAKE

THE SMELL OF THIS CAKE, mingled with the rich aroma of the coffee my mother served with it, is the essence of my boyhood weekends. Saturday mornings, my brothers and sister and I would be encouraged to forfeit a chance to sleep past dawn, awakened by this glorious aroma. I'd rush to the kitchen to dance from foot to foot, pestering my mother about when it would come out of the oven. Waiting for it to cool was a torture that even a slice of homemade soda bread with Mum's preserves and our farm's butter wouldn't quiet.

I'd watch while she frosted the top with buttercream frosting flavored with Camp coffee essence. Before she'd cut it, I got the job of dotting the top with walnut halves for decoration.

MAKES
1 LARGE LAYER CAKE

12 tablespoons (1½ sticks) / 173 grams unsalted butter,
at room temperature, plus more for buttering pans

¾ cup / 140 grams all-purpose flour, plus more for flouring pans

¾ cup / 170 grams superfine sugar

½ teaspoon vanilla extract

2 ounces / 30 grams mild instant coffee powder

3 large eggs

Preheat the oven to 350°F / 180°C. Butter and flour two 8-inch / 20-centimeter layer cake pans and set aside.

Using a wooden spoon, cream together the butter and sugar in a large mixing bowl until well combined and fluffy. Add the vanilla and stir.

In a small bowl, sift together the flour and instant coffee. In a separate small bowl, beat the eggs. Alternately add the wet ingredients, the dry ingredients, and the beaten egg to the large bowl, stirring well after each addition. Finally, stir in 2 teaspoons of warm, but not hot, water.

Divide the mixture evenly between the prepared cake pans. Bake for 20 minutes, or until skewers inserted into the center of the cakes come out clean.

Let cool in the pans on cooling racks for 30 minutes. Once cool, tip out the cakes onto the racks to cool completely. Fill or frost with your favorite frosting, and decorate with walnut halves, if desired. Serve immediately or store in an airtight tin or plastic cake keeper for up to 2 days.

HARMONY CAKE

THERE'S SOME IN NORTHERN IRELAND—Belfast, in particular—that call this dessert "Irish War Cake," because it can be made without using eggs, which can be hard to come by outside a farm when rationing takes place in times of troubles and emergencies. Given the hopefulness of the recent historic handshake between Queen Elizabeth and former Irish Republican Army commander Martin McGuinness, I prefer a more optimistic name for my version of this treat, so I'm calling it Harmony Cake. Every time I make it, I consider it a wish for peace on this earth. It's so quick and easy you can whip it up for last-minute guests, and it keeps beautifully. May all who gather to eat it enjoy the sweetness of the treat, and of one another's company!

MAKES
ONE 9 x 12-INCH / 23 x 30-CENTIMETER CAKE

8 tablespoons (1 stick) / 113 grams unsalted butter,
at room temperature, plus more for buttering pan

4 ounces / 113 grams raisins

2 ounces / 56 grams walnuts

1¾ cups / 210 grams all-purpose flour

1 cup / 200 grams granulated sugar

½ teaspoon salt

1 teaspoon baking soda

½ teaspoon ground cinnamon

½ teaspoon freshly grated nutmeg

¼ teaspoon ground cloves

Preheat the oven to 350°F / 175°C. Butter a 9 x 12-inch / 23 x 30-centimeter cake pan and set aside.

In a large, heavy-bottomed saucepan over high heat, boil 2 cups of water and add the raisins. Lower the heat to a simmer and cook the fruit for 15 minutes. Remove the saucepan from the heat, add the butter, and allow the mixture to cool. Once cool, add the walnuts, flour, sugar, salt, baking soda, cinnamon, nutmeg, and cloves and mix with a wooden spoon or paddle, taking care not to overwork the batter.

Spread the batter into the prepared pan. Bake for about 30 minutes. Test the cake by inserting a metal skewer into the center. If it doesn't come out clean, continue baking in 5-minute increments until you get a clean skewer. Tip the cake out onto a wire rack and allow it to cool completely before serving. Store in an airtight tin or plastic cake keeper for up to 5 days.

YOUNG MASTER NOEL'S FIRST ORANGE CAKE

MY FIRST SOLO SUCCESS IN THE WORLD OF BAKING at the tender age of thirteen was with an orange cake very much like this one. My mother allowed me to eat my whole creation on my own, without sharing: a big event in a household of six children. Suffice it to say, just because one is allowed to do something, doesn't always mean one should! I still have memories of the bellyache. Regardless, I think this is a lovely cake, if you can bring yourself to savor it with a bit of restraint.

MAKES
ONE 8-INCH / 20-CENTIMETER LAYER CAKE

8 ounces (2 sticks) / 225 grams unsalted butter,
at room temperature, plus more for buttering pans

1 cup / 200 grams granulated sugar

4 large eggs

1½ cups / 180 grams self-rising flour

1 tablespoon baking powder

Zest of 1 orange

FILLING AND TOPPING

5½ tablespoons / 85 grams unsalted butter, at room temperature

2 cups / 200 grams confectioners' sugar, sifted

2 tablespoons / 30 milliliters freshly squeezed orange juice

Finely grated rind of 1 orange

Recipe continues

Preheat the oven to 350°F / 175°C. Lightly butter two 8-inch / 20-centimeter cake pans and line them with baking parchment.

Combine the butter, sugar, eggs, flour, baking powder, and orange zest in a large mixing bowl and beat with an electric mixer on high speed for about 2 minutes, until just mixed.

Divide the mixture evenly between the prepared pans and level the surface with rubber spatula dipped in water. Bake for about 25 minutes, or until the cakes are well risen and golden. The tops of the cakes should spring back when pressed lightly with a finger. Allow the cakes to cool in the pans for 15 minutes, then run a small palette knife or butter knife around the edge of the pans to free the sides of the cakes. Turn out the cakes onto cooling racks, peel off the parchment, and leave them to cool completely. Choose the cake with the better top, then put the other cake top side down onto a serving plate.

To make the filling and topping, beat together the butter, confectioners' sugar, orange juice, and orange rind until very fluffy, using an electric mixer on high speed, about 10 minutes. Spread half of the orange cream on the first layer and place the other cake on top, with the top facing up, and spread the rest of the orange cream on top, leaving the sides bare.

Serve immediately, or store the cake in an airtight tin or plastic cake keeper in the refrigerator for up to 3 days.

CARROT CAKE

CARROTS HAVE BEEN USED IN SWEET PUDDINGS since medieval times. These humble dirt jewels contain more natural sugar than any vegetable apart from the sugar beet. The world over, they're generally inexpensive to buy and easy to grow.

In my home country, carrots are a dependable staple. Like all of Ireland's root veg, carrots survive happily under the soil, unbothered by such weather conditions as cold snaps and ferocious coastal winds. Prized in cakes for their sweetness, carrots also add a lovely texture, contributing to a firm but moist cake with an open crumb.

The extra sweetness in this cake comes from golden syrup, a pale treacle with a distinctive buttery taste. Outside the United Kingdom, it may be a bit hard to find, but its distinctive flavor adds so much that to some people, it's worth tracking down. For a substitute, try either equal parts of maple syrup and honey, or two parts light corn syrup to one part light molasses.

MAKES
1 LARGE LAYER CAKE

CAKE

Butter for buttering pans

3½ cups / 350 grams all-purpose flour, plus more for flouring pans

¾ cup / 300 milliliters sunflower oil

1 cup / 200 grams brown sugar, packed

4 large eggs

6 ounces / 175 grams golden syrup, or either 3 ounces 90 milliliters each maple syrup and honey, or 4 ounces / 120 milliliters light corn syrup plus 2 ounces / 60 milliliters light molasses

2 teaspoons ground cinnamon

1 teaspoon ground ginger

1 teaspoon baking soda

1¼ cups / 225 grams grated carrot

⅔ cup / 50 grams dry unsweetened shredded coconut

⅓ cup / 25 grams chopped walnuts

FROSTING

10 ounces / 300 grams cream cheese

1 cup / 100 grams confectioners' sugar

Grated zest of 2 large oranges, reserving about a tablespoon to decorate

---

Preheat the oven to 350°F / 180°C. Butter and flour two 8-inch / 20-centimeter round layer cake pans and set aside.

In a large mixing bowl, whisk together the oil, brown sugar, eggs, and golden syrup, until moistened, taking care not to overwork the batter.

In a medium mixing bowl, sift together the flour, cinnamon, ginger, and baking soda.

Slowly add the dry ingredients to the wet mixture, stirring as you go. Then gently fold in the grated carrot, coconut, and walnuts.

Divide the mixture evenly between the prepared cake pans. Bake for 40 to 50 minutes, or until a skewer or fork inserted into the center comes out clean.

While the cake bakes, make the frosting: beat the cream cheese, confectioners' sugar, and orange zest together in a large bowl for 7 or 8 minutes, until smooth, using an electric mixer set on high speed. Let the cake pans cool on cooling racks for an hour. Then tip out the cakes onto cooling racks and allow them to cool completely before frosting and decorating with the reserved orange zest. Slice and serve immediately, or store in an airtight tin or plastic cake keeper for up to 1 week.

RHUBARB CAKE

ON THE TELEVISION SHOW *Great British Menu,* I served a dessert called Trio of Rhubarb, and I'm surprised at how often people remember it and ask for the recipe. Rhubarb is one of those ingredients that inspires devotion in those who love it.

My dad was partial to this simple sweet, no doubt owing to the abundance of rhubarb on his land when he was a boy. Together with some such farm staples as flour, sugar, and dairy, rhubarb enjoyed an elevated status for such a simple ingredient. In lean times, his people relied on creativity to make something special out of nothing special. Both my parents ate this as children, dished straight out of the oven. At its heart, this treat is little more than jam on scones, or a glorified pie. Serve it warmed with whipped cream, and it becomes a delicacy.

MAKES
6 SERVINGS

6 tablespoons (¾ stick) / 80 grams unsalted butter at room temperature, plus more for buttering pan

3 cups / 340 grams all-purpose flour, plus more for dusting

1 teaspoon baking soda

½ teaspoon salt

1¼ cups / 250 grams granulated sugar, divided, plus more for sprinkling

1 large egg

¾ cup / 175 milliliters buttermilk

4 cups / 700 grams chopped rhubarb

Juice of 1 small lemon

1 medium-size egg white, whisked

Preheat the oven to 350°F / 175°C, and butter a 10-inch / 25-centimeter deep pie plate.

Sift the flour, baking soda, and salt into a large mixing bowl. Add ¼ cup / 50 grams of the sugar and rub in the butter until crumbly, using your hands.

In a small bowl, beat the egg together with the buttermilk and add this to the flour mixture, stirring to make a shaggy dough.

Turn out the dough onto a lightly floured work surface and knead it gently. Divide the dough into 2 balls.

Using a rolling pin, roll out 1 dough ball and use it to line the pie dish. Spoon in the rhubarb and sprinkle it with the remaining 1 cup / 200 grams of sugar and the lemon juice. Roll out the second dough ball to make the top crust. Brush the rim of the bottom crust with water, then lay on the top and pinch the edges together all around. Glaze the top with the beaten egg white and sprinkle it with sugar. Using a butter knife, cut vents in the top crust. Bake for 45 minutes to 1 hour, until the crust is lightly browned and the fruit is soft and bubbling. Serve warm, or store in the refrigerator for up to 1 week.

BAKEWELL TART

MY MUM USED TO MAKE BAKEWELL TARTS with her own homemade jam. Originating in Bakewell, England, the tart has been adopted and welcomed into Irish homes and bakeries. It's not easy to make, but it's a humble and honest pudding. It's not too sweet, or gooey, and the nuts keep the flavor grounded and the texture solid. The idea behind blind-baking the pastry case and brushing it with egg is to ensure that the hard shell will hold the moist filling without absorbing it, thus avoiding what some chefs call "soggy bottom."

MAKES
8 SERVINGS

1¼ cups / 150 grams all-purpose flour,
plus more for dusting

5⅓ tablespoons / 80 grams cold, unsalted butter, cubed,
plus more for buttering pan

Pinch of salt

2 to 3 tablespoons very cold water

1 egg white, lightly beaten

FILLING

2 tablespoons raspberry jam

6 tablespoons plus 2 teaspoons / 150 grams unsalted butter,
at room temperature

¾ cup / 150 grams superfine sugar

4 medium-size eggs, plus 1 egg, divided

1½ cups / 150 grams ground almonds

Zest of 1 medium-size lemon

2 tablespoons sliced almonds

Preheat the oven to 325°F / 170°C.

Place the flour, butter, and salt into a large bowl. Rub the butter into the flour with your fingertips until the mixture resembles coarse breadcrumbs, working as quickly as possible to prevent the dough from becoming warm. Add 2 tablespoons of the water to the mixture, and, using a cold knife, stir until the dough binds together, adding more cold water a teaspoon at a time if the mixture is too dry. Wrap the dough in plastic wrap and chill for at least 15 minutes or up to 30 minutes.

Roll out the pastry on a lightly floured board to ¼-inch / 6-millimeters thick. Butter and then line an 8-inch / 20-centimeter deep tart tin with the pastry. Prick the base all over with a fork. Chill in the refrigerator for 15 minutes. Line the tart shell with parchment paper and fill with dried beans or pie weights. Bake for 15 minutes, or until the pastry is a pale golden color. Remove the beans, lightly brush the inside of the pastry case with the egg white, and bake for a further 5 minutes, or until light golden brown.

For the filling, spread the raspberry jam onto the base of the pastry shell. Leave to cool. Cream the butter and sugar together until pale in color, using an electric mixer on high speed. In a separate bowl, beat 3 of the eggs together with the yolk of the fourth egg. Add the egg mixture to the butter mixture a little at a time. Gently fold in the ground almonds and lemon zest. Pour the mixture into the cooled pastry shell and gently level the surface to fill the whole tart evenly. Beat the egg white and brush the top of the pasty with it. Bake for 20 minutes. Sprinkle the flaked almonds onto the surface and bake for a further 20 minutes, or until golden and set.

SWEET IRISH PANCAKES

IF YOU TAKE TEA IN A TRADITIONAL IRISH HOUSE, it's not unheard of to be offered "a bit of pancake." Usually these thick and hearty skillet pastries have been cooked in advance and served cold, with butter and jam on the side. I like to offer mine with homemade Apple and Sultana Purée (page 32), and a heaping spoon of the kind of rich clotted cream that'll leave a sheen on the lips.

MAKES ABOUT
24 PANCAKES

2 cups plus 1 tablespoon / 250 grams all-purpose flour

2 teaspoons / 10 milliliters baking powder

½ cup / 100 grams granulated sugar

1¼ cups / 300 milliliters whole milk

1 large egg

Pinch of salt

Butter, for buttering griddle

Sift the flour and baking powder together into a large mixing bowl, then add the sugar, milk, egg, and salt, and whisk together thoroughly, forming a smooth, thick batter.

Heat a lightly buttered griddle or heavy nonstick skillet. To cook the pancakes in batches, drop small amounts of the batter onto the pan, spacing them well apart. Once the bubbles on the surface of the pancakes begin to pop, turn them over with a spatula and cook briefly on the other side. Keep warm in a low oven if serving immediately, or allow them to cool and seal them in an airtight container if storing them in the pantry for later.

FRESH FARM – FREE RANGE

rthy
hter)

HEN & DUCK EGG

6 QUAIL EGGS
£1.00

20 LARGE
EGGS
£2.44

FREE RANGE
LARGE EGGS
* £1.20
PER...
* 6 *
EGGS
FROM VERY HAPPY HENS!
*

FREE RANGE
MED. EGGS
* £1.00
PER...
* 6 *
EGGS
FROM VERY HAPPY HENS!
*

FREE RANG
FRESH FARM DUCK E
FOR
* £2.00

BOXTY POTATO BREAD PANCAKES

BACSTAÍ OR *ARÁN BOCHT TÍ* IN IRISH means "poorhouse bread." As a dish cobbled together from peasant food leftovers, made without yeast, and cooked humbly on the griddle, boxty has sustained the poor and the farm-bound since the nineteenth century.

At Rock Cottage, electricity came in 1968, and, before that, my mum tells me they cooked on the same fire where they warmed themselves. An iron skillet hung above the flame, and that's where the simple and hearty breads, such as boxty, were baked.

For light, airy potato bread, be sure to use floury potatoes, such as long whites, russets, or Idahos. Part pancake, part hash browns, part bread roll, the potato boxty is a versatile bread that complements any meal, night or day.

MAKES
4 LARGE PANCAKES

2 large floury potatoes, peeled

1 cup / 225 grams cooked and mashed floury potatoes
(from 2 to 3 whole potatoes, depending on the size; peel before mashing)

1 cup / 120 grams all-purpose flour, plus 1 tablespoon for dusting

½ teaspoon baking powder

½ teaspoon salt

3 tablespoons salted butter, melted and cooled

Milk for thinning the dough, as needed

Grate the raw potato over a double layer of cheesecloth and then wring out the grated potato over a bowl, catching the liquid: This will separate into a clear liquid with starch at the bottom. Pour off and discard the liquid, then scrape out the starch with a rubber spatula and mix it with the grated and mashed potatoes.

Sift together the flour, baking powder, and salt and mix into the potatoes with the melted butter, adding a little milk if necessary to make a pliable dough. Turn out the dough onto a lightly floured surface and knead lightly.

Divide the dough into 4 parts and form round flat cakes about ½-inch / 1.3-centimeters thick. With the back of a knife, cut a cross into each round, extending almost to the edges, without cutting it through. Heat a large griddle or heavy skillet until hot. Dust the pan with flour, then place a dough round marked-side down onto the pan. Cook over medium heat for 3 to 5 minutes. Turn the round over, and repeat on the other side for 2 to 3 minutes. Let cool on a cooling rack, and store in an airtight container.

• Top with crème fraîche, lox, and thinly sliced scallion
for a new twist on Russian cuisine.

• Pair with Irish stew instead of soda bread as a vehicle to mop up gravy.

• Melt sharp Cheddar cheese, sliced onion, and Dijon mustard
between 2 pancakes for a grown-up grilled cheese sandwich.

CLASSIC IRISH FARLS

Different versions of folklore tell the tale that circular bread loaves were cut into quarters, or farls, for good reason. Depending on who's telling the tale, the X-shaped scoring that divided a round into four farls was meant to keep thoughts of the Cross of Christ in mind. Another explanation was that the sign of the cross kept fairies from the bread. Most dramatically, some say it was employed to let evil spirits out of the bread. The likely reason is that bread cut into quarters is easier to serve or transport and that the cross cut into the top of the loaf helps the bread rise.

It's thought that the word *farl* is a shorter form of *fardel,* a Lowland Scots term for a three-cornered cake or the fourth segment of a round, and that the language was carried down to Northern Ireland.

TRADITIONAL IRISH SODA BREAD

THE PROVERB, "GIVE A MAN A FISH and you'll feed him for a day; teach a man to fish and you'll feed him for a lifetime," was given proper weight in my family. I'm filled with gratitude that my parents gave me practical tools for life, such as how to plant a drill of potatoes or rhubarb, how to pick blackberries, how to preserve by hand, how to organize and tidy a kitchen. Learning to cook has provided me with hours of pleasure, proud independence, and a living I love. I've spent a lot of time in the kitchen with my niece Gemma, trying to pass on what her gran and granddad taught me. One of our first lessons was soda bread: a simple and somewhat fail-proof challenge. I'm proud to say she mastered it in a flash, and we've since moved on to more complicated lessons. It's a joy to watch the confident ownership she shows when cooking meals for the whole family.

MAKES
1 ROUND MEDIUM-SIZE LOAF OR 4 FARLS

---

2 cups / 280 grams all-purpose flour, plus more for dusting

1 teaspoon salt

1 teaspoon cream of tartar

1 heaping teaspoon / 10 grams baking soda

1 cup / 236 milliliters buttermilk

Olive oil or rapeseed oil, for oiling pan

In a large mixing bowl, combine all the dry ingredients. Using your hand, make a well in the flour and pour in the buttermilk. Mix lightly with a fork until a sticky dough is formed, being careful not to overwork it.

Turn out the dough onto a very well floured surface and form it into a ball. If the dough is extremely sticky, flour your hands or sprinkle a small amount of flour onto the top. Knead gently 3 or 4 times. Form the dough into a ball, flatten it to about ½-inch / 1.3-centimeters thick, and cut it into quarters.

In a hot, lightly oiled iron skillet (pour in enough oil to just coat the bottom), cook the bread over medium heat for about 8 minutes, allowing it to brown slightly. Then turn it once and continue to cook for about 8 minutes, until the bread is barely browned on both sides and makes a hollow sound when tapped. Store in a breadbox or an airtight tin for up to 5 days.

TRADITIONAL IRISH SODA BREAD WITH A HINT OF CURRY

WHEN THE IRISH (OR THE ENGLISH OR AMERICANS, for that matter), think of curry powder, we're in fact actually thinking of garam masala, a Northern Indian spice mixture with a name loosely translated as "warm spice mixture." True Indian curry powder, common in the south of India, is made from fresh curry leaves (called *karivepalai, kari patta,* or *meetha neem*).

Of course you can buy the spice premixed at supermarkets or specialty stores, but it's so easy to make and so much more economical that I urge you to give it a whirl. That way, you can showcase your own tastes and personality with the components and proportions. Some of the most common spices included are cumin seeds, coriander seeds, cinnamon, black pepper, cloves, and cardamom pods. I have my own version (see page 234) but I mix it up from time to time and improvise.

MAKES
1 ROUND LOAF

1¼ cups / 170 grams all-purpose flour, plus more to dust

1¼ cups / 170 grams self-rising flour

½ teaspoon salt

1 teaspoon mild curry powder

½ teaspoon baking soda

1¼ cups / 290 milliliters buttermilk

Preheat the oven to 400°F / 200°C and lightly flour a baking sheet.

In a large mixing bowl, combine the flours, salt, curry powder, and baking soda and stir gently with a fork. Using your hand, make a well in the center of the dry ingredients and pour in the buttermilk, mixing with a fork to form a soft dough, taking care not to overwork it.

Turn out the dough onto a lightly floured surface and knead 3 or 4 times. If the dough is sticky, sprinkle flour onto your hands or onto the dough. Form it into a round that will fit onto your prepared baking sheet, and press it on to the sheet. Cut a cross on the top and bake for about 30 minutes, or until the loaf sounds hollow when tapped. Store in a breadbox or airtight tin for up to 5 days.

WHEATEN
SODA BREAD

THIS VERSION IS A HEALTHFUL AND TOOTHSOME standard family bread that keeps beautifully when wrapped tightly or stored in an airtight container. It begs to be served with sweet butter and jam or alongside a hearty meat dish dripping with gravy. You can premix the dry ingredients and store them in a canister, adding the butter and buttermilk later, if you prefer, for fresh hot bread in the wink of an eye.

MAKES
TWO 8 X 4-INCH / 20 X 10-CENTIMETER LOAVES

2 tablespoons / 28 grams cold salted butter,
plus more for buttering pans

3¼ cups / 450 grams coarsely ground whole wheat flour

2 teaspoons salt

2 teaspoons baking soda

2½ cups / 225 grams old-fashioned rolled oats

1 tablespoon sunflower seeds

2½ cups / 700 milliliters buttermilk

Preheat the oven 400°F / 200°C. Butter two 8 x 4-inch / 20 x 10-centimeter loaf pans and set them aside.

Sift the flour into a large mixing bowl with the salt and baking soda. With your hands, work in the butter until you have a crumbly mixture. Stir in the oats and sunflower seeds, using a large, wooden mixing spoon. Add the buttermilk a little at a time, mixing well. This batter should be on the wet side.

Divide the batter evenly between the prepared pans. Bake for 40 to 50 minutes, or until the tops are golden brown and the loaves springs back when gently pressed with your hand. Turn the loaves out of the pans and return them to the oven directly onto the oven racks for 10 more minutes to crisp the outside, then transfer them to cooling racks to cool completely. Store in a breadbox or airtight tin for up to 5 days.

CARAWAY AND RAISIN BROWN BREAD

I LOVE OFFERING SLABS OF THIS nutty and crumbly bread slathered with Irish butter alongside velvety soups made from carrots, leeks, or whatever vegetable is in season. The caraway seeds spice up this workaday bread with a pungent, dill-like flavor and a vague whiff of licorice, and the raisins lighten the loaf with a touch of fruity sweetness.

MAKES
ONE 8 x 4-inch / 20 x 10-centimeter loaf

1⅔ cups / 240 grams all-purpose flour, plus more for flouring pan

⅔ cup / 110 grams raisins

1⅓ cups / 180 grams whole wheat flour

2 teaspoons caraway seeds

1 teaspoon baking soda

¾ teaspoon salt

1¼ cups / 295 milliliters buttermilk

Preheat the oven to 425°F / 220°C. Lightly flour a baking sheet and set it aside.

Put the raisins in a small bowl, and cover with warm water. Allow them to soak until plump, about 15 minutes. Drain.

Using a fork, mix the flours, caraway seeds, baking soda, salt, and raisins in a large bowl, and, with a fork, mix in enough buttermilk for the mixture to moisten.

Gather the dough into a ball and turn it out onto a floured surface. Knead the dough for a few minutes. You want the dough to keep its shape, but take care not to overwork it, or it will turn tough. Once it is smooth and clings together, stop kneading.

Form the dough into a round about 2-inches / 5-centimeters high and place it on the baking sheet. Using a butter knife, cut a 1-inch / 2.5-centimeter-deep cross into the dough, cutting almost to the edge. Bake for 30 minutes, or until the bread is golden brown and sounds hollow when tapped with your finger. Store in a breadbox or an airtight container for up to 5 days.

TRADITIONAL TREACLE BREAD

WHEN I'M ASKED TO ADVISE BEGINNERS on what recipes to start with, I tell them, "Start with something you can manage, and that will turn out well, like soda bread or treacle bread." Back when my niece Gemma was a young girl, I thought I'd teach her to cook. She told me she didn't like to because it dirtied the kitchen! I got her started with her first soda bread. Next, we tackled Treacle Bread, the dark-colored soda bread flavored with dark treacle, which, to those of you unfamiliar, is a bit like blackstrap molasses. Dark treacle both sweetens and adds a bitter, distinctive flavor to this basic bread, and like Guinness is a unique, particular taste beloved of the Irish. Inside of 10 minutes, Gemma had done a stellar job and had a fine loaf to pop in the oven. Just as important as the measuring and the mixing is cleaning as you go, and we worked as if we were in a restaurant kitchen. Today, she's not only a great cook, she leaves no mess, and I daresay that pleases her mum as much as do the delicious treats my niece serves.

MAKES
6 TO 8 SERVINGS

2½ cups / 300 grams all-purpose flour, plus more for dusting

½ teaspoon salt

½ teaspoon granulated sugar

1¼ cups / 300 milliliters buttermilk, plus more as needed

3 tablespoons dark treacle, warmed (if you can't find treacle, you can use 2 tablespoons molasses plus 1 tablespoon honey)

Preheat the oven to 400°F / 200°C and lightly flour a baking sheet.

In a large mixing bowl, combine the flour, salt, and sugar and stir lightly with a fork. Make a well in the center of the dry ingredients, using your hand. In a separate bowl, mix the buttermilk and treacle together and whisk. Pour the buttermilk mixture into the well of the dry ingredients and mix quickly with a large fork to form a soft dough. If the dough seems too stiff, you can add a bit of buttermilk, a very small amount at a time, taking care not to make the dough too wet or sticky.

Turn out the dough onto a lightly floured surface and knead briefly, taking care not to over-work it. Form it into a round that will fit onto your prepared baking sheet. Flatten the dough slightly before pressing it onto the prepared baking sheet. Cut a shallow cross on the top, extending almost to the edges, and bake for about 30 minutes, or until the round sounds hollow when tapped. Let cool on a cooling rack. Store in a breadbox or in an airtight tin for up to 5 days.

NOEL'S
GLUTEN-FREE BREAD

MY FIRST RULE OF HOSPITALITY is to put guests at their ease. When serving meals, one of the most generous things a host can do is to make sure each and every person has something delicious to eat that suits both taste and dietary needs. I like to offer alternatives when guests can't eat like the rest of the crowd. Sometimes, these tasty "specialty" offerings beckon to the larger curious population. Who doesn't occasionally order a kosher or vegetarian meal on an airplane, even when we don't face restrictions? It's fun to try something new!

That's how I feel about this bread. If you're looking for yeasty white bread, you'll be disappointed. But, if you're looking for a different taste and texture, and you believe that variety is the spice of life, rotating the grains from which you make your breads can turn dull sandwiches into a culinary adventure.

MAKES
ONE 9 X 5-INCH / 23 X 7-CENTIMETER LOAF

1½ cups / 200 grams brown rice flour

1½ cups / 200 grams potato flour

3.5 ounces / 100 grams soy flour

1 teaspoon salt

1 (¼-ounce / 7-gram) package active dry yeast

1½ teaspoons honey

1½ teaspoons extra-virgin olive oil

1¾ cups / 400 milliliters hot, but not boiling, water

Butter, for buttering pan

1 teaspoon baking soda

2 teaspoons cream of tartar

In a large mixing bowl, sift together the rice, potato, and soy flours with the salt. Scoop one quarter of the mixture into a separate bowl and set aside. Stir the yeast into the greater mixture left in the bowl and make a well in the center, using your hand. Add the honey, olive oil, and hot water to the well, and stir by hand until you have a smooth, thick batter. Cover the bowl with plastic wrap and allow it to rest it in a warm place for 30 minutes to activate the yeast.

Preheat the oven to 400°F / 200°C. Butter a 9 x 5-inch / 23 x 7-centimeter loaf pan and set it aside.

Using a fork, lightly mix the baking soda and cream of tartar with the reserved flour mixture, then sift it on top of the yeast batter. Stir gently until all the ingredients combine, forming a soft dough. Turn the batter into the prepared loaf pan. It will be quite wet. Bake for 25 to 30 minutes, or until firm, crisp, and golden brown. Turn out onto a cooling rack to cool. Slice and serve when cooled, or store in a breadbox or airtight tin for up to 3 days.

DULSE BREAD

DULSE, ALSO KNOWN AS DILLISK, DULCE, sea lettuce flakes, and *creathnach*, is a red algae that grows along the northern coasts of the Atlantic and Pacific oceans, where it's used as a traditional food. Locals in Northern Ireland gather it for home use, as it is free and plentiful. Dulse can be found throughout the country, for the picking or at markets, and it is traditionally sold at the Ould Lammas Fair in Ballycastle.

Commercially available dried dulse (usually sold in the U.S. among Asian ingredients in grocery stores and health-food or whole food markets) is eaten as is for snacking, or is ground into flakes or a powder. Many now tout it for its health-giving properties, as it's high in minerals and vitamins and packed with fiber. As a side dish, or an ingredient in baked goods, dulse is a widely popular food in Ireland and, along with Guinness, is often given credit for the long lives and twinkling eyes of its inhabitants.

MAKES
ONE 8 x 4-INCH / 20 x 10-CENTIMETER LOAF

8 tablespoons (1 stick) / 113 grams butter, melted,
plus more for buttering pan

2 tablespoons dulse, finely chopped

4 medium-size eggs

1 large carrot, peeled and grated

1 small zucchini, peeled and grated

¼ cup / 50 grams granulated sugar

½ teaspoon salt

2 cups / 250 grams all-purpose flour

¼ teaspoon baking powder

Preheat the oven to 275°F / 140°C. Butter an 8 x 4-inch / 20 x 10-centimeter loaf pan. Place the chopped dulse into a fine-mesh strainer and soak in a bowl of warm water for 10 minutes. Once soaked, pat it dry with a clean tea towel.

In a large mixing bowl, combine the dulse, eggs, carrot, zucchini, sugar, butter, and salt. Fold in the flour and baking powder, then turn the mixture into the prepared loaf pan.

Bake for about 50 minutes, or until a skewer inserted into the middle comes out clean. Once baked, set the entire pan on a cooling rack to cool for 30 minutes. Once cooled, turn out the loaf on the rack and allow it to cool fully before slicing. Store in a breadbox or an airtight tin for up to 5 days.

GUINNESS AND BACON
BREAD

WHEN YOU WANT FRESH, SAVORY BREAD for a winter's evening meal but you're short on time, this loaf fits the bill. It's almost a meal in itself. I like to serve it with puréed soups, such as butternut squash or potato and leek.

MAKES
ONE 9 x 5-INCH / 23 x 7-CENTIMETER LOAF

Bacon grease, to grease the pan
(or olive oil if you don't have it on hand)

8 ounces / 230 grams Irish streaky rashers or meaty sliced bacon

3 cups / 360 grams all-purpose flour

1 tablespoon dark brown sugar, packed

1 tablespoon baking powder

1 (12-ounce / 360-milliliter) bottle Guinness

4 tablespoons (½ stick) / 60 grams butter, melted

Preheat the oven to 375°F / 190°C. Grease a 9 x 5-inch / 23 x 7-centimeter loaf pan.

Fry half of the bacon in a skillet until it's crispy, then set it aside, allowing it to drain in a single layer on top of sheets of brown paper (draining on a paper towel will make it soggy). Reserve the bacon grease in the pan.

In a bowl, sift together the flour, sugar, and baking powder. Stir in the reserved bacon grease and the Guinness and stir well. Stir in the fried bacon crumbles and melted butter.

Chop the remainder of the uncooked bacon into very small pieces and sprinkle them on top of the raw loaf. Bake it for 40 to 45 minutes, until puffed and golden. Let cool slightly before removing from the pan, then turn out onto a cooling rack to cool slightly more. Slice and serve warm, or store in the refrigerator for up to 5 days, warming in the oven or toasting before serving.

WALNUT AND CHEDDAR LOAF

THIS SAVORY LOAF IS WELL AND TRULY IRISH. It's hearty, earthy, dense, and offers just the slightest hint of bitterness: It's not bread for the faint of heart, and that's probably why it's beloved of my people. It comforts with its wholesomeness while offering a subtle tang from the flavors of the Cheddar and the mustard. This bread will linger in the memories of the guests who eat it in your home.

MAKES
ONE 8 x 4-INCH / 20 x 10-CENTIMETER LOAF

---

6 tablespoons (¾ stick) / 85 grams unsalted butter,
at room temperature, plus more for buttering pan

1½ cups / 210 grams all-purpose flour

½ cup / 75 grams whole wheat flour

1 teaspoon dry mustard

¼ teaspoon salt

½ teaspoon baking powder

½ teaspoon baking soda

2 teaspoons granulated sugar

4 ounces / 113 grams Cheddar cheese, grated

½ cup / 60 grams chopped walnuts

2 large eggs

1 cup / 240 milliliters low-fat buttermilk

Recipe continues

Preheat the oven to 375°F / 190°C. Lightly butter an 8 x 4-inch / 20 x 10-centimeter loaf pan and set it aside.

Combine the flours, mustard, salt, baking powder, baking soda, and sugar in a food processor, then pulse the mixture 4 or 5 times. Add the butter to the bowl of the food processor and process for another 15 seconds, or until the mixture becomes coarse and crumby. Set aside 1½ tablespoons / 22 milliliters of the cheese and 1½ tablespoons / 22 milliliters of the walnuts for the topping and add the rest to the food processor, pulsing about 10 times, until mixed.

In a small bowl, beat the eggs with a fork, then add the eggs and the buttermilk to the mixture in the food processor, and process for 15 seconds, or until the dough is soft.

Pour the dough into the prepared pan and smooth the top with a rubber spatula that has been dipped in cold water. Top with the reserved cheese and walnuts. Bake for 40 to 45 minutes, or until a skewer inserted into the center comes out clean.

Remove from the oven and let cool in the pan on a cooling rack for 15 minutes, then tip out the cake and cool directly on the rack before slicing and serving while still warm, or store in a breadbox or airtight tin for up to 5 days.

NOEL'S WAY

• Spread slices with cream cheese and layer on good Irish smoked salmon.

• Toast thin slices and serve with savory omelets,
stuffed with garlic and bacon.

• Round out simple tomato soup with
warm buttered slices sprinkled with sea salt.

SMOKY BACON AND CHEESE BLOOMER

I LOVE BREAD. I LOVE EATING IT AND I LOVE MAKING IT. Bread is served at every meal in a traditional Northern Irish house, and I can't remember many meals where I've skipped it. I've taught bread baking master classes for RTÉ TV and at Castle Leslie. I can make fancy breads, and I can make simple. This classic loaf is called a bloomer. Bloomers are rolled up thick and long, and slashed across the top. As a loaf of this shape bakes, the cuts open up and "bloom," resulting in a very crisp crust. I like this one because it's easy to make, and very flavorful.

MAKES
1 LARGE LOAF

---

3 to 4 slices bacon or streaky rashers

1 teaspoon active dry yeast

⅔ cup / 150 milliliters warm, but not hot, water

⅔ cup / 150 milliliters cold water

4 ounces / 110 grams smoked Irish Blarney cheese
(or smoked Gouda, if you can't find it), grated

4 ounces / 100 grams Corleggy cheese (or ricotta salata,
if you can't find it), crumbled

3½ cups / 500 grams all-purpose flour,
plus more for shaping

½ cup / 50 grams whole wheat flour, plus more for dusting

2 teaspoons salt

Canola oil

Recipe continues

Fry the bacon in a skillet until it's crisp and dry it on layers of parchment or brown paper (paper towels will make it soggy). Once it's cool, crumble it into small pieces and set it aside.

In a large mixing bowl, combine the yeast with the warm water and allow it to proof for 10 minutes. Add the cold water, stir, then crumble in the smoked cheese and Corleggy cheese and mix well. Add the flours and salt, then mix everything to a smooth dough. Stir in the crisp bacon pieces, then cover the bowl with a clean tea towel and let it rise for 10 minutes.

Lightly oil a large mixing bowl, tip in the dough, and give it a light, 10-second knead. Let it rise for 10 minutes, then repeat this rise and light knead twice more at 10-minute intervals. Once the rise-and-knead cycle is complete, cover the bowl with the tea towel and let it rise for about an hour, or until it doubles in size.

Lightly flour a work surface and tip out the dough onto it. Pat the dough into a ½-inch / 1.3-centimeter-thick rectangle, then starting from the top right-hand corner, roll it up very tightly. Place the roll seam-side down on a baking sheet lined with parchment paper, cover with a clean tea towel, and let it rise for an hour.

Preheat the oven to 425°F / 220°C. Fill a heatproof baking dish halfway with water and set it on the lowest rack.

After the dough has risen for an hour, lightly rub flour on the loaf, using your hands, then make shallow, diagonal cuts along the top with a knife.

Put the baking sheet on the middle rack of the oven (above the pan of hot water) and bake for about 40 minutes, until the crust is golden brown. Tip it out onto a wire cooling rack and allow it to cool for 10 minutes, then slice and serve warm, or store in the refrigerator for up to 5 days, warming in the oven or toasting before serving.

PLAIN SCONES

IT'S HARD TO NAIL DOWN THE IMAGE of the perfect scone. Across Ireland, you'll find them in a variety of shapes and sizes, some made with buttermilk, some with cake flour, and some fashioned after soda bread. A fellow's opinion of the best type of scone likely boils down to what his granny set before him at the table. For my taste, the fluffier a scone is, the better. I like to eat plain scones—made with my recipe here—in the morning, savory scones with hearty and warming stews for midday dinner, and sweet scones with milky tea at teatime.

MAKES
8 SCONES

¾ cup / 175 milliliters milk

1 teaspoon vanilla extract

1 teaspoon freshly squeezed lemon juice

3 cups / 350 grams self-rising flour,
plus more for dusting

¼ teaspoon salt

1 teaspoon baking powder

6 tablespoons (¾ stick) / 85 grams cold unsalted butter,
cut into cubes

3 tablespoons granulated sugar

1 medium-size egg

Recipe continues

Preheat the oven to 400°F / 220°C, and put a baking sheet inside to warm.

Heat the milk in the microwave or in a small saucepan on the stove for about 30 seconds until it's warm but not hot, taking care not to scald or boil it. Add the vanilla and lemon juice to the milk and set it aside.

Combine the flour, salt, and baking powder in a large mixing bowl and mix lightly with a fork. Add the butter and rub it in to the dry ingredients with your fingers until the mixture looks like fine crumbs. Next, add the sugar to the crumb mixture and mix it in with your fingers.

Using your hand, make a well in the dry mixture, then add the milk mixture and combine it quickly with a fork—it will seem wet at first.

Scatter some flour onto a work surface and tip out the dough. Sprinkle the dough with a little more flour, then fold the dough over 2 or 3 times, until it's a little smoother. Pat the dough into a round about 1½-inches / 4-centimeters thick. Dip a 2-inch / 5-centimeter round biscuit cutter (smooth-edged cutters tend to cut more cleanly, giving a better rise) into some flour. Cut out 4 scones, then gently press the remaining dough into a round and cut 4 more scones.

In a small bowl, lightly beat the egg, then lightly brush the tops of the scones with the egg wash and place them carefully on the warm baking sheet. Bake for about 10 minutes, or until risen and golden on the top. Serve warm, or store in a breadbox or airtight tin for up to a week.

SIMPLE DROP SCONES

DROP SCONES ARE NOT WHAT THEY SOUND LIKE to American ears. Also known as Scotch Pancakes, they don't much resemble traditional scones. Instead, they're like hearty pancakes. These skillet-fried treats are easy to make but manage to look quite impressive, so this is a grand recipe to make with small children. Often, my nieces and nephews and I will cook these up together on Sunday mornings to treat the family. Even though drop scones are traditionally for breakfast, there's nothing stopping you from making a double batch, so you can top leftovers with ice cream and chocolate sauce once the sun goes down!

MAKES
1 DOZEN SCONES

2 cups / 240 grams all-purpose flour

2 tablespoons granulated sugar

1 teaspoon baking powder

Pinch of salt

2 large eggs

1 cup / 250 milliliters milk

2 tablespoons / 25 grams unsalted butter, melted

Canola oil, for oiling pan

Sift the flour, sugar, baking powder, and salt into a large mixing bowl and break the eggs into it. Start adding the milk gradually to the flour mixture, beating it as you go. Slowly add the rest of the milk and the melted butter, until the batter is smooth, thick, and creamy.

Lightly oil the bottom of a large, heavy skillet with the oil, then ladle in a dollop of batter, which should spread out to about the size of your palm. Allow the bottom to turn golden brown, about 2 minutes, then flip the scone with a spatula. Allow the other side to cook for 2 to 3 minutes, or until risen and browned, then serve right out of the pan warm, or cool them on a cooling rack and store them in an airtight tin for up to 5 days.

CHOCOLATE AND WALNUT SCONES

IF YOU ASK THEM THAT KNOW ME WELL, you'd hear that I'm a fairly clean-living sort. You'd also hear—so I may as well admit—that I'm a chocoholic. At the Lough Erne Resort, in Enniskillen, County Fermanagh, I offer these chocolate-walnut scones for afternoon tea in the Garden Hall. I won't tell you how many from my batches never make it onto a silver tray.

MAKES
10 SCONES

1¾ cups / 200 grams all-purpose flour,
plus more for dusting

¼ cup / 45 grams granulated sugar

2 teaspoons baking powder

½ teaspoon salt

8 tablespoons (1 stick) / 113 grams cold unsalted butter,
cut into ½-inch / 1.3-centimeter cubes

6 ounces / 175 grams dark, bittersweet
chocolate chips or chunks (1 cup)

¾ cup / 100 grams toasted coarsely broken walnuts

½ cup / 120 milliliters buttermilk

1 large egg

1½ teaspoons vanilla extract

Recipe continues

Preheat the oven to 375°F / 190°C.

In a large mixing bowl, stir together the flour, sugar, baking powder, and salt. Using your fingers, crumble the butter into the dry mixture until you have a rough crumb, like tiny marbles coated in sand, then add the chocolate and walnuts and stir until mixed.

In a medium bowl, stir together the buttermilk, egg, and vanilla. Slowly add the buttermilk mixture to the flour mixture and mix it with your hands, just until the dough comes together, taking care not to overwork it.

With lightly floured hands, tip out the dough onto a floured work surface and press it into a sheet about 1-inch / 2.5-centimeters thick.

Using a sharp-edged pastry cutter, or a drinking glass if you don't have one, cut circles in the dough. After you've cut as many as you can, pull the remaining dough together and repeat until all the dough is used.

Bake the scones on an ungreased baking sheet for 15 to 20 minutes, or until lightly browned on top. Place the baking sheet on a cooling rack for 5 minutes, then transfer the scones to the rack to cool slightly. Serve while still warm, or store in a breadbox or an airtight tin for up to 5 days.

ORANGE AND OAT SCONES

SIMPLE AND CHEERY, SCONES ARE ALWAYS WELCOME on a platter of treats for cream tea. They're not quite as upmarket as cookies, and not as workaday as bread rolls. Filling and sweet, these orange and oat scones stand alone as breakfast. Because they've whole wheat flour and a generous portion of oats, I can almost convince myself they're a health food!

MAKES
8 SCONES

---

2 cups / 240 grams whole wheat pastry flour

1 cup / 120 grams all-purpose flour, plus more for dusting

½ cup / 100 grams turbinado or raw sugar, plus more for sprinkling

2 teaspoons baking powder

1 teaspoon baking soda

8 ounces (2 sticks) / 225 grams cold unsalted butter, cut into small pieces

1 tablespoon freshly squeezed orange juice

2 cups / 180 grams old-fashioned rolled oats

Zest of 1 orange

1 cup / 240 milliliters buttermilk, plus more as needed

1.5 ounces / 45 grams dried currants

Preheat the oven to 350°F / 175°C. Line a baking sheet with parchment paper.

Combine the flours, turbinado sugar, baking powder, and baking soda in the bowl of a food processor. Add the butter and orange juice and pulse 15 to 20 times, until it forms a rough crumb, like tiny marbles coated in sand. If you don't have a food processor, mix the dry ingredients, then cut in the butter, using a pastry cutter or 2 butter knives pulled in opposite directions. Turn out the dough into a large mixing bowl, then lightly mix in the oats and orange zest. Stir in the buttermilk and currants until just moistened and then form the dough into a ball. If the dough is too crumbly to stick together, stir in more buttermilk, a spoonful at a time, taking care not to overwork the dough, or it will turn tough.

On a floured work surface, form the dough into an 8-inch / 20-centimeter round. Cut the round into 8 wedges and lay them onto the prepared baking sheet, spacing apart evenly. Sprinkle the tops with turbinado sugar.

Bake for 12 to 15 minutes, or until the bottoms are deeply golden. Serve warm, or store in a breadbox or an airtight tin for up to 5 days.

POTATO CINNAMON ROLLS

MY FAMILY ALWAYS "PUSHED OUT THE BOAT," as we say in Ireland, when my dad's brother, Monsignor John McMeel, would come to stay. My mother felt honored to have a man of the cloth among us, so she taught my brothers, sister, and me to lay out nicely folded napkins, wipe glasses before setting them out, and, of course, to offer the very best food.

Fragrant cinnamon rolls were just the thing for the mornings when he woke up at Rock Cottage. Their spicy-sweet smell filled the house in the morning before he'd say Mass to the multiple friends and relatives who'd come to hear it.

I love this recipe because the bit of potato changes the dough, making it less glutinous and feathery light. I can honestly say they're like a little slice of heaven.

MAKES
1 DOZEN ROLLS

1 small floury potato, peeled and cut into
1-inch / 2.5-centimeter chunks

1½ teaspoons salt, divided

4½ cups / 540 grams all-purpose flour,
plus more for kneading and shaping

1 cup / 200 grams granulated sugar

2¼ teaspoons active dry yeast

12 tablespoons (1½ sticks) / 173 grams unsalted butter,
at room temperature, divided, plus more for buttering pan

1 large egg

Canola oil, for oiling bowl

1 tablespoon ground cinnamon

2 cups / 200 grams confectioners' sugar

3 tablespoons whole milk

1 teaspoon vanilla extract

In a medium saucepan over high heat, cover the potato with water by ½ inch / 1.3 centimeters and add ½ teaspoon of the salt. Cover the saucepan, bring the water to a boil, and cook the potato until it is fall-apart tender, for 10 to 15 minutes.

Meanwhile, in a large mixing bowl, combine the flour, ½ cup / 100 grams of the granulated sugar, the yeast, and the remaining 1 teaspoon of salt.

Drain the potato, reserving 1¼ cups / 300 milliliters of the starchy cooking liquid, and put the potato through a ricer, discarding the skin. Add 4 tablespoons / 60 grams of the butter to the cooking liquid and stir until fully melted. When the butter mixture cools, add it to the dry ingredients along with the potato and the egg. Stir the batter with the dough hook attachment of a stand mixer on medium speed or by hand until smooth and fully combined.

Knead the dough with the dough hook or turn it out onto a lightly floured surface and knead it by hand until it feels smooth and elastic, adding small amounts of flour (only as necessary) to keep the dough from sticking.

Oil a large bowl with canola oil, place the dough inside, and turn it over to coat it lightly. Cover the bowl with a clean tea towel and let the dough rise for about an hour, or until it doubles in size.

Butter a 13 x 9-inch / 32 x 22-centimeter baking dish. Punch down the dough, then transfer it to a floured surface. Using a rolling pin, roll the dough into a rectangle about 8 x 12 inches / 20 x 30 centimeters. Spread the remaining 8 tablespoons / 113 grams of butter over the surface of the dough. Combine the remaining ½ cup / 100 grams of sugar with the cinnamon and sprinkle this mixture in a thin, even layer over the butter. Starting from one of the long sides, roll up the dough as tightly as possible. Cut the roll into 12 slices and lay them in the buttered pan, cut-side up.

Cover the pan with a clean tea towel and let the rolls rise for about an hour, until they're doubled in size.

While the rolls rise, preheat the oven to 350°F / 175°C. Slide them into the oven and bake for about 45 minutes, until golden brown on top. Meanwhile, in a large mixing bowl, whisk together the confectioners' sugar and milk, then whisk in the vanilla. Let the cinnamon rolls cool slightly, then drizzle on the icing and serve warm, or store in an airtight tin or plastic cake keeper for up to 3 days.

BUTTERNUT SQUASH AND DUBLINER CHEESE MUFFINS

IT'S NO COINCIDENCE THAT IRELAND IS KNOWN for its excellent dairy products. The abundant green grass that paints our isle emerald sustains the hungry cows that bless us with their creamy milk. Local cheese makers spin it into delicious Dubliner cheese, with the sharpness of Cheddar, the nuttiness of Swiss, and the bite of Parmesan. It's widely available around the world, but, in a pinch, feta would be good instead.

MAKES
1 DOZEN MUFFINS

---

1 tablespoon unsalted butter for buttering pan

2 cups / 255 grams of ½-inch / 1.3-centimeter cubes of butternut squash (from 1½ medium-size squash)

2 tablespoons canola oil

Salt and freshly ground black pepper

1 large handful baby spinach, chopped

1 tablespoon chopped fresh parsley

1 tablespoon chopped fresh sage

3 tablespoons chopped walnuts, toasted

5 ounces / 150 grams Dubliner cheese, cubed

2 teaspoons English mustard

2 large eggs, lightly beaten

¾ cup / 180 milliliters milk

2 cups / 240 grams all-purpose flour

1 tablespoon baking powder

1 teaspoon salt

Preheat the oven to 450°F / 230°C and put the rack in the high middle. Line a baking dish with foil. Butter a 12-hole muffin pan.

In a large mixing bowl, coat the squash with oil and toss. Add salt and pepper and toss again, then pour the squash into the prepared baking dish. Arrange so that there's space between the cubes and bake for 25 minutes, or until fork-tender. Set aside to let cool.

In a large mixing bowl, combine three quarters of the baked squash with the spinach, parsley, sage, walnuts, two-thirds of the cheese, and all of the mustard and mix well.

In a separate bowl, beat the eggs and milk together and add slowly to the squash mixture, stirring gently.

Sift the flour and baking powder onto the squash mixture and fold together, using a rubber spatula, taking care not to overwork the batter.

Spoon the mixture into the prepared pan, filling each hole three quarters full, top each muffin with a bit of the reserved baked squash and remaining Dubliner cheese. Bake for 20 minutes, or until the tops and sides of the muffins are lightly browned and the muffins have set. Let the entire pan cool on a cooling rack for 10 minutes, then turn out the muffins onto the rack to cool slightly before serving, or store in the refrigerator for up to 5 days, warming in the oven before serving again.

HERB AND ONION FOCACCIA

ASK ME WHAT I REMEMBER MOST about any given trip abroad, and I'll describe the local bread. It's amazing what something so simple can convey about a region's people, customs, and terrain. The local milk, the strains of wheat, and the traditional spices of a place give a dialect to one of humanity's most basic foods. From an early age, I had the privilege of experiencing the cuisines of other cultures through travel. As an All-Ireland Championship Irish Dancer, I experienced the joy of eating my way through Hungary, Italy, Germany, Scotland, Wales, and the United States. I like this loaf as a nod to central Italy, with my Irish fingerprints all over it.

MAKES
8 TO 10 SERVINGS

4½ cups / 540 grams all-purpose flour, plus more for dusting

2¼ teaspoons instant yeast,
or 1 (¼-ounce / 7-gram) package active dry yeast

4 tablespoons olive oil, divided,
plus more for bowl, pan, and drizzling

Pinch of salt

1 cup / 240 milliliters warm, not hot, water

1 medium-size yellow onion, thinly sliced

1 tablespoon coarse sea salt

1 medium-size tomato, thinly sliced

In the bowl of a stand mixer, combine the flour, yeast, 2 tablespoons of the olive oil, and the salt on medium speed. Add the water, and, using the dough hook, knead until you have a soft dough ball. Transfer the dough to an oiled bowl, cover it with a clean tea towel, and allow it to rise for about an hour, or until it doubles in size.

Heat the remaining 2 tablespoons of olive oil in a large, heavy skillet over low heat. Add the onion, cover, and cook, stirring occasionally, for about 20 minutes, until the onion is golden brown.

Tip out the dough onto a floured surface, and knead it gently. Shape the dough into a round no more than ¾-inch / 2-centimeters thick and place it on an oiled baking sheet.

Using your fingertips, press pits into the surface of the flattened dough, making it look like a bumpy pizza crust. Drizzle the round with olive oil and sprinkle it generously with sea salt. Push the caramelized onion into the pits and cover the surface with tomato slices. Cover the loaf with a clean tea towel and allow it to rise for 30 minutes.

Meanwhile, preheat the oven to 400°F / 200°C. Bake the bread for 10 to 15 minutes, until puffy and browned on top. Tip the loaf out of the pan, and serve it warm or let it cool on a cooling rack. Store in a breadbox or a brown paper bag on the counter for up to 2 days.

NOEL'S WAY

- Top with sausage crumbles and shredded cheese and broil
until browned, for a special pizza.

- Serve at room temperature with cold slices of mozzarella and thin-sliced salami,
for an open-faced Italian sandwich. Top with oil and vinegar.

- Cut it into soldiers, and serve with my Easiest Garlic Oil (page 134)
for top-shelf breadsticks.

CHAPTER THREE

CONDIMENTS, DRESSINGS, AND KETCHUPS

KEEP RUNNING TILL YOU CROSS
THE FINISH LINE

At Rock Cottage, my parents taught us kids that no job is finished until it's finished. These words were never said, but the idea was modeled daily.

A skilled stonemason, my father left standing monuments to this idea in the form of walls and buildings. Almost meditative in his work, he sparked an idea, planned it out, and toiled without stopping. As the Irish say, "A castle is built a stone at a time." With him, when a thing was done, it was truly done. He wasn't a man to leave loose ends. My mother is the same way. Even with six children and a husband to care for, she didn't skip steps or fall short. Pies were topped with artistic vents or pretty latticework. Napkins were ironed. She didn't go to bed until the last guest was tucked in tight.

I owe my success as a chef to the knowledge and practice of this principle. By working in top-class restaurants from Chez Panisse to the Watergate Hotel, to Castle Leslie, I've learned how to master cheffy techniques and to present food in refined, sophisticated ways. That said, I'll never forget the field I was foaled in. Basics must be the best. After that, it comes down to the last detail: the right herb to flavor croutons for soup, a spun-sugar cage to top a pudding, a ramekin of homemade salsa to flank blackened monkfish. It's a matter of showing care up to the finishing touch, including pairing the perfect condiment with a simple dish to turn it into something special without gilding the lily.

MY GREEN PASTE

IN PAST DECADES, PEOPLE SCOFFED when they heard the words "Irish cuisine," joking about boiled meat and unadorned potatoes. I'm not going to deny that I like a bit of plain farm-style comfort food, but the chefs (and home cooks!) of Ireland have embraced world cuisine. Between the influence of the diverse immigrants who've made this land their adopted home and tips and tricks gleaned from the Internet, all of our tables are globally inclined. Here's a spicy sauce I call "My Green Paste." I like to think of it as a condiment without borders.

MAKES ABOUT
2 CUPS / 480 MILLILITERS PASTE

1 large chile pepper (I suggest a serrano if you like heat,
or a jalapeño if you like it slightly milder)

10 to 15 tomatillos

2 tablespoons olive oil for sprinkling

½ large white onion, chopped

1 garlic clove, chopped

Juice of 2 limes

¼ cup / 60 grams chopped fresh cilantro leaves

1 teaspoon salt

1 teaspoon freshly ground black pepper

1 ripe avocado, peeled, pitted, and quartered

Holding the chile pepper in heatproof tongs, pass it back and forth through the flame on your stove's gas ring until the flesh is charred, then place the whole pepper in a resealable plastic bag. Allow it to steam until the skin is soft and can be rinsed off under running water. Rinse carefully, pulling off the blackened skin, then remove the seeds, using a paring knife, and chop the chile pepper finely.

Preheat the broiler on high. In a large saucepan half-full of boiling water immerse the tomatillos, blanching them, working in batches if necessary. Strain in a colander, and, once cool, remove the green skins with your hands. Cut the tomatillos in half and arrange them cut-side up on a baking sheet lined with foil. Drizzle them with the olive oil. Roast them under the broiler for 5 to 7 minutes, until they are slightly caramelized.

In a blender or food processor, whizz the tomatillos, chile pepper, onion, and garlic until the mixture is smooth. Add the lime juice, cilantro, salt, black pepper, and avocado. Pulse until smooth, then ladle the mixture into clean jars and store in the refrigerator for up to 2 days.

RHUBARB KETCHUP

HARDY AND HEALTHFUL, THIS STUNNING GARNET and emerald gift of nature is a useful early crop. Tradition tells us to sweeten it and use it for jams, compotes, and pastry fillings. Given its natural astringency, however, there's no reason that rhubarb shouldn't take a starring role in savory fare.

No one will mistake this tangy and sweet sauce for the bottled tomato ketchup we've come to expect with our burgers and chips down at the pub. I wouldn't put it in the chutney camp, either. I like to think of it as a delicious cross between a marmalade, a ketchup, and a steak sauce. Unique and flavorful!

MAKES ABOUT
1½ CUPS / 350 MILLILITERS KETCHUP

---

2 tablespoons / 25 grams salted butter

2 cups / 300 grams rhubarb,
chopped into ½-inch / 1.3-centimeter pieces

½ small onion, chopped finely

2 garlic cloves, peeled and minced

2 tablespoons light brown sugar, packed

2 tablespoons red wine vinegar

2 tablespoons tomato paste

2 tablespoons olive oil

Pinch of freshly ground black pepper

In a small, heavy-bottomed saucepan, melt the butter. Add the rhubarb and stir until the rhubarb pieces soften. Add the onion and garlic and sauté with the rhubarb pieces for about 2 minutes, allowing them to sweat, taking care not to overbrown.

Add the sugar, vinegar, tomato paste, olive oil, and pepper and cook over medium heat for 10 minutes, or until the rhubarb begins to disintegrate, falling apart easily when mashed with the back of a spoon. Reduce the mixture until it's the consistency of a commercial ketchup. Remove the pan from the heat and set aside, allowing it to cool for about 30 minutes. Once the mixture is cool, purée it until smooth, using a stick blender or in the carafe of a standing blender. Once puréed, ladle into clean jars and store in the refrigerator for up to 4 weeks.

GREEN TOMATO KETCHUP

YOU KNOW THE OLD SAYING, "If life gives you lemons, make lemonade." That's how I feel about green tomatoes. Sure, I could try all the tricks to ripen them: cut half a ripe tomato and set it under my plants; put the green ones in a paper bag with a ripe apple; harvest regularly, taking care not to pick them before they've matured and are sure never to ripen.

Rather than have a zebra change its stripes, I like to appreciate nature's gifts for what they are. When it became clear to my mum and dad that my twin brothers, Owen and John, who'd endured a difficult birth, wouldn't walk, talk, and learn like other children, they changed their expectations. Instead of fretting over fitting them into a mold or pattern, they found ways to help my brothers develop what is unique, special, and precious about them. Our parents taught the rest of us to appreciate Owen and John for exactly what they are. Every day with them has been a gift.

So, when I hold a green tomato in my hand, I don't waste hours wishing it were a red one. Instead, I focus on the firmness of its flesh, the pale yellow-green hue of its skin, the slightly tart flavor and the almost grassy aroma. Green tomatoes are simply different than red ones: not better, not worse. Different.

MAKES ABOUT
2 PINTS / 950 MILLILITERS KETCHUP

¾ cup / 180 milliliters cider vinegar

2 tablespoons mustard seeds

1 tablespoon allspice berries

2 teaspoons coriander seeds

2 whole cloves

1 teaspoon dried red chile flakes

1 mild chile pepper (such as a banana pepper),
seeded and minced

1 bay leaf

2 sticks cinnamon

2 medium-size white onions, chopped

1 stalk celery, chopped

5 sweet peppers, seeded and minced

2 tablespoons olive oil

3 garlic cloves, peeled and minced

8 medium-size green tomatoes, chopped

½ cup / 90 grams light brown sugar, packed

1 tablespoon salt

1 tablespoon freshly ground black pepper

1 tablespoon Tabasco sauce

In a small saucepan, combine the vinegar, mustard seeds, allspice, coriander seeds, cloves, chile flakes, chile pepper, bay leaf, and cinnamon sticks and bring to a boil. Cook for 1 minute, then remove from the heat and set aside.

In a large, heavy-bottomed pot over medium heat, fry the onions, celery, and sweet peppers in the olive oil until soft, adding the garlic for the last minute of cooking, being careful not to overbrown it. Add the tomatoes, and the brown sugar, and 1 cup / 240 milliliters of water to the vegetables and continue to cook over medium heat, stirring regularly, until the tomatoes soften and fall apart and the mixture starts to get bubbly and foamy. Lower the heat to low and simmer the mixture for an hour, stirring occasionally.

Using a colander with large holes, strain out the large pieces from the now-cool vinegar mixture and discard. Pour the vinegar mixture into the pot that contains the tomato mixture. Purée the sauce with a stick blender, or blend or process in small batches in a blender or food processor. Continue to cook the thinned sauce for another 30 minutes, or until you like the consistency. Add the salt, pepper, and Tabasco sauce.

Ladle into hot, sterilized jars (see page 17) and store in the refrigerator for up to 4 weeks.

SPICY TOMATO AND DILL KETCHUP

IN THE LATE SUMMER BEFORE THE HECTIC MONTHS leading up to the holidays, I love to fill my kitchen with the fresh, earthy smell of this sauce: It's my twist on the universally loved condiment that is tomato ketchup. It's inexpensive if you work when the tomatoes are abundant (also when they're at their flavorful best!) and it's so much tastier and more nuanced than bottled commercial ketchup.

MAKES ABOUT
2 PINTS / 950 MILLILITERS KETCHUP

---

6 large ripe tomatoes, peeled and chopped

1 large yellow onion, diced

3 large garlic cloves, crushed

3 teaspoons black peppercorns

3 teaspoons mustard seeds

3 allspice berries

3 whole cloves

2 teaspoons celery seeds

2 teaspoons smoked paprika

½ teaspoon ground chile pepper

2 bay leaves

1 small bunch fresh dill, chopped

½ cup / 90 grams brown sugar, packed

½ cup / 120 milliliters white vinegar

Juice of 1 lemon

1 teaspoon salt

Recipe continues

In a large stockpot, simmer the tomatoes, onion, garlic, peppercorns, mustard seeds, allspice berries, cloves, celery seeds, paprika, chili powder, and bay leaves for 1 to 2 hours, stirring occasionally, or until the liquid has reduced by about one-third.

Remove the pot from the heat, remove the bay leaves, and allow the mixture to cool briefly. Blend until smooth directly in the stockpot, using a stick blender, or blend or process in small batches in a blender or food processor. Press the puréed tomato mixture through a wire-mesh strainer or fine sieve, extracting as much juice as you can, and transfer the juice back to your stockpot.

Add the dill, brown sugar, vinegar, lemon, and salt, and cook the mixture over medium heat for another 75 to 90 minutes, until it is the consistency of a commercial tomato ketchup. Ladle into hot, sterilized jars (see page 17) and store in the refrigerator for up to 4 weeks.

SPICY DIPPING MUSTARD

TANGY, SPICY, AND LOW IN CALORIES, this sauce adds loads of flavor to any simple dish. I serve it in ramekins alongside pretzels, crackers, and raw vegetables for a waist-conscious cocktail-hour offering. For those who don't mind a bit of decadence, I suggest pouring it over a block of cream cheese, Brie, or other soft, mild cheese and serving with warm rounds of baguette. If you like your mustard really hot, eat this on the sooner side, as the pungency lessens the longer it keeps. For a smoother taste, let it rest for a week.

MAKES ABOUT
1 CUP / 240 MILLILITERS MUSTARD

6 tablespoons / 45 grams mustard seeds

½ cup / 60 grams dry mustard

¼ cup / 60 milliliters cider vinegar

½ cup / 120 milliliters white wine

2 teaspoons salt

2 tablespoons honey

2 tablespoons prepared horseradish

2 tablespoons chopped fresh parsley

2 tablespoons chopped fresh thyme leaves

Grind the mustard seeds for a few seconds in a spice or coffee grinder, or by hand with a mortar and pestle until coarsely ground. Pour the ground seeds into a large mixing bowl, add the dry mustard, and stir lightly with a fork.

Add the vinegar and wine, then stir again lightly. Add the salt, honey, horseradish, parsley, and thyme and mix well. When everything is incorporated, ladle the mixture into clean jars and store in the refrigerator for up to a month.

TRADITIONAL WHOLE-GRAIN MUSTARD WITH STOUT

MADE IN THE TRADITIONAL MANNER, this is not your everyday yellow mustard. This piquant mustard offers the aroma of roasted barley from the Guinness, along with the sharp tang of the vinegar. Fans of strong and unusual mustards will appreciate the substantial texture of this condiment, along with the pleasant pop of the mustard seeds.

MAKES ABOUT
2 CUPS / 480 MILLILITERS MUSTARD

⅔ cup / 120 grams mustard seeds,
yellow and brown mixed

2 teaspoons salt

½ cup / 120 milliliters Guinness stout

2 tablespoons honey

¼ cup / 60 milliliters cider vinegar

1 teaspoon turmeric

1 teaspoon coarsely ground black pepper

Grind half of the mustard seeds for a few minutes in a blender, food processor, or spice mill, or by hand with a mortar and pestle. Be careful if you are using a mortar and pestle: If you go too fast, the mustard seeds will spring and fly from the bowl. Slowly does it.

In a medium mixing bowl, combine the ground mustard, whole mustard seeds, and the salt. Add the Guinness and honey and stir well. Cover and let sit for 30 minutes. Mix in the vinegar, turmeric, and pepper. Pour into a clean jar and allow it to rest in the refrigerator for at least a week or 2 before eating.

NOEL'S WAY

• Use as a sauce for slow-cooked brisket, done in a Dutch oven with a root veg.

• Whiz 1 tablespoon with a cup of cream cheese in a food processor,
and serve as a cracker spread.

• Stir a little into a pot of mashed potatoes, and serve
as a side dish with juicy pot roast.

HONEY MUSTARD
DIPPING SAUCE

WARM AND SPICY, THIS DIPPING SAUCE served with practically any food holds its own against a fortifying mug of dark stout or ale on a snowy evening. Complex, with sweet flavors from the honey and orange juice vying against the tart tang of the vinegar and surprising heat from cayenne and black pepper, this sauce livens up any plain food that can serve as a canvas for its color. I strongly suggest pairing it with stick-to-the-ribs foods, such as mozzarella sticks, pretzels, or simple farmhouse cheeses on crackers, or smearing it on a pork roast or hen before a slow oven-roasting. Bottled in an attractive jar, tied up with a ribbon, this sauce makes a welcome hostess gift in lieu of the expected bottle of wine or box of chocolates.

MAKES ABOUT
1 CUP / 240 MILLILITERS SAUCE

¾ cup / 180 milliliters smooth Dijon mustard

1 tablespoon red wine vinegar

1 tablespoon freshly squeezed orange juice

1 tablespoon honey

2 teaspoons prepared horseradish

1 garlic clove, finely minced

Pinch of cayenne pepper

Pinch of salt

Pinch of freshly ground black pepper

Combine the mustard, vinegar, orange juice, honey, horseradish, garlic, cayenne, salt, and black pepper in a large mixing bowl. Using a whisk, mix thoroughly until the sauce is uniform and has a smooth consistency. Pour into a clean jar, and store the refrigerator for up to 1 week.

SIMPLE CHINESE DRESSING

I LIKE THE PLAIN ELEGANCE OF THIS DRESSING and like to have it on hand for marinating chicken, to top crisp lightly cooked vegetables, and for green salads. It's light and earthy at the same time and lends depth and complexity to plain vegetables. Being Irish, I love it atop raw shredded cabbage as a side salad. If you're a fan of heat, you can add ½ teaspoon of dried chile flakes to spice things up.

MAKES ABOUT
2½ CUPS / 600 MILLILITERS DRESSING

1½ cups / 350 milliliters Asian sesame oil

½ cup / 120 milliliters rice wine vinegar

1 tablespoon soy sauce

1 garlic clove, minced

2 teaspoons sesame seeds, measured whole, then crushed

In a medium bowl, whisk together the oil, vinegar, soy sauce, garlic, and crushed sesame seeds, then decant the sauce into a clean bottle or jar and store in the refrigerator for up to 2 days.

FLAVORED AND INFUSED
OILS AND VINEGARS

Vinegars

To add fresh, bold flavors to ordinary salad dressings and marinades, homemade herb- and fruit-infused vinegars offer a lovely base. These aromatic concoctions are gorgeous to look at and delicious to eat. Inexpensive and simple to make, they're a welcome addition to your own pantry shelf and a welcome treat when given as gifts to the adventurous home cooks in your circle.

For fresh and tangy flavors, craft them with bright and sunny fruits, such as cranberries and raspberries, or the peel of oranges, grapefruits, or lemons. For deeper and more complex nuances, try fresh herbs and fragrant spices.

Homemade infused vinegars are generally considered safe to use without processing because vinegar naturally cures foods, contains antimicrobial properties, and prevents the growth of such bacteria as the one that causes botulism. To ensure safety, vinegar solutions must be 5 percent acidity or higher—the formula of those commonly sold in supermarkets.

Once you've made and mixed a favorite flavor combination, store your vinegar in the refrigerator or a cool, dark place. If properly prepared, flavored vinegars will remain tasty for up to 3 months in cool room storage and 6 months in the refrigerator. Use your common sense: If you see signs of mold or fermentation (such as bubbling, cloudiness, or sliminess) in your flavored vinegar, throw it away and make a fresh batch.

Oils

Everyone loves a starter of Italian bread dragged through a dish of garlicky, herbed olive oil. And we can have our cake, and eat it, too, as long as we follow some safe-handling guidelines.

All things grown in soil can harbor bacteria, and that bacteria can thrive in oil. If you prepare and store flavored oils properly, however, you can enjoy them safely. Make infused oils fresh and refrigerate them for use within two days. You can freeze them on the first day if you want them to last longer. Ingredients dried in a food dehydrator are the safest bet as infusions. Fully dried tomatoes in oil are less of a safety concern than are fresh items because the pH of tomatoes is generally 4.6 or lower, and because the low water content discourages growth of botulism. Fully dried herbs are similarly safe, because of their low water level. Even with fully dried tomatoes and herbs, it's wise to follow the cold-storage guidelines for all infused oils.

Any oils exposed to air, sunlight, and heat can become rancid. Although rancidity won't make you sick in the short run, over time it can clog arteries and harm healthy cells. Be aware that rancidity and toxic bacteria don't travel hand in hand. Botulism can be present without the taint of off odors, colors, or smells. Similarly, oil can be rancid without the presence of bacteria, but as rancidity signals improper storage, it should signal you to toss the oil.

CRANBERRY VINEGAR

as a tangy meat marinade or drizzled over grilled poultry or chops. Once you've infused it, try cooking it down slowly over very low heat to make a reduction.

MAKES ABOUT
2 CUPS / 480 MILLILITERS VINEGAR

3 ounces / 80 grams dried cranberries

2 tablespoons granulated sugar

¾ cup / 180 milliliters red wine vinegar

Pinch of salt

In a saucepan, combine the cranberries, sugar, vinegar, and salt with ¾ cup / 180 milliliters of water and bring the mixture to a boil. Lower the heat to medium-low and simmer for 5 minutes. Transfer the sauce to a large, nonreactive mixing bowl and let cool.

In a blender, purée the ingredients on high speed. Transfer the mixture to a clean jar, cover tightly, and refrigerate for 2 weeks, gently shaking the jar every few days to distribute the flavors.

Strain the vinegar through a fine-mesh sieve, and then through a colander lined with a coffee filter. Decant the vinegar into a clean bottle and store it in the refrigerator for up to 2 months.

SAVORY HERB AND GARLIC VINEGAR

THE DELICIOUS AROMA ALONE IS REASON ENOUGH to invest the few minutes it takes to make this vinegar, but it's the flavor that will lure you into making batch after batch. I like to pour a little into meat-and-vegetable stir-fries, with a small dash of olive oil as a healthy way to boost flavor while limiting fat.

MAKES
2 CUPS / 480 MILLILITERS VINEGAR

1 small bunch fresh basil

8 sprigs fresh thyme

4 sprigs fresh rosemary

2 cups / 500 milliliters Champagne vinegar

1 garlic clove, thinly sliced

Peel of 1 lemon, chopped

Pinch of salt

Thoroughly rinse the basil, thyme, and rosemary and then pat them dry with paper towels. Chop the herbs coarsely and set them aside.

In a nonreactive saucepan over low heat, warm the vinegar until hot but not simmering, then remove it from the heat. Combine the chopped herbs, garlic, lemon peel, and salt in a large glass jar. Pour in the hot vinegar and allow it to cool.

Cover the jar tightly and refrigerate for 2 weeks, gently shaking the jar every few days to distribute the flavors.

Strain the vinegar through a fine-mesh sieve, and then through a colander lined with a coffee filter. Decant the vinegar into a clean bottle or jar and store it in the refrigerator for up to 2 months.

EASIEST
GARLIC OIL

GARLIC WAS USED SPARINGLY IN IRISH RECIPES FOR CENTURIES, despite the fact that it grows well in most parts of the country. In fact, many old-fashioned recipes from our Isle call for no more than a quarter- or half-clove of garlic. In the past half-century or so, my country-men have come to embrace this humble but flavorful bulb, having been wooed by the world cuisines introduced by immigrants and the culinary revolution that's taken place through our formerly isolated island's connection through television and the Internet.

MAKES
1 CUP / 240 MILLILITERS OIL

1 large head garlic

1 cup / 240 milliliters extra-virgin olive oil

Separate the head into cloves. Using a broad, flat chef's knife, cut off the base and smash each clove. Peel the cloves.

Transfer the garlic to a medium saucepan, add the olive oil, and cook over medium-low heat until bubbles form around the cloves, 3 minutes.

Cover, lower the heat to low, and cook for 10 minutes. If the garlic begins to brown or the oil begins to smoke, remove the pan from the heat and allow it to cool for 10 minutes, then set it back over low heat and cook until golden.

Once golden, remove the pan from the heat and pour the mixture into clean jars, leaving a ½-inch / 1.3-centimeter headspace if you plan to freeze.

To store, refrigerate the mixture immediately and keep for no more than 2 days, or freeze for up to 6 months.

RASPBERRY AND MINT
VINEGAR

THIS FLAVOR COMBINATION WILL WAKE YOU UP with a pucker-up tang from raspberries and wine vinegar, balanced with the eye-opening herbal finish of mint. It pairs well with either sliced, raw onion or cooked, cubed beets as a marinade, turning them into delicious condiments to serve with barbecued meats, or spicy bean dishes. Or try it for deglazing a pan after frying lamb chops and serving it alongside the main course in a jug, for drizzling or dipping.

MAKES
2 CUPS / 480 MILLILITERS VINEGAR

2 cups / 480 milliliters white wine vinegar

2 cups / 250 grams fresh raspberries

15 fresh mint leaves, chopped coarsely

In a nonreactive saucepan over low heat, warm the vinegar until hot but not simmering, then remove it from the heat and set it aside.

Combine the berries and mint in a large glass jar. Pour in the hot vinegar, then set it aside to cool.

Cover the jar tightly and refrigerate for 2 weeks, gently shaking the jar every few days to distribute the flavors.

Strain the vinegar through a fine-mesh sieve, and then through a colander lined with a coffee filter. Decant the vinegar into a clean bottle and store it in the refrigerator for up to 2 months.

NOEL'S WAY
• Sprinkle over melons chunks and top with finely chopped mint,
a shake of sea salt, and a sprinkle of sugar.

• Chop a head of cabbage and a large carrot finely, and cover with this vinegar
and ½ cup of olive oil. Store in the fridge in a lidded container,
shaking daily, for a week. Serve salted.

• Combine with canned diced tomatoes, chopped onion, and ketchup
and use it as a marinade for pot roast.

LEMON-INFUSED OLIVE OIL

IN IRELAND, WE LOVE THE TASTE OF CITRUS FRUIT, and each Christmas I hear stories from the generation before me about how precious it was to receive an orange in the toe of a stocking. There was a time when cooking with lemons signified wealth, as our cool climate doesn't readily support the cultivation of the trees. Nowadays, lemons are quite common, but that doesn't stop us from pausing to delight in a glass of fresh-squeezed lemonade, or savoring the wedge that's served with a fillet of sweet Atlantic cod.

MAKES
1 CUP / 240 MILLILITERS OIL

2 lemons

1 cup / 240 milliliters olive oil

Sterilize a bottle or tall jar that holds slightly more than 1 cup / 240 milliliters (see page 17). Using a vegetable peeler or paring knife, carefully strip 1 lemon of its zest. Try to keep each strip long and wide, and avoid gathering any of the bitter white pith. Stuff zest strips into your bottle and set it aside.

Zest the second lemon and set it aside.

In a medium saucepan set over medium-high heat, slowly warm the olive oil until a few small bubbles start to form. If the oil starts smoking, remove the pan from the heat and allow it to cool for 10 minutes. Add the zest from second lemon to the warm olive oil, remove it from the heat, and let it steep for 30 minutes.

Using a wire-mesh strainer (and a funnel, if needed), carefully strain the lemon-infused oil over the uncooked strips of lemon zest into the bottle, making sure not to include any of the cooked lemon zest. Don't overfill, and try to leave a ½-inch / 1.3-centimeter headspace, if you plan to freeze the oil.

To store, refrigerate the oil for up to 1 week, or freeze for up to 6 months.

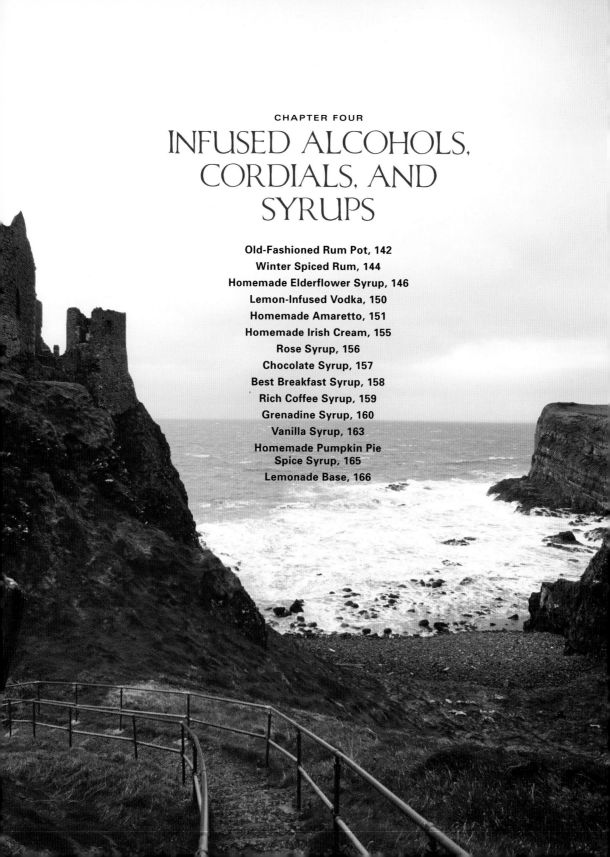

CHAPTER FOUR

INFUSED ALCOHOLS, CORDIALS, AND SYRUPS

TO HEALTH

"*S*láinte!*"

Pronounced "SLAWN-cha," it's what we say in Ireland when we toast one another with spiced rum or a glass of homemade Irish cream over ice. It means "health," and, honestly, I don't think there's a more important wish to make for another. After his ninety-four years of a rich and productive life, we lost my father this past fall. As we said to each other at the wake, "The longer you have him, the longer you want him."

The very bright side is that my father lived out his days in his own home, on his own land, with my mother, his deeply beloved wife, right up to the very end. He was fit and sharp to the last, and my family agrees that this was a tribute to the way he lived. He used his mind and body in his work. He ate simple, fresh foods garnered from the farm, and prepared by my mother's hands. He was grateful.

Health.

That's my toast to all holding this book.

"*Sláinte!*"

OLD-FASHIONED RUM POT

THIS AROMATIC RUM FEATURES FRUITY DEPTH and a spicy bite. Served straight up, on the rocks, or splashed in Coca-Cola, it's a showstopper and a definite walk off the beaten path compared to a pint or a glass of chardonnay. I recommend doubling and tripling the batches if you plan to give it as gifts.

MAKES
1 QUART / 950 MILLILITERS RUM POT

---

2 large apples, washed, cored, and cut into chunks

2 large pears, washed, cored, and cut into chunks

4 plums, washed, pitted, and cut into chunks

10 black peppercorns

10 whole cloves

5 cinnamon sticks

1 quart / 1 liter light or golden rum

If you have a large jar with a tight-fitting lid, combine the apples, pears, plums, peppercorns, cloves, cinnamon sticks, and rum in that. If not, combine all the ingredients in a very clean stockpot with a lid. Make sure that all the ingredients are covered with the spirits, as the alcohol is a preservative.

Allow the ingredients to infuse for 2 weeks in the refrigerator. After 2 weeks, strain the mixture through a colander and discard the solids.

Strain it again through a colander lined with cheesecloth to remove any fine sediment, and decant it into a clean glass jar. Store in a cool, dark place and use within 6 months, for peak flavor.

WINTER SPICED RUM

WARM UP YOUR WINTER'S GATHERINGS with a special latte, a fizzy soda-based cocktail, a grown-up cola, or a tea-and-lemon toddy. What's so special about those, you ask? The aromatic addition of homemade Winter Spiced Rum. I think it's just the thing when we're chilled to the bone and need some cheer.

MAKES ABOUT
1 QUART / 950 MILLILITERS SPICED RUM

1 vanilla bean, split lengthwise
and seeds scraped

1 slice orange zest,
about the size of your thumb

1 slice lemon zest,
about the size of your thumb

1 cinnamon stick

2 allspice berries

3 whole cloves

3 black peppercorns

⅛ teaspoon freshly grated nutmeg

1 slice fresh ginger, about the size of your thumb

1 quart / 1 liter light rum, such as Bacardi or Myers

If you have a very large jar, sealable with a two-part canning lid and rubber seal or cork, combine the vanilla bean, orange zest, lemon zest, cinnamon stick, allspice berries, cloves, peppercorns, nutmeg, ginger, and rum in that. If not, combine all the ingredients in a large, very clean stockpot with a lid. Make sure that all the ingredients are covered with the spirits, as the alcohol is a preservative.

Allow the ingredients to infuse for 2 weeks in the refrigerator. After 2 weeks, strain the mixture through a colander and discard the solids.

Strain it again through a colander lined with cheesecloth to remove any fine sediment, and decant it into a clean glass jar. Store in a cool, dark place and use within 6 months, for peak flavor.

NOEL'S WAY

• Warm the spiced rum on the stove, and serve in mugs
with lemon slices and cinnamon sticks.

• Heat equal parts apple cider and cranberry juice,
and serve it with a shot of the spiced rum.

• Scoop vanilla ice cream onto a slice of Cinnamon-Sugar Quick Bread Mix (page 270),
and drizzle with Winter Spiced Rum, warmed in a saucepan with
1 tablespoon of good-quality butter.

WINTER RUM AND GINGER

Want to drive away winter sluggishness?
Awaken your senses with this extra-snappy version of a Moscow Mule.

MAKES
1 SERVING

2 ounces / 60 milliliters Winter Spiced Rum

2.5 ounces / 75 milliliters ginger beer

Dash of aromatic bitters

Combine the Winter Spiced Rum, ginger beer, and aromatic bitters
over ice in a clear, glass tumbler, and stir briskly with a long spoon.

HOMEMADE
ELDERFLOWER SYRUP

WITH SUBTLE AND COMPLEX FLAVORS that are both floral and fruity, elderflower lends a celebratory, sophisticated feeling to nonalcoholic party drinks. Intrepid foragers should know that the bush is often found in abundance in abandoned lots and fields, and its blooms are ripe for your plucking. I love these flowers for their light, muscatlike scent. While growing up, it was easy for us to find fresh elderflowers during the short window when they bloomed. A word of caution: Avoid brownish or yellowish blossoms. They can emit a musky odor that smells worryingly of cat wee!

This recipe also works well with dried elderflowers. Nowadays dried elderflowers are easy to come by at natural food stores or in bulk bins, on the Internet, and at wine-making or home-brewing supply stores. Adding fizzy water to this syrup makes the perfect sparkling drink for the health-conscious who occasionally want to skip caffeine or alcohol, or for the mother-to-be at her own shower. It's also a nice way to honor the "designated drivers," those selfless souls at the party who surely deserve more than just plain sparkling water or commercial canned soda.

MAKES ABOUT
2 QUARTS / 2 LITERS SYRUP

20 to 25 elderflower umbels (the bunches that make up
one "flower" comprised of tiny flowers)

Zest and juice of 3 lemons

Zest and juice of 1 naval orange

4½ cups / 900 grams sugar

Working over a sink, give the elderflower plants a shake by sharply snapping your wrist and whacking the flowers on the bottom of the sink. This will help rid the plants of any dead leaves or clumps of dirt.

Place the flowers in a colander and gently rinse off the umbels, inspecting them for insects or debris and removing any that you find by picking them out with your fingers. Separate the small elderflower florets from their stems with kitchen scissors or using your hands. Collect them in a large glass bowl or other nonreactive container (do not use cast iron, copper, or aluminum). Add the citrus zest and juice to the bowl.

Combine 1 quart / 1 liter of water and the sugar in a large pot over high heat, and bring it to a boil while stirring constantly. Once the sugar has completely dissolved and the liquid turns syrupy, pour the hot syrup over the flowers in the bowl and stir.

Cover the bowl loosely with a clean tea towel, and let it rest at room temperature for 3 days. After 3 days, strain the mixture through a colander and discard the solids.

Return the strained syrup to a large pot and bring it to a boil over medium-high heat. Skim off any scum from the boiling mixture, using a slotted spoon. Strain the syrup through a colander lined with cheesecloth to remove any remaining fine sediment.

Decant the syrup into sterilized jars (see page 17), and store in the refrigerator for up to 4 weeks.

NOEL'S WAY

• Freeze the syrup in ice cube trays,
then transfer the cubes into resealable freezer bags to thaw
and enjoy in batches over the course of a year.

• Drizzle a tablespoon of syrup into white wine
or sparkling wine for a fragrant cocktail.

• Add a spoonful of syrup to heavy whipping cream
before whipping it for an aromatic dessert topping to use
with sorbet or angel food cake.

MAKE YOUR OWN
FLAVORED ALCOHOLS

Infusing spirits is a nice way to get flavor without the bulk of physical garnishes weighing down your drink. We refer to the flavor component that gets transferred from herbs, spices, and other foods as an essential oil. Essential oils don't break down in water. Therefore, the most concentrated flavors will suspend in alcohol even after the solids are long gone.

Vodka is an excellent candidate for infusing as it has an understated natural flavor of its own. If you like playing potion master, think about the basic flavors that complement sprits like whiskey and rum to create your own delicious concoctions.

Getting Started

STEP 1: **Choose a spirit**. Your base alcohol provides the foundational flavor for your infused spirit. Picking a smooth-tasting, middle-of-the-road-quality alcohol is a good idea. It's a waste of money to infuse top-quality spirits with flavorings, but the cheapest of the bunch are too harsh, and may have objectionable flavors that will compete with your add-ins. If you're not sure that you'll like a certain combination, work in micro-batches, or use less expensive spirits the first time out of the gate.

STEP 2: **Choose add-ins**. Most people start with herbs, spices, or fruit. Then branch out if you're bold. You could try coffee beans, cacao nibs, chile peppers, scraped vanilla beans, or shelled nuts. Make sure to use only fresh ingredients, and check them for mold, age spots, and dirt before plunging them into your alcohol.

STEP 3: **Combine**. Start with sterilized jars with tight-fitting lids. Mason jars work well. If you know you'll use a large batch of a particular blend, make it in a huge jar, as I do with my rum pot. If you want to make multiple flavors or if you are tentative about a taste, then you can always work with several smaller jars and make multiple flavors at once. Thoroughly wash fresh produce or pick over your ingredients, place them in sterilized jars (see page 17), and fill them with spirits. Make sure the ingredients are completely submerged, as alcohol is a natural preservative.

STEP 4: **Infuse.** Store your jar in a cool, dark place (I just chuck mine into the fridge) and shake it every couple of days to help the infusion along. Infusion time varies from 3 days to 2 weeks, depending on the strength or delicacy of the add-ins. You can taste-test at any point along the road.

STEP 5: **Strain and store.** Once the flavor peaks, remove the add-ins. I advise two strainings. For the first, use a fine-mesh wire strainer and discard the solid ingredients. Next, line a colander with a coffee filter or clean cheesecloth and strain out any remaining sediment. Decant the strained spirits into a sterilized jar (see page 17), store in a cool, dark place, and use within 6 months, for peak flavor.

Preparing Your Add-Ins

Soft berries: Remove leaves, wash, and leave whole.

Cranberries: Wash and score the skins with a paring knife.

Cinnamon and other spices: Use whole sticks, pods, and cloves, not ground spices. Rinse in a colander before using.

Pineapple, mango, and papaya: Wash, core or pit, and cut into chunks.

Citrus: Wash and slice thinly, discarding pips, or use only thick strips of zest with no pith.

Vanilla beans: Wash and cut lengthwise.

Coffee beans: Rinse in a colander, use whole. Do not use ground coffee.

Fresh herbs: Wash and use whole (stems and all).

Hot peppers: Wash and cut in half.

Cacao nibs: Rinse in a wire-mesh strainer, use whole.

LEMON-INFUSED VODKA

I COULD TASTE THE LEMON IN THE VODKA after a week but chose to leave it for three weeks before using. When I opened the jar lid, I was overwhelmed with the most gorgeous aroma of lemon filling the air. Completely intoxicating. The vodka takes on the most perfect shade of light yellow as well.

MAKES ABOUT
1 QUART / 950 MILLILITERS LEMON VODKA

1 quart / 950 milliliters vodka (choose a brand with a neutral flavor)

6 medium-size lemons, washed and cut into eighths

Combine the vodka and lemon pieces in a large jar and seal it tightly.

Store the jar in the refrigerator for 2 weeks, shaking occasionally to marry the flavors.

After 2 weeks, strain the mixture through a colander and discard the solids.

Strain it again through a colander lined with cheesecloth to remove any fine sediment, and decant it into a clean glass jar. Store in a cool, dark place and use within 6 months, for peak flavor.

NOEL'S WAY

• Freeze until it's thick, and serve as shots at a summer garden party.

• Fill a tall glass with cranberry juice and ice, and float the lemon vodka on top.

• Mix with fresh blueberries, ice, and cream, and blend for a frozen cocktail.

• To turn this into the classic Italian digestif limoncello, dissolve 2 cups / 400 grams of sugar in 2½ cups / 595 milliliters of boiling water, let cool, then add to the infused vodka. Let it rest for 2 weeks in the refrigerator, then serve over ice.

HOMEMADE AMARETTO

THE WORD *AMARETTO* IS THE DIMINUTIVE OF the Italian word *amaro*, which means "bitter." This word isn't far off from the Italian word *amore*—meaning "love"—so this liqueur enjoys a strong link with romance. The sweeter side of amaretto makes it a natural to link to chocolate, almonds, and other nuts. The bitterness lends itself well to savory dishes: I like it on roasted chicken or in amandine sauces for fish, asparagus, and string beans.

MAKES ABOUT
1 QUART / 950 MILLILITERS AMARETTO

½ cup / 60 grams whole, blanched almonds

1 vanilla bean, split

1 cup / 200 grams granulated sugar

¾ cup / 135 grams light brown sugar, packed

1 teaspoon vanilla extract

1 tablespoon pure almond extract

Pinch of salt

2½ cups / 595 milliliters vodka

Preheat the oven to 350°F/ 175°C. Line a baking sheet with foil and spread the almonds in a single layer. Toast the almonds, stirring occasionally, until light brown and fragrant, then let them cool. Once cool, chop them coarsely and set aside.

Wash the vanilla bean, and, with the point of a knife, slit it lengthwise. Do not remove the seeds. Set the bean aside with the almonds.

Combine the sugars with 1½ cups / 360 milliliters of water in a saucepan over medium heat. Heat until the mixture boils and the sugar dissolves. Remove from the heat and add the almonds, the vanilla bean, the vanilla and almond extracts, and the salt. Let the mixture cool for about an hour. Stir in the vodka. Pour it into a clean jar, and store in the refrigerator for 2 weeks. After 2 weeks, strain it through a colander and discard the solids.

Strain it again through a colander lined with cheesecloth to remove any fine sediment, and decant it into a clean glass jar. Store in a cool, dark place and use within 6 months, for peak flavor. (Reserve the vanilla pod to make vanilla sugar; see page 152.)

NOEL'S WAY

• Soak ladyfingers in the amaretto, and layer them in your favorite trifle.

• Heat and add the amaretto to an equal part of hot tea for an exotic toddy.

• Add a tablespoon of the amaretto to cappuccino
for an après-dinner coffee.

MAKE YOUR OWN
VANILLA SUGAR

Chocolate is known as a flavor that drives women wild and brings grown men to their knees. Vanilla takes a red-headed stepchild–style backseat that I've never found fair. Pure vanilla offers a tropical aroma and unique, robust flavor that's the smell of lush rain forests in Costa Rica, Tahiti, or Hawaii, where the beans are grown. Sure, an upmarket bottle of vanilla extract serves its purpose, but there's no comparing that with the real deal. Keeping vanilla sugar on hand is a clever home cook's secret weapon. Homemade vanilla sugar is beautifully shelf-stable and when substituted spoon for spoon for regular sugar in recipes, it pays for the very little labor and time invested in making your own.

How to Buy Vanilla Beans

You may blanch at the price of a single bean, but one bean can impart a lot of flavor and aroma, so the cost per part winds up being quite affordable.

Get your beans at a specialty store, as turnover is key for freshness. Look for a strong aroma and an oily outer pod. Reject any beans that smell or look mildewed. If your store only stocks beans in glass vials, look closely at the packaging. Reject any with faded labels, old sell-by dates, or broken freshness seals.

Homemade Vanilla Sugar

Pour 2 cups / 400 grams of sugar into a large, metal mixing bowl. (You can use whatever ratio suits you; I like using 1 large bean to 2 cups of sugar.)

Wash 1 vanilla bean and cut it in half lengthwise. Using the tip of a very sharp paring knife, pry open each half of the bean, exposing the shiny, oily, deep black seeds. They resemble caviar, and are nearly as precious. Holding the bean flat against your cutting board, scrape out the seeds.

Work all the seeds into the sugar with your thumb and forefingers. The more you mix, the more aromatic your sugar will be.

Place the empty pods in a sterilized jar (see page 17) and cover with the sugar, leaving at least a ½-inch / 1.3-centimeter headspace. Seal and store in a cool, dark place. Every day or so, turn and shake the contents of the jar to help the vanilla oil mix with the granules of sugar.

After 2 weeks, use and enjoy!

HOMEMADE IRISH CREAM

AS AN ICE-CREAM TOPPING OR A COFFEE SYRUP or served on the rocks, Irish cream never fails to turn the moment into a party. Rich, creamy, and decadent, it's embarrassingly easy to make, and it packs a huge wallop in the "impress your friends" category, eliciting moans and demands for the recipe. This recipe calls for Chocolate Syrup (page 157), but a quality, store-bought brand will work just fine. It's up to you whether you choose to keep the secret of its simplicity or share it with your fans.

MAKES
2 QUARTS / 1.9 LITERS IRISH CREAM

---

2 large egg yolks

2 (14-ounce / 397-gram) cans sweetened condensed milk

2 cups / 480 milliliters heavy whipping cream

¼ cup / 60 milliliters strong brewed coffee
(preferably French or Italian roast)

3 tablespoons Chocolate Syrup (page 157)

1 tablespoon vanilla extract

1 tablespoon almond extract

Pinch of salt

2½ cups / 600 milliliters Irish whiskey

In a large mixing bowl, whisk the egg yolks for 2 minutes, or until they're thick and lemon-colored. Add the sweetened condensed milk, cream, coffee, chocolate syrup, vanilla, almond extract, and salt until the mixture is smooth and uniform. Next, whisk in the whiskey.

Funnel into sterilized jars or bottles (see page 17), and store in the refrigerator for up to 2 weeks.

ROSE SYRUP

PRIZED THE WORLD OVER FOR FLAVORING TEAS and perfuming desserts, rose essence offers a delicious floral fragrance and a refreshing, if somewhat acquired, taste. I like using both the petals and hips of the plant, for a combination of delicacy and depth.

Bake this syrup into madeleines for a whiff of floral sweetness Add a few drops to lemonade to conjure up the exotic feel of Middle Eastern fare. Stir it into a glass of icy-cold milk as a tribute to the cuisines of India and Malaysia. Mixed with seltzer, this syrup mimics the nonalcoholic Champagne substitute used to toast the winners of the Abu Dhabi and Bahrain Grand Prix. If you've a garden, grown without pesticides, use its bounty to make this syrup fresh. If not, food-grade rose petals and hips are easy to come by from specialty tea shops, wholesale herb purveyors, and sources on the web, and you can substitute both dried petals and hips cup for cup for fresh.

MAKES ABOUT
3 CUPS / 750 MILLILITERS SYRUP

3 large handfuls fresh or dried unsprayed rose petals, gently washed

1 handful fresh or dried rosehips, washed and coarsely chopped

1½ cups / 300 grams superfine sugar

Juice of ½ lemon

In a large, nonreactive pot over high heat, bring 3 cups / 750 milliliters of water to a boil and add the rose petals. Lower the heat, cover the pan with a tight lid, and let the mixture stand overnight. The next day, strain the mixture through a fine-mesh strainer into a large bowl, reserving the water and discarding the petals.

Place the rosewater back into the same pot and add the rose hips. Bring the mixture to a boil, then turn off the heat and cover with a tight lid. After an hour, strain the mixture through a colander and discard the solids, reserving the water.

Strain again through a fine-mesh strainer lined with a coffee filter or cheesecloth to remove the sediment, reserving the water. Transfer the infused water back to the pot, and, over very low heat, stir in the sugar and lemon juice, heating until the sugar dissolves but never allowing the mixture to boil. Pour into a clean large glass jar and refrigerate for up to 3 weeks.

NOEL'S WAY

• Drizzle over vanilla yogurt and sprinkle with fresh raspberries.

• Beat into softened butter to make an aromatic spread for waffles blanketed in confectioners' sugar.

• In a tall, chilled glass, add equal parts whole milk and seltzer, and add 2 tablespoons of the rose syrup for a soda fountain–style refresher.

CHOCOLATE SYRUP

IF YOU'VE GOT THIS RICH, CHOCOLATY SYRUP in your pantry, you can whip up a surprisingly wicked dessert from just about anything. Combine it with ice cream and milk to make a thick and creamy milk shake. If you've pound cake, drizzle it over the cake for added moistness and a jolt of complementary flavor. Warm it with peanut butter for a salty-sweet topping. As many different ways as I use this, I think I like it best stirred into a cold, creamy glass of dairy-fresh, full-fat Irish milk.

MAKES ABOUT
2 CUPS / 475 MILLILITERS SYRUP

½ cup / 60 grams unsweetened cocoa powder

2 cups / 200 grams sugar

Pinch of salt

½ teaspoon vanilla extract

In a medium saucepan over medium heat, combine the cocoa powder with 1 cup / 240 milliliters of water, stirring to dissolve the cocoa. Add the sugar and stir to dissolve.

Bring the mixture to a boil and cook for 5 minutes over medium heat, stirring with a wooden spoon to keep it from boiling over. Lower the heat to a simmer and add the salt and vanilla. Ladle into smaller, sterilized jars (see page 17), and store in the refrigerator for up to 2 weeks.

BEST BREAKFAST SYRUP

TO MAKE GUESTS FEEL AT HOME WHEN THEY AWAKEN, there's nothing like the smell of sizzling bacon, piping hot tea and coffee, and a bit of pancake on the griddle. It's how I was taught to put friends and family at their ease at Rock Cottage, and how I like doing it today in my own home. This sweet, spicy, apple-fragrant syrup is the icing on the cakes, so to speak.

MAKES ABOUT
2 CUPS / 480 MILLILITERS SYRUP

½ cup / 100 grams granulated sugar

½ cup / 90 grams dark brown sugar, packed

2 cups / 475 milliliters apple cider

2 teaspoons ground cinnamon

Pinch of freshly grated nutmeg

Pinch of salt

2 tablespoons freshly squeezed orange juice

2 tablespoons cornstarch

4 tablespoons (½ stick) / 60 grams unsalted butter

In a medium, heavy-bottomed saucepan over medium heat, combine the granulated sugar, brown sugar, apple cider, cinnamon, nutmeg, salt, orange juice, and cornstarch.

Bring the mixture to a low boil, stirring constantly. Once the syrup boils, lower the heat to low and stir in the butter. Continue to cook, whisking until the butter is completely melted and the sauce has thickened, 2 to 3 minutes. Ladle the syrup into a glass jar and store in the refrigerator for up to 3 weeks.

RICH COFFEE SYRUP

NOT MUCH HARDER TO EXECUTE than brewing your morning coffee, this syrup is a brilliant add-in for livening up all sorts of drinks and pick-me-up treats. On warm summer mornings I like to stir a few tablespoons into a tall glass of milk and ice cubes, for an ultra-quick iced coffee that rivals Starbucks. Pair it with Homemade Chocolate Syrup in a glass with equal parts seltzer and milk, and you'll have an invigorating version of a New York egg cream. For true coffee lovers, this syrup is magic when ladled over a scoop of vanilla ice cream. And my favorite way: stirred into a postsledding mug of cocoa and topped with whipped cream for Hot Mocha Deluxe.

MAKES ABOUT
2 CUPS / 480 MILLILITERS SYRUP

1½ cups / 120 grams coarse-grind, dark-roasted coffee

¾ cups / 150 grams sugar

In a medium saucepan, bring ½ cup / 40 grams of the ground coffee and 3 cups / 750 milliliters of water to a boil. Once the mixture reaches the boiling point, immediately turn off the heat. Allow it to cool for an hour.

Strain the mixture through a fine-mesh strainer lined with coffee filters set over a large mixing bowl. This is a slow process and can only be done a little at a time. Once the contents of the pan have been strained, discard the coffee grounds, rinse the pan, and return the liquid to the pan.

Add ½ cup / 40 grams of the remaining ground coffee to the strained liquid and bring to a boil. Repeat the straining through a fine-mesh sieve lined with coffee filters. Combine the last ½ cup ground coffee with the strained liquid in the pan, bring to a boil, then strain.

Heat the coffee infusion over very low heat, taking care not to boil it. Stir in the sugar until it dissolves, then funnel the syrup into a large, clean glass bottle and store in the refrigerator for up to 4 weeks.

GRENADINE SYRUP

JUST READING THE LABEL on commercially bottled grenadine makes my head spin. There's no call for buying the bottled version of this simple syrup, when it' so easy to make at home, the fresh and natural way. This ruby-hued, sweetly tart liquid is a grand addition to drinks, owing to both its color and taste. I prefer to hand juice pomegranates rather than to buy bottled juice. It's dead easy to do, once you get the hang of it. But if you go the store-bought route because you need a time-saver, choose a good-quality brand and your guests likely won't taste the difference.

MAKES ABOUT
2 CUPS / 480 MILLILITERS SYRUP

---

2 cups / 480 milliliters pomegranate juice,
freshly juiced preferred (see page 162 for juicing tips)

1 cup / 200 grams granulated sugar

1 teaspoon freshly squeezed lemon juice

½ teaspoon salt

Combine the pomegranate juice, sugar, lemon juice, and salt in a medium saucepan over medium-low heat. Simmer gently, but do not boil, stirring constantly until the sugar melts.

Once the sugar is melted, remove the syrup from the heat, and allow it to cool slightly, for about 10 minutes, then decant to a clean bottle or jar and seal. Store in the refrigerator for up to 2 weeks.

NECTAR OF THE GODS: EXTRACTING THE JUICE FROM POMEGRANATES

Pomegranates are like a secret to be unlocked. It's well worth the effort, though, because the fresh juice is an entity unto itself. Get started by harvesting the precious seeds: You need to free them from the skin and pith. Cut a pomegranate in half through its equator. Holding 1 pomegranate half over a large mixing bowl, smack it hard on the skin side of the fruit. The exquisite seed gems will fall right out into the bowl.

There are a number of ways to juice the fruit—pick your favorite.

- Place the seeds in a resealable plastic bag and lightly smash them with a rolling pin. Don't roll hard enough to pulverize the seeds. There are chemicals inside them that might make your juice taste bitter. Strain through cheesecloth to remove the seeds, and reserve the juice.

- Whiz the seeds in a blender, then strain through cheesecloth, if the thought of the bitterness isn't a bother to you.

- Use a food mill, then discard the leftover pulp, reserving the juice. The same idea about the bitterness applies here.

- Ream the 2 halves of the fruit on a powerful citrus juicer, without removing the seeds first. It's kind of like juicing citrus fruit.

VANILLA SYRUP

THIS SYRUP IS FRAGRANT AND PURE, and anything but boring. Drizzle it over fresh fruit salads or baked fruits, or use to flavor milk or elegant summer cocktails made with light rum.

MAKES ABOUT
2 CUPS / 480 MILLILITERS SYRUP

---

2 cups / 400 grams granulated sugar

2 vanilla beans, split lengthwise

1 teaspoon vanilla extract

1 strip lemon zest, about the size of half your thumb

In a medium, heavy-bottomed saucepan over low heat, combine the sugar, vanilla beans, and lemon zest and add 2 cups / 480 milliliters of water. Heat, stirring occasionally, until the sugar is dissolved and the liquid is fragrant, about 15 minutes.

Remove the pan from the heat and let the mixture cool to room temperature. With a slotted spoon, remove the vanilla beans and lemon zest. Discard the lemon zest. Scrape the seeds from the vanilla bean into the liquid and discard the pods (or add to a jar of vanilla sugar; see page 152). Pour into a clean glass bottle and refrigerate for up to 4 weeks.

HOMEMADE PUMPKIN PIE SPICE SYRUP

THE WARMING SPICES OF AUTUMN fill my mind with thoughts of mulled wine, fragrant coffees, and spiced cider: the very things to ward against the season's chill. This tasty basic syrup can be blended with tea and spirits for toddies, or added to rich coffee for a sophisticated espresso-bar delight, or to creamy drinking chocolate.

MAKES ABOUT
1 CUP / 240 MILLILITERS SYRUP

1 cinnamon stick

5 allspice berries

2 whole cloves

1 cup / 200 grams granulated sugar

¼ cup / 60 milliliters Irish whiskey

½ cup / 75 grams cooked pumpkin from one small pumpkin,
or use canned pure pumpkin

1 teaspoon grated fresh ginger

1 whole vanilla bean, scraped and chopped

In a medium, heavy-bottomed saucepan over medium-heat, combine the cinnamon stick, allspice berries, and cloves. Warm the spices, stirring them constantly with a wooden spoon so that they don't burn, for about 1 minute, or until you smell the spices. As soon as you smell them, turn them out of the pan onto some paper towels, to allow them to cool, or else they'll scorch. (You'll be adding them back to the pan with the other ingredients.)

Add the sugar, whiskey, pumpkin, ginger, vanilla bean, 1 cup / 240 milliliters of water, and the toasted spices, and bring the mixture to a light simmer. Remove the pan from the heat and allow it to cool. Let it rest, loosely covered with a clean tea towel, in a cool corner for a day, then strain the syrup through a colander and discard the solids.

Strain again through colander lined with cheesecloth, to remove any remaining fine sediment. Ladle into smaller, clean jars and store in the refrigerator for up to 4 weeks.

LEMONADE BASE

THERE ARE FOLKS IN MY COMMUNITY and in my family who have never touched a drop of alcohol, so my people get creative with our festive, celebratory drinks. One that was popular across the board was homemade lemonade, made from sunny-fresh citrus. We'd have it at our church suppers at Our Lady of Lourdes, which were always high teas featuring turkey rolls, cold corned beef, coleslaw, and tomato and onion salads. It quenched thirst on warm spring days when we were lucky enough to get sun at Easter, and brought the promise of summer when we suffered spring drear. Here's my recipe for the base I like to keep in the kitchen. In the wink of an eye, I can have a fresh pitcher ready to offer to thirsty travelers.

MAKES ABOUT
2½ CUPS / 600 MILLILITERS LEMONADE BASE

---

2 cups / 400 grams granulated sugar

¼ cup / 60 milliliters honey

2 cups / 475 milliliters freshly squeezed lemon juice
(from 8 to 12 medium-size lemons)

Zest of 1 lemon

In a medium, heavy-bottomed saucepan over medium-high heat, combine the sugar and honey with ½ cup / 120 milliliters of water and bring to a boil. Remove the pan from the heat and stir in the lemon juice and zest. Ladle into smaller, sterilized jars (see page 17), and store in the refrigerator for up to 4 weeks.

To make lemonade, mix with still or fizzy water to your taste. I like a proportion of 2 cups / 480 milliliters of water to ⅓ cup / 80 milliliters of this syrup.

TIPS FOR ZESTING
AND SQUEEZING LEMONS

If you learn these handy skills for handling lemons, you can store them in your arsenal for years of impressive and efficient kitchen execution. What's good for the lemon is good for the lime, as they say, so you can apply these techniques to any citrus fruit.

EASY ZESTING

1. Start with an unwaxed, washed lemon (preferably organic) and a citrus zester.
2. Hold the lemon in the palm of your hand from tip to tail, so that one side touches your little finger and the other touches your thumb.
3. Hold the zester against a flat cutting board at an angle, bearing down to hold it steady.
4. With a long, fluid stroke, push the lemon's peel against the zester from tip to tail while rotating your wrist. Grate only the very outer part of the zest, so that you don't dig into the white pith under the colored part of the outer lemon skin.
5. Repeat this motion, spinning and making long strokes one next to the other (like mowing a lawn), until you've stripped all the oily, aromatic zest from outside the lemon, leaving you with a naked white lemon, which you can then juice as usual.

EASY JUICING

1. Start with room-temperature fruit. If you're taking the lemons from the refrigerator, plunge them into hot water from the tap and allow them to soak for a few minutes, or put them in the microwave for 15 seconds.
2. Pressing with the flat of your hand, roll the fruit on a hard surface, such as a tabletop. This breaks apart the sections, allowing the individual pulp cells to burst with ease.
3. Cut each lemon lengthwise into quarters or eighths, from tip to tail, then squeeze each section individually between your thumb and forefinger.
4. To harvest every last drop, use the tines of a large fork to scrape inside the peel and break open any last, stubborn cells.

CHAPTER FIVE

PICKLED DELIGHTS

THE GIFT
OF NECESSITY

Pickling, like canning, was born of necessity. Pickling sustained the family pantry and allowed the poorest of the poor to eat vitamin-rich fruits and vegetables, even when the soil was frozen. Under the loving care of Ireland's home cooks, pickling has blossomed into something more than its humble origins might have predicted. Elevated from chore to art, pickling not only preserves just-harvested gems from the garden, it changes their nature.

Simply adding ingredients found in any solid kitchen, such as sugar and vinegar and fat, can transform the flavor and texture of such basic foods as cucumbers, ham, and cabbage. Take it a step further, as most Irish do, and you can apply techniques and traditions from other lands, such as India, Germany, and the southern United States. Suddenly, with a little bit of folk wisdom, countless bushels of green tomatoes have new possibility.

PICKLED COURGETTES

THE FRENCH CALL IMMATURE MARROWS **COURGETTES**, and so do we Irish. You might know them as zucchini, but, as they say, a rose by any other name is still as sweet, and so is this easy-to-grow, verdant beauty. They're close relatives of squashes and pumpkins, and they thrive in Ireland even in the harshest summers. With all that welcome abundance, enterprising and thrifty home gardeners and cooks are constantly on the hunt for ways to use and keep this staple vegetable in the kitchen.

I love to flavor this versatile condiment with cilantro leaves (which we Irish call coriander), for their lemony, peppery, herbal taste that hints at arugula and mint. Pickled zucchini are both spicy and sweet, and are delicious served as a spread on fresh crusty bread, as a side dish to strong and gamey roast meats, or ladled over steamed vegetables.

MAKES ABOUT
1 CUP / 240 MILLILITERS PICKLED ZUCCHINI

1 mild chile pepper (I suggest ancho or poblano), finely chopped

Small bunch of fresh cilantro (also called coriander), freshly chopped

2 cups / 480 milliliters rice wine vinegar

3 tablespoons light brown sugar

4 garlic cloves, crushed

1 tablespoon Thai fish sauce (*nam pla*)

1 small zucchini (or *courgette*, for some), cut into ½-inch / 1-centimeter slices

In a medium saucepan over medium-low heat, combine the chile pepper, cilantro, vinegar, brown sugar, garlic, and fish sauce and simmer for 10 minutes, allowing the flavors to blend.

Turn off the heat and add the zucchini slices to the brine. Cover and allow the mixture to stand for 30 minutes. Ladle into a small, clean jar and refrigerate for at least a week before eating. This will keep in the refrigerator for up to 1 month.

SWEET AND SOUR
FIG PICKLE

ORIGINALLY FOUND IN SYRIA, PERSIA, AND NORTH AFRICA, many varieties of figs prosper only on rocky hillsides exposed to direct sun. For that reason, homegrown figs are less common, but not unheard of, in Ireland's cooler, darker clime. The good news about fig trees is that where they survive, you'll reap crops with regularity and virtually no maintenance. If nestled away from the harsh winds, fig trees can take root, persevere, and thrive, just like the Irish who cultivate and tend to them. Delicious as they are, there is a limit to the number one can eat from the tree. This pickle is a delightful and different accompaniment for cold meats and cheeses.

MAKES
2 CUPS / 480 MILLILITERS FIG PICKLE

---

1 cup / 240 milliliters red wine vinegar

½ cup / 100 grams granulated sugar

6 whole cloves

1 cinnamon stick

½ lemon

½ orange

1 pound / 450 grams fresh figs, washed and stems removed

In a medium saucepan over high heat, bring the vinegar, sugar, cloves, cinnamon stick, lemon half, and orange half to a boil, then lower the heat to low and simmer, covered, for 10 minutes. Add the figs and simmer gently for another 10 minutes.

Remove the pan from the heat and allow the mixture to cool overnight, covered, in the refrigerator. The next day, bring the mixture back to a boil, then lower the heat and simmer for 30 minutes, until the figs are soft enough to mash with a spoon. Remove the lemon and orange halves and discard.

Mash the figs with the back of a spoon, transfer them to a clean, glass jar, and pour the pickling liquid over them. Store in the refrigerator for up to 2 weeks.

NOEL'S WAY

• Serve with spicy-sweet pork sausages, brought to a crackling crisp,
and a side of lentils.

• Add dried chile flakes, to your taste, for figs with a kick.

• Pair with nutty cheeses, such as Gouda, Asiago, or Single Gloucester, for an après-dinner cheese board, and serve alongside a pinot noir or sauvignon blanc.

WATERMELON RIND PICKLES

SUGARY SWEET, WITH A SURPRISING TANG, and lovely to look at in the jar, watermelon rind pickles offer the welcoming consistency of a perfectly ripe pear. Watermelons themselves are rare birds in Ireland, and, once I get my hands on one, I want to enjoy it to the fullest. You can chop the pickle into a tuna or chicken salad for a cool summer lunch, or use it as a side dish for salty broiled ham steaks or roast pork with raisins. The recipe is very easy, if a bit time-consuming. It's a sure winner every time, though, and people can't help eating twice or three times a normal portion. Double the recipe!

MAKES ABOUT
FOUR 1-PINT / 475-MILLILITER JARS PICKLE

---

1 small watermelon, such as Sugar Baby (about 2½ pounds)

1 cup / 300 grams pickling salt

1 large lemon, thinly sliced and seeded

1¼ cups / 250 grams granulated sugar

2 cups / 450 milliliters white vinegar

20 whole cloves

4 cinnamon sticks, broken into small pieces

26 allspice berries

Slice the watermelon, carving out the pink flesh for eating later. With a paring knife, cut off and discard the patterned green outer skin from the rind, leaving the more tender, light green part of the rind. Cut that into 1- to 2-inch- / 2.5- to 5-centimeter chunks. Place the chunks in a large mixing bowl and fill with cool water to cover. Stir in the salt, swishing to dissolve. Cover and let it sit overnight in a cool, dark place.

The next day, drain and rinse the rind. Place it in a large stockpot and cover it with fresh water. Bring the pot to a boil over high heat and cook for about 10 minutes, or until just tender, checking frequently to avoid overcooking, which will give the pickles a rubbery texture. Drain the rinds and pack them, along with the lemon slices, into 4 hot, sterilized 1-pint / 475-milliliter canning jars (see page 17).

In the same pot, combine the sugar, vinegar, cloves, cinnamon, and allspice berries, and 3 cups / 720 milliliters of water. Bring the mixture to a boil and boil it for 7 to 8 minutes, until slightly thickened and syrupy. Remove the pan from the heat, stir thoroughly, then pour the syrup over the rinds, leaving a ½-inch / 1.3-centimeter headspace. Cover the jars loosely until they are cool, then screw down the lids. Store in the refrigerator for up to 2 weeks.

PICKLED BEETS

COULD THERE BE ANYTHING AS PRETTY as brilliantly colored magenta beets flanked by red onion in a jar? Rich in iron and loaded with fiber, beets offer the total package: delight for the senses and fortification for the body. I designed this mild pickle especially for my friends who shy away from sharp and pungent flavors. Spoons full of this stunning side dish couple perfectly with delicate egg mayonnaise (or egg salad, as the Americans call it) sandwiches, chicken salad, or buttered bread with cucumber slices.

MAKES
TWO 1-PINT / 475-MILLILITER JARS BEETS

---

3 medium-size beets

1 small red onion, peeled and sliced into half-moons

½ garlic clove, peeled and coarsely chopped

⅔ cup / 160 milliliters white vinegar

1 teaspoon sea salt

1 teaspoon granulated sugar

2 allspice berries

3 whole cloves

2 black peppercorns

1 bay leaf

Pinch of celery seeds

Pinch of mustard seeds

Preheat the oven to 400°F / 200°C. Wash the beets and remove any long roots or leaves, then wrap each beet in a layer of foil. Place the packets on a baking sheet, leaving plenty of space in between them, and bake for 1 hour.

Unwrap each packet and check for doneness. If the beets are not fork-tender, rewrap and bake in 15-minute increments. Remove the beets from the foil and set them aside to cool. When they are cool enough to handle, peel and slice into ¼-inch / 6-millimeter slices.

In a large stockpot, combine the onion, garlic, vinegar, salt, sugar, allspice berries, cloves, peppercorns, bay leaf, celery seeds, and mustard seeds. Bring the mixture to a boil, then lower the heat and simmer for 15 minutes.

Pack the beets into 2 hot, sterilized 1-pint / 475-milliliter jars (see page 17), and ladle the hot liquid over them, leaving a ½-inch / 1.3-centimeter headspace. Seal using the hot water bath (see page 43) for 30 minutes. Store for up to 1 year in a cool, dark place.

PICKLED PEARL ONIONS

TRUE PEARL ONIONS HAVE SOMETHING in common with garlic—they've only one storage leaf, making them easy to peel. Commonly found in Germany, Italy, and the Netherlands, they're less common in the supermarkets of other countries. Prized for pickling, pearl onions are enjoying more attention in today's atmosphere of DIY, and it's becoming easier to find them in organic and farmers' markets. Pearl onions are generally sweeter and more tender than other varieties of white onion, making them perfect to plop in a cocktail. If you can't lay your hands on true pearl onions, there's no reason why you can't substitute tiny, new onions of any stripe for this pickle.

MAKES
TWO 1-PINT / 475-MILLILITER JARS ONIONS

About 4 cups / 500 grams trimmed pearl onions

3 cups / 720 milliliters white vinegar

¾ cups / 150 grams granulated sugar

1 tablespoon kosher salt

1 tablespoon celery seeds

1 tablespoon yellow mustard seeds

6 whole cloves

1 lemon, cut into 8 wedges

Fill a large bowl with cold water and ice cubes and set it aside. Fill a large stockpot with water and bring it to a boil over high heat. Place a few onions at a time in a fine-mesh strainer. Plunge the strainer into the boiling water for 30 seconds, then dip it into the ice water to blanch the onions. Let them cool in the water.

With a very sharp paring knife, remove the tip and tail of the onions and peel off the outside layer. Repeat the process until all the onions are peeled, then set them aside.

In a large, covered stockpot over high heat, combine the vinegar, sugar, salt, and 1 cup / 240 milliliters of water and bring to a boil. Boil for 5 minutes. Add the onions and bring the mixture back to a boil, then lower the heat and simmer for 5 minutes, or until they are just tender when pricked with the tip of a sharp knife. Add the celery seeds, mustard seeds, cloves, and lemon wedges to the pot, stir, bring back to a boil, and cook for 5 more minutes.

Using a slotted spoon, transfer the onions to hot, sterilized jars (see page 17), and cover with the pickling liquid, dividing the lemon wedges between the jars, leaving a ½-inch / 1.3-centimeter headspace. Seal using the hot water bath (see page 43) for 5 minutes. This should keep for up to 6 months in a cool, dark place, if properly sealed.

FARM-STYLE CUCUMBER PICKLES

YOU KNOW IT'S SUMMER IN IRELAND when the cucumber plants start popping. A single plant can produce 30 to 40 cucumbers, so savvy home gardeners make sure to include a few out back each year. Leaving the cucumbers too long before picking discourages the plants from producing more, so it's best to get 'em while they're hot, so to speak. If you're planning to can, this scheme works out perfectly, as the smaller, newer cucumbers make the best pickles. Follow this favorite recipe of mine and you'll have tart and crunchy bites of July sunshine, even in the cold of winter.

MAKES
TWO 1-PINT / 475-MILLILITER JARS PICKLES

---

10 to 12 small cucumbers

2½ cups / 600 milliliters white vinegar

2 tablespoons kosher salt

4 teaspoons dill seeds

4 small garlic cloves

16 black peppercorns

Wash the cucumbers well. Using a paring knife, slice off the tip and tail of each. In a medium saucepan over high heat, combine the vinegar, salt and 2½ cups / 600 milliliters of water and bring the mixture to a boil.

Sterilize 2 jars (see page 17), and while they're still hot, add 2 teaspoons of the dill seeds, 2 of the garlic cloves and 8 of the peppercorns to each jar.

Pack in the cucumbers as tightly as you can without crushing them and pour the boiling brine into the jars, leaving a ½-inch / 1.3-centimeter headspace. Seal using the hot water bath (see page 43) for 30 minutes. This should keep for up to 1 year in a cool, dark place, if properly sealed.

PLOUGHMAN'S PICKLE RELISH

IN NEARLY EVERY PUB, YOU'LL FIND THE OFFERING of a ploughman's lunch on the menu. A simple cold meal, the basic components generally include crusty bread, cheese, relish or chutney, and perhaps a bit of seasonal fruit. The selection varies, though, so you might also be treated to slices of cold meat or pâté, a boiled egg, and some salad or crudités.

The origins of the classic ploughman's lunch are pretty straightforward. When it came time to plow the far reaches of farmland, a man could wind up miles from home, and it made no economic sense to waste daylight hours walking home for a meal. Farm wives would pack an inexpensive lunch, cobbled together from such homemade staples as loaves of bread, jars of pickles, and wheels of cheese. The hearty and nutritious lunch kept well without refrigeration, didn't need to be reheated to be tasty, and provided all the protein and calories a hardworking farmhand needed to sustain him.

I have to be honest, my life as a chef doesn't demand that kind of backbreaking labor, but I still love a rustic lunch of this sort. And the icing on the cake is the fragrant, dark pickle relish that I heap on every bite.

MAKES ABOUT
1 QUART / 950 MILLILITERS RELISH

3 medium-size carrots, peeled and diced

1 medium-size rutabaga (swede), peeled and diced

5 cloves garlic, peeled and minced

1 medium-size head cauliflower, finely chopped

4.5 ounces / 130 grams dried dates, finely chopped

2 large onions, finely chopped

2 medium-size tangy apples, finely chopped

2 medium-size zucchini (courgettes), finely chopped

20 small, fresh gherkins, finely chopped

2 cups / 360 grams dark brown sugar, packed

1 teaspoon salt

Juice of 1 large lemon

1½ cups / 360 milliliters malt vinegar

1 tablespoon Worcestershire sauce

2 tablespoons mustard seeds

1 teaspoon ground allspice

1 teaspoon cayenne pepper

In a large, heavy-bottomed saucepan, bring the carrots, rutabaga, garlic, cauliflower, dates, onions, apples, zucchini, gherkins, brown sugar, salt, lemon juice, vinegar, Worcestershire, mustard seeds, allspice, and cayenne pepper to a boil, then lower the heat and cook on a low simmer for about 2 hours, until the vegetables are tender.

Ladle into hot, sterilized jars (see page 17), leaving a ½-inch / 1.3-centimeter headspace. Seal using the hot water bath (see page 43) for 15 minutes. This should keep for up to 1 year in a cool, dark place, if properly sealed.

NOEL'S WAY

- Spread atop a wheel of soft Brie, and serve with Rye Crackers (page 260).
- Set a ramekin of this pickle out on your cheese board, to use for an aromatic spread.
- Combine with Dubliner Cheese in a food processor, for a quick party spread.

HOW IS PICKLING SALT DIFFERENT FROM KOSHER SALT AND TABLE SALT?

Pickling salt shares qualities with table salt, but it lacks the iodine and certain anticaking additives that can turn pickles dark and cloud the liquid in which they rest. Pickles made with table salt would still be as tasty, but you take the chance that they wouldn't be as pleasing to the eye.

Once you've bought the stuff, you can feel free to use it as you would ordinary table salt, remembering that without the anticaking agent, it might go lumpy on your table if the air in your hometown is damp. If you don't mind putting a few grains of rice in your salt cellar or shaker, this won't be a problem. If you can't get pickling salt, choose kosher salt over table salt when you can. Like pickling salt, kosher salt contains no iodine. Some brands of kosher salt contain yellow prussiate of soda, an anticaking agent. If possible, go with the brands free of it. Don't panic if that's all you can get your hands on. Unlike table salt, kosher salt won't cloud your pickle juice.

WALNUT PICKLE

IF YOU ARE UNFAMILIAR WITH THE TART and earthy joy of pickled walnuts, it may interest you to hear a passage by Charles Dickens, from *The Pickwick Papers,* in which a man is literally brought back from the dead by the mere thought of one: "The first faint glimmerings of returning animation were his jumping up in bed, bursting out into a loud laugh, kissing the young woman who held the basin, and demanding a mutton chop and a pickled walnut. He was very fond of pickled walnuts, gentlemen." I don't mind telling you, gentleman *and ladies,* that I'm also quite fond of them, especially on my Christmas table, served alongside a strong Stilton or Huntsman cheese, or served with a simple ploughman's lunch. The best walnuts for pickling—technically called drupes—are harvested around June (to be eaten the following Christmas, if you can keep them that long!), and can be picked green before the shell has formed inside. You can test for this by pricking the nuts with a needle; the best place to check is the stem end. Brined and allowed to air dry before pickling, these trufflelike morsels turn dark brown or black, offering a distinctive look in their jars or surrounding a piping hot and fragrant rib of beef.

This recipe is well and truly easy, but I don't want to lead you down the garden path. It's a multistep process, stretched out over the course of three weeks, but the results are well worth the trouble.

MAKES
1 POUND / 455 GRAMS PICKLED WALNUTS

1 pound / 455 grams fresh (green) young walnuts

1 cup salt, divided

1 cup / 240 milliliters cider vinegar

2½ cups / 450 grams light brown sugar, packed

¼ teaspoon ground allspice

2 whole cloves

1 cinnamon sticks

1 coin-size slice fresh ginger

4 black peppercorns

Wearing rubber gloves, wash each walnut and pierce each 3 or 4 times with the tines of a fork. Clear juice will ooze out—beware! It will stain a deep espresso color, so take care to wear an apron, and never to let it sit on light-colored countertops.

Stir ½-cup of salt until dissolved into 1 quart / 1 liter of water in a large mixing bowl. Add the walnuts, cover the bowl loosely with plastic wrap, and soak the walnuts for 1 week in a cool place. After 1 week, drain and repeat the brining process. After the second week, drain the walnuts and spread them out in a single layer, with space between them for air to circulate, to dry. If you can do this in the sun, with the walnuts on a drying screen, it would be ideal. Barring that, old towels or sheets stretched over a bench in a shed or garage is a close second. If all else fails, you can dry them on the countertop on thick layers of brown paper or grocery sacks, in the corner of your kitchen. Caution! They will stain.

Let the walnuts rest for 4 or 5 days (longer if the weather is very damp), turning them frequently to prevent mildew, until they all turn black. Once black, they are ready to pickle.

Combine the vinegar, brown sugar, allspice, cloves, cinnamon, ginger, and peppercorns in a large pot over high heat. Bring to a boil, then lower the heat to a simmer and add the walnuts. Simmer over medium heat for 20 minutes.

Remove the walnuts and pickling liquid from the heat and use a slotted spoon to transfer the walnuts into hot, sterilized jars (see page 17). Ladle on the hot liquid, leaving a ½-inch / 1.3-centimeter headspace. Seal using the hot water bath (see page 43) for 30 minutes. This should keep for up to 1 year in a cool, dark place, if properly sealed.

SAFE PICKLING PRACTICES

As with canning, pickling can be an excellent way to preserve foods. Pickling is also a lovely way to process foods to get that distinctive mix of flavors: salty, tangy, and pungent.

There are two basic ways to pickle food: in vinegar, as with cucumber pickles, or by brining to encourage fermentation, as with Korean kimchi. Both ways will extend the life of your favorite fresh foods, and both will turn them into delicious treats.

Because pickling is a craft to be studied, and different foods react differently in different environments, I'm offering small-batch recipes for normal meal-to-meal consumption, and I'm relying on the pickling to make the food delicious, not to preserve it for great lengths of time. Part of the pleasure of the recipes I've included here is that you can make small batches of a variety of seasonal foods to enjoy soon after or share with friends and family. Of course, many of these recipes lend themselves to large-batch canning. If you've fresh foods in bulk, there's no reason not to double or even triple these recipes and put the foods up to be stored in your pantry.

PICKLED EGGS

THE HUMBLE PICKLED EGG ENJOYS A DEVOTED FOLLOWING as a poor man's delicacy and ubiquitous pub food. And why not? Pickled eggs are a low-fat, high-protein, tasty snack with roots in such admirable virtues as economy and innovation. Sure, the pickling spices, vinegar, and salt have handy preservation attributes, but they also offer intense savory flavor that can stand up to a mug of beer or a plate of smoked meats and sharp cheeses. I like to add beets to mine, not only for the sweet, earthy flavor, but also for the sunset-pink hue that extends from white to yolk.

MAKES
**1 DOZEN EGGS (A LITTLE MORE THAN
1 QUART- / LITER-SIZE JAR)**

12 eggs

1 medium-size white onion, peeled and sliced into half-moons

2 garlic cloves, peeled and halved

2 cups / 480 milliliters red wine vinegar

1 medium-size beet, washed, peeled and chopped into chunks

⅓ cup / 60 grams dark brown sugar, packed

1 tablespoon salt

6 black peppercorns

Place the eggs in the bottom of a large pot, cover with cold water, and bring to a boil over high heat. Once boiling, remove the pot from the heat, cover, and set aside. Let the eggs stand untouched for 17 minutes. Plunge the eggs into cold water, then let them cool for 15 minutes. Gently peel the eggs, taking care not to puncture or tear the whites, and making sure all traces of shell are removed. Set the peeled eggs aside in a bowl.

Meanwhile, in another large pot over high heat, combine the onion, garlic, vinegar, beets, brown sugar, salt, and peppercorns and bring them to a boil. Cover and simmer for 15 minutes, stirring once to make sure the sugar and salt dissolve. Cool the brine by setting the pot either in the refrigerator or on the back porch, if it's winter. Once the brine is cool, ladle it from the pot into a pitcher.

Sterilize one 1-quart / 1-liter jar (see page 17) and fill the jars with the eggs and onion slices, packing them in tightly without crushing the eggs. Pour the brine slowly into the jars, allowing it to seep down and fill the spaces between the eggs and onions. Tightly cover with the jar lids, and refrigerate for at least 2 weeks, for the flavors to fully infuse.

A simple fact of Irish farm life is that if you waste nothing, you want for nothing. In lean times, falling back on what you've put aside has always meant survival. Today, it's hard to think of a fresh egg as a treat, but, in hard times of the past, through months of eating dried, salted, and canned food, the taste buds of our forefathers must have yearned for something that tasted immediate and bursting with just-opened flavor. If you were lucky enough to have a hen or two in the days before iceboxes and refrigerators, stockpiling eggs when there was a glut was the sensible thing to do.

Starting with fresh eggs no more than a few days old got the ball rolling. Discarding any egg with a crack or a flaw was crucial, as one bad egg could spoil a whole store. Next, the shells were carefully washed with warm water and soap. Then, the eggs were coated with melted lard or butter and left on a clean cloth to thoroughly dry: the greasy film kept the eggshells essentially airtight. Finally, the eggs were buried in the earth, layered in cloth in a chest in the cellar, or submerged in salt and stored in a cool place kept them safe for future use. It makes the corner supermarket sound like a palace of wonders, does it not?

GREEN TOMATO PICKLE SPREAD

WHEN YOUR SUMMER GARDEN IS SIGHING its last breath, and the tomatoes languishing on the vines show no signs of ripening in time to join your salad bowl, ingenuity is called for. Don't get me wrong, though. As much as I love a ripe red tomato, there's also a special place in my heart for crunchy, thick-walled, vegetal green tomatoes. I especially enjoy them for the way they lend themselves to pickling: They'll stand up to floating preserved in vinegar without ever losing their integrity. Serve this tangy-sharp pickle alongside grilled meats or as a sandwich topping, or take jars along on a picnic with cold fried chicken and potato salad.

MAKES
TWO **1-PINT** / 475-MILLILITER JARS PICKLE SPREAD

12 medium-size green tomatoes, peeled, seeded, and coarsely chopped

½ medium head green cabbage, coarsely chopped

1 small red bell pepper, seeded and diced

1 large stalk celery, diced

1 small yellow onion, diced

¼ cup / 75 grams kosher salt

⅓ cup / 60 grams light brown sugar, packed

2 teaspoons mustard seeds

1 teaspoon celery seeds

1¼ cups / 300 milliliters white vinegar

2 teaspoons prepared horseradish

Place the tomatoes, cabbage, pepper, celery, and onion in a large bowl and cover them with the salt. Allow the mixture to stand for 15 minutes, then mix them thoroughly and transfer them to a colander and let them drain for 4 hours.

Press the vegetables to force out the liquid, then transfer them to a large, heavy-bottomed pot and bring to a simmer over low heat. Cook for 5 minutes. Add the brown sugar, mustard seeds, celery seeds, vinegar, and horseradish and simmer for 15 minutes, or until all of the vegetables are tender but not mushy.

Ladle the mixture into hot, sterilized jars (see page 17), and cover with the pickling liquid, leaving a ½-inch / 1.3-centimeter headspace. Seal using the hot water bath (see page 43) for 5 minutes. This should keep for up to 6 months in a cool, dark place, if properly sealed.

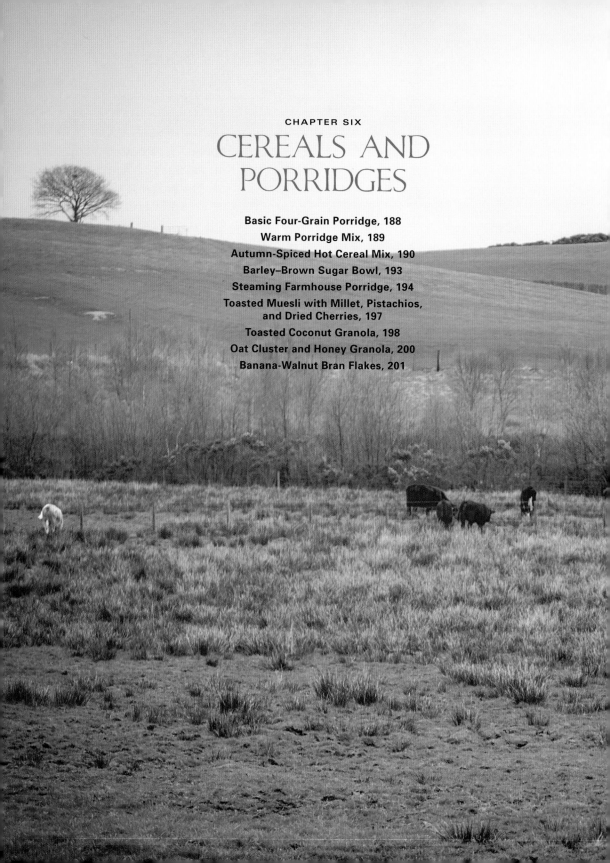

CHAPTER SIX

CEREALS AND
PORRIDGES

TRUE IRISH PORRIDGE

The cool temperatures and damp climate of Ireland promote the slow ripening of the oat crop. It enables the oats to draw the goodness from the soil and yield up a crop with fuller, plumper grains that benefit from the poor drainage and the flooded fields. Barley and rye also managed to survive, if not flourish. Wheat, while available since ancient times, fared less well. Bread was seen as a luxury. The population was sustained on a food called stirabout, a thick paste of cooked grain blended water that was left in the pot for as many days as it took to consume. Wealthier households might have tarted it up a bit with dairy, such as milk and butter or buttermilk, and sweetened it with honey or treacle.

I was weaned on this old-fashioned, homey, and basic thin porridge. Inexpensive, filling, and nutritious, it lined my belly most mornings as I set off to school. I find it comforting to this day. I have to admit that when I eat it now, I like a bit of Honeyed Whiskey Butter or imported maple syrup on top. I am a chef, after all.

BASIC FOUR-GRAIN PORRIDGE

A WARM, SUSTAINING BOWL OF THIS PORRIDGE fills my belly so nicely that elevenses will come and go, and lunchtime will arrive before I have a thought about snacking. For times when a plate of bacon and eggs might weigh me down and I need more than sweet pastry to get me through the day, I like to treat my body and my taste buds to this healthful blend.

MAKES ABOUT
8 SERVINGS

1 cup / 90 grams old-fashioned rolled oats

1 cup / 100 grams rolled rye

1 cup / 100 grams rolled barley

1 cup / 100 grams rolled spelt

To make the cereal mix, combine all the ingredients in a lidded, airtight container, leaving at least a three-fingers' width of space at the top. Make sure the lid is secured, then shake, turn, and roll the container to mix. This mix will keep for up to 6 months in a cool, dark place.

To make hot cereal, combine 1 part mix with 2 parts water in a heavy-bottomed saucepan and bring to a boil over medium-high heat. Once it boils, lower the heat, cover, and continue to cook over low heat until it reaches a thick, porridgelike consistency.

NOEL'S WAY

• For a healthful boost of omega-3 fatty acid,
add ½ cup / 60 grams of ground flaxseeds.

• To sweeten the pot, add 4 ounces / 120 grams of dried banana chips,
dried cherries, or sultanas.

• For a tropical twist, add 2 ounces / 60 grams of chopped,
dried pineapple and 4 ounces / 120 grams of unsweetened
shredded coconut, toasted or raw.

WARM PORRIDGE MIX

MY STRONGEST CHILDHOOD MEMORIES ARE LINKED TO SMELLS. Burning peat at dusk, a hot iron on a starched shirt on a Sunday morning, the rosebushes along the fence in June. A smell I'll forever associate with my home is apples and cinnamon, and I suppose that's why I created this morning blend featuring that delicious pairing. When the good Armagh Bramleys came ready for harvest, we had them in abundance. My mother and sister cooked them into everything from pies to turnovers to applesauce. I can just smell Mum's tart, deep and rich, baked and served in the earthenware dish reserved for that use. Always with a touch of cinnamon.

MAKES ABOUT
20 SERVINGS

6½ cups / 600 grams old-fashioned rolled oats

1½ cups / 180 grams dry milk powder

5 ounces / 150 grams dried apples, chopped

1 cup / 200 grams granulated sugar

¼ cup / 45 grams dark brown sugar, packed

1½ tablespoons ground cinnamon

1 teaspoon salt

¼ teaspoon freshly grated nutmeg

¼ teaspoon ground cloves

To make the cereal mix, combine all the ingredients in a lidded, airtight container, leaving at least a three-fingers' width of space at the top. Make sure the lid is secured, then shake, turn, and roll the container to combine. This mix will keep for up to a month in a cool, dark place.

To make hot cereal, combine 1 part mix with 2 parts water in a heavy-bottomed saucepan and bring to a boil over medium-high heat. Once it boils, lower the heat, cover, and continue to cook over low heat until it reaches a thick, porridgelike consistency.

AUTUMN-SPICED HOT CEREAL MIX

I'M NOT OPPOSED TO BUYING A BOX OF CEREAL at the supermarket and pouring it into a bowl, but I'm always left wanting. Not because I can truly make dry cereal better than a factory can, but because I haven't found one featuring almonds, dates, and apples. I made one of my own, using a basic box of four-grain cereal that you'd find at any well-stocked grocery. While I was at it, I fine-tuned the spices to make a slightly better blend.

MAKES ABOUT
10 CUPS / 900 GRAMS CEREAL MIX

---

3 cups / 270 grams old-fashioned rolled oats

3 cups / 270 grams heart-healthy 4-grain cereal

2 tablespoons wheat germ

5 ounces / 150 grams dried dates, chopped

5 ounces / 150 grams dried apples, chopped

3 ounces / 80 grams prunes, chopped

1 cup / 125 grams almonds, chopped

1 cup / 180 grams light brown sugar, loosely packed

2 tablespoons ground cinnamon

1 tablespoon ground ginger

1 teaspoon ground cloves

1 teaspoon salt

In a large, airtight container with a lid, combine the oats, 4-grain cereal, wheat germ, dates, apples, prunes, almonds, brown sugar, cinnamon, ginger, cloves, and salt, leaving at least a three-fingers' width of space at the top. Make sure the lid is secured, then shake, turn, and roll the container to combine. This mix will keep for up to 6 months in a cool, dark place.

For hot cereal, bring 1 cup / 240 milliliters of water to a boil in a medium saucepan over high heat. Stir in ¾ cup / 125 grams of the mix. Remove from the heat, cover, and let stand for 10 minutes before serving.

A WORD ABOUT OATS

Types and designations of raw oats can be confusing, as some terms refer to the origins of the cereal grain, some to the way the grains were processed, and some to the way you're meant to cook them.

You can generally find whole oats only in health food stores, bulk food stores, or on the Internet. This type takes the longest to cook, but is richest in fiber and nutrition, and fans (like me!) enjoy their nutty flavor and toothsome texture.

Process your oats one step further by cutting them into pieces, and you've got steel-cut oats, which are also commonly called pinhead oats, Irish oatmeal, or porridge oats. Some might call this variety Scottish oats, but I beg to differ. In England, Scandinavia, and the United States, this type is considered a specialty item and you'll have to look for them in upscale markets, import grocers, or health food stores.

Scottish oats contain whole groats, like the steel cut, but are ground into uneven pieces rather than cut with a blade. This results in crushed bits, yielding a bowl of porridge that's creamier and less grainy than Irish oatmeal.

Rolled oats, sometimes called old-fashioned oats, are what the English, Americans, and Scandinavians consider basic oatmeal. To produce this style of cereal grain, the groats are steamed and then rolled into flakes. The greater surface area on the flakes helps them cook longer. Rolled oats make for a very creamy bowl of hot cereal that's less chewy and blander than the less processed types.

If you pressed rolled oats even flatter and steam them even longer, you'll wind up with quick-cooking oats. Even flatter and even longer? Instant oatmeal. These final two have a less firm texture that some describe as watery. It's an advantage for some oat lovers, and a drawback for others.

For the most part, people like their bowl of hot oatmeal the way they like it, which is generally the way their mum served it when they were children. But for cooking, different styles offer different perks, so it's great to be familiar with the whole gamut.

BARLEY–BROWN SUGAR BOWL

WHOLE-GRAIN BARLEY CONTAINS EIGHT AMINO ACIDS, and is shown to help regulate blood sugar. It's packed with fiber and it tastes good. Barley did the work of a journeyman in our house, stretching food to feed all the hungry mouths at the table. It rounded out and fortified beef and vegetable soup, plumped up apple-barley pudding, and was the cornerstone of stuffing for roast chicken.

MAKES ABOUT
8 SERVINGS

½ cup / 60 grams pearl barley

½ cup / 60 grams bulgur wheat

½ cup / 45 grams old-fashioned rolled oats

½ cup / 90 grams dark brown sugar, packed

2 teaspoons ground cinnamon

½ teaspoon salt

2.5 ounces / 75 grams raisins

½ cup / 55 grams slivered almonds

Mix the barley, bulgur wheat, oats, brown sugar, cinnamon, salt, raisins, and almonds in a large, tightly lidded container and shake well to combine, leaving at least a three-fingers' width of space at the top. Make sure the lid is secured, then shake, turn, and roll the container to combine. This mix will keep well for up to 1 year in a cool, dry, dark place.

To make hot cereal, combine 1 part mix with 2 parts water in a heavy-bottomed saucepan and bring to a boil over medium-high heat. Once it boils, lower the heat, cover, and continue to cook over low heat until it reaches a thick, porridgelike consistency.

STEAMING FARMHOUSE PORRIDGE

THERE'S AN OLD IRISH PROVERB, "He who has water and peat on his own farm has the world his own way." This simple breakfast dish is a sort of living practice of that sentiment. It's inexpensive, packed with nutrition, and easy to make. In short, it's good enough, and good enough is sweet beyond measure.

MAKES ABOUT
8 SERVINGS

2 cups / 180 grams old-fashioned rolled oats

1 cup / 90 grams wheat farina (semolina)

½ cup / 45 grams oat bran

2.5 ounces / 75 grams raisins

½ cup / 90 grams dark brown sugar, packed

2 tablespoons ground cinnamon

To make the cereal mix, combine all the ingredients in a lidded, airtight container, leaving at least a three-fingers' width of space at the top. Make sure the lid is secured, then shake, turn, and roll the container to combine. This mix will keep for up to a month in a cool, dark place.

To make hot cereal, combine 1 part mix with 2 parts water in a heavy-bottomed saucepan and bring to a boil over medium-high heat. Once it boils, lower the heat, cover, and continue to cook over low heat until it reaches a thick, porridgelike consistency.

WHOLE-GRAIN BASICS

Your choice of cooking method can transform the textures of different grains.

FLUFFY Covering the pot and abstaining from peeking or stirring creates a firmer, fluffier texture and keeps larger grains (such as barley) intact. This method relies on steam to puff up the individual grains like a rice pilaf.

In a heavy pot, bring water and salt to a boil. Using a fork, lightly stir in the grains, and return the mixture to a boil. Lower the heat to low, and simmer covered as directed. Then turn off the heat and allow the pot to rest, covered, for 5 minutes. Just before serving, fluff with a fork.

CREAMY Use more water for this method, and cook the grains longer so they will break down. Frequent stirring helps, resulting in a more uniform texture. Smaller grains and larger grains that have been cut, such as steel-cut oats, work better with this technique that results in a porridge.

In a heavy pot, bring water and salt to a boil. Using a whisk, stir in the grains, and return the mixture to a boil. Lower the heat to low, and simmer covered, for the proper amount of time, stirring often and vigorously. Then turn off the heat and serve immediately.

SUGGESTED COOKING TIMES FOR COMMON WHOLE GRAINS

GRAIN (½ CUP)	WATER	TIME
Amaranth	1 cup	15 minutes
Barley, pearl	1¼ cups	20 minutes
Barley, hulled	1½ cups	30 to 40 minutes
Buckwheat	1 cup	7 to 12 minutes
Bulgur wheat	1 cup	5 to 10 minutes
Millet	1¼ cups	10 to 15 minutes
Oats, quick-cooking	1¼ cups	5 minutes
Oats, rolled	1¼ cups	10 minutes
Oats, steel-cut	1½ cups	20 to 40 minutes
Oats, groats	1½ cups	30 minutes
Polenta	1½ cups	10 minutes
Quinoa	1 cup	7 to 10 minutes
Rye	1½ cups	30 minutes
Spelt	1½ cups	30 minutes

TOASTED MUESLI WITH MILLET, PISTACHIOS, AND DRIED CHERRIES

I KEEP MILLET ON MY SHELF FOR GUESTS on gluten-free diets. Dressed up with crunchy pistachios and wine-scented dried cherries, it's almost luxurious. This recipe tastes nice enough for the saintly to eat dry, but I'm Irish born and bred, so I have mine with a splash of heavy cream.

MAKES ABOUT
10 SERVINGS

2 cups / 180 grams whole millet

2 cups / 180 grams old-fashioned rolled oats

1 cup / 150 grams roasted pistachios, chopped

½ cup / 120 grams unsweetened shredded coconut

½ cup / 120 milliliters honey

1 tablespoon coconut oil

1 teaspoon salt

5 ounces / 140 grams dried cherries

Preheat the oven to 325°F / 160°C. Spread the millet onto a baking sheet and bake on the middle rack for 10 minutes. Toss, then bake for another 10 minutes. The edges will be a little brown. Allow it to cool, then transfer it to a small bowl on the countertop, pour boiling water over the top, and cover it loosely. Let it rest for 30 minutes, or until it's fork tender, then drain it.

In a large mixing bowl, combine the drained millet, oats, pistachios, and coconut flakes and set the mixture aside.

In a small saucepan over medium-high heat, bring the honey, oil, and salt to a boil. Remove it from the heat and pour it over the millet mixture, then stir gently until combined.

With a rubber spatula, spread the mixture in a thin layer onto a rimmed baking sheet and bake for 10 minutes. Stir and flip the muesli and bake for another 10 minutes, repeating this process in 5-minute increments until it is toasted golden brown. Remove it from the oven and allow it to cool. Stir in the dried cherries. Serve immediately with milk or yogurt, or store in an airtight container for up to 6 months in a cool, dry place.

VARIATIONS

• Add dark chocolate chunks to the cooled mix, for a sweet and healthful trail snack.

• Substitute sultanas, raisins, or dried cranberries for the cherries, or enjoy a medley.

TOASTED COCONUT GRANOLA

CHEWY AND CRUNCHY AT THE SAME TIME, this sweet cereal is like a breakfast dessert. Pour milk on top, sprinkle it on yogurt, or eat it by the handful.

MAKES ABOUT
5 CUPS / 500 GRAMS GRANOLA

---

1 cup / 240 grams unsweetened shredded coconut

3 cups / 270 grams old-fashioned rolled oats

½ cup / 75 grams cashews, chopped

4 tablespoons honey

3 to 4 tablespoons olive oil

1 tablespoon vanilla extract

1 tablespoon almond extract

1 teaspoon kosher salt

Preheat the oven to 350°F / 175°C. Spread the coconut onto a baking sheet in a thin layer. Bake it until barely brown, about 5 minutes. It's usually done when you can smell it. Remove the toasted coconut from the oven and set it aside to cool, and lower the oven temperature to 300°F / 150°C to preheat for the next step.

In a large mixing bowl, combine the oats, cashews, and toasted coconut. Warm the honey, oil, vanilla, almond extract, and salt in a small saucepan over medium heat until just simmering. Simmer for 5 minutes, taking care not to let it boil, then remove the pan from the heat.

Pour the honey mixture over the oat mixture and stir well with a wooden spoon until the dry ingredients are coated. Spread this mixture in a thin layer over a large baking sheet and bake for 10 minutes, then stir and flip the mixture. Repeat the 10-minute baking time, then stir again, repeating until the granola is well toasted. (This usually takes about 50 minutes total baking time.)

Once toasted, let the granola sit on the baking sheet, stirring occasionally. When cooled, the granola stays fresh in the refrigerator for about a month, or at room temperature for about 2 weeks.

OAT CLUSTER AND HONEY GRANOLA

HOLISTIC HEALTH EXPERTS SAY THAT IF YOU EAT the local honey, you won't suffer allergies. I suppose we owe a great debt of gratitude to those bees that process the spoils of the flowers they vaccinate us against. Every year, I like to go to the Honey Show at Florence Court, near my home in Fermanagh. You can't get much closer to the source of your food than meeting the bee who made it.

MAKES ABOUT
10 CUPS / 900 GRAMS GRANOLA

10 cups / 900 grams old-fashioned rolled oats

2 tablespoons canola oil

1 teaspoon salt

1¼ cups / 300 milliliters honey

Preheat the oven to 350°F / 175°C.

In a large bowl, stir together the oats, oil, salt, and honey until the oats are evenly coated. Spread everything out onto a large baking sheet and bake for 30 minutes, taking it out every 5 minutes to flip and stir, until the mixture is golden brown. Allow it to cool before serving, or store it in an airtight container for up to 6 months.

BANANA-WALNUT BRAN FLAKES

FOR THOSE WHO LIKE SWEET BREAKFASTS, I recommend a bowl of this blend. To me, it tastes just like banana bread. If you're feeling decadent, toss in a handful of chocolate chips before serving.

MAKES
8 SERVINGS

3 tablespoons chopped walnuts

3 to 4 tablespoons dried banana chips

½ cup / 50 grams wheat bran

½ cup / 70 grams whole wheat flour

2 tablespoons granulated sugar

¼ teaspoon baking powder

¼ teaspoon salt

⅓ cup / 80 milliliters milk

Honey, for drizzling

Preheat the oven to 350°F / 175°C.

Combine the walnuts and banana chips in a food processor and process for 1 minute, until the mixture is the texture of pebbly sand.

In a large mixing bowl, sift together the wheat bran, flour, sugar, baking powder, and salt. Add the milk, ¼ cup / 60 milliliters of water, and walnut mixture and mix well. Prepare 2 sheets of parchment paper, and turn out the dough onto it. Break the dough into 2 equal parts.

Cover the dough with clear plastic wrap. Roll out the dough with the plastic wrap covering it. You want the dough to be as thin as possible; you're actually creating a giant cereal flake. Remove the plastic wrap and place the dough (on the parchment) on a large baking sheet. Drizzle with the honey.

Bake for 10 minutes, checking often as thin dough burns easily. Remove the sheet from the oven and allow it to cool on a cooling rack. Repeat with the remaining dough. Lower the oven temperature to 275°F / 135°C. After both giant bran flakes have completely cooled, crack them into lots of smaller flakes. Arrange the flakes on a large baking sheet and bake at the lower temperature for 20 minutes, stirring every 5 minutes. If they're still moist, continue to bake in 5-minute increments, checking often, until they're dry and crisp.

Remove the pan from the oven and place on a cooling rack to cool. Store the flakes in a sealed container for up to 2 weeks.

CHAPTER SEVEN

POTTED
AND CURED

THE REDISCOVERY
OF TRADITION

A lot of people have been noticing in recent years that there's a new way of thinking about food in Ireland, and they're right. Forward-thinking pioneer Myrtle Allen has not only dedicated her life to putting the emphasis back on sourcing locally, and practicing traditional arts in growing, cooking, and storing food, she's opened her house and heart to anyone who cares to learn what she has to teach.

I've taken up the mantle of such revolutionaries as Myrtle and Alice Waters and Paul Rankin. Revolutionary, yes. But also I'm simply traditional. I'm driven because I truly believe I've my own contribution to make, dragging forward the practical, old farm ways I learned into the twenty-first century.

I have patience to offer. I spend money on trees for my land, knowing that they'll help me leave the earth a better place than I found it. I plant perennial bulbs, hoping that future generations will be wooed to tend the land by the beauty of their seasonal cycles.

It's true that I'll likely never have to rely on drying beef or potting prawns to survive the winter. But that doesn't mean I don't want to be linked with them who had to, or to carry it forward to those who might again.

NOEL'S JERKY FOR BEGINNERS

THE SECRET TO THIS JERKY is to slice the meat very thinly and trim the fat. Here's a chef tip for you: Always put a damp tea towel under your cutting board to keep it from sliding. That's particularly important for jerky: The thinner the meat, the better it'll dry, and the longer it'll keep. Cut carefully with a very, very sharp knife to get paper-thin slices. You can flavor jerky many ways, but I think of this as my "meat and potatoes" recipe.

MAKES ABOUT
1 POUND / 500 GRAMS DRIED JERKY

3 pounds / 1.5 kilos top round London broil

Olive oil, for marinating

White vinegar, for marinating

3 teaspoons salt

2 teaspoons coarsely ground black pepper

1 teaspoon garlic powder

Cut the meat into thin strips, then lay the strips in a large, flat, shallow bowl with a lid, or into a flat glass casserole dish that you can tightly cover with foil or plastic wrap. Drizzle on enough olive oil to moisten each strip of meat, and toss. Next, pour in enough white vinegar to cover all the pieces of meat.

Cover the bowl or casserole tightly, and allow it to rest in the refrigerator for at least 4 hours, or overnight.

After the meat has marinated, combine the salt, pepper, and garlic powder in a large bowl. Using your hands, lift each strip of meat out of the marinade individually, and hold it over the marinade bowl, allowing the excess oil and vinegar mixture to run off, about 5 seconds per strip. Dredge the meat strips in the dry spice mixture. Rub the spice mixture into each meat strip, then let them rest in the spice mixture bowl, covering the bowl loosely with foil. Refrigerate for 24 hours.

Preheat the oven to 180°F / 80°C, and take out 1 of the racks.

The next day, working in batches of strips that will fit in a single layer on your oven rack, remove the strips from the dry spice mixture, and lay them directly on the oven rack so that air can circulate around them. Place a foil-lined baking sheet under the meat to catch the drippings. Return the remaining meat to the refrigerator until you have space on the oven rack.

Bake each batch for up to 6 hours, checking for doneness at regular intervals. When the meat is fully dry, remove the rack and allow the meat to cool completely before storing in an airtight container in the refrigerator or freezer. The jerky should last up to 6 months in the refrigerator and a year in the freezer.

PORK CRACKLINGS

THESE ARE THE ORIGINAL HOMEMADE JUNK FOOD. Those with heart problems and high blood pressure may want to steer clear, but, to everyone else, I urge you to indulge in this beloved treat from my childhood at least once a year. The best part of pork cracklings is this: If you make friends with your butcher, and ask nicely, he's likely to hand over as much pork skin as you can handle, free of charge.

MAKES
8 SERVINGS

---

2 teaspoons kosher salt

1½ teaspoons fennel seeds

½ pound / 1 kilo pork fatback with skin,
fat cut to ⅓-inch / 75-millimeters thick

Pulse the salt and fennel in a spice grinder or mash with a mortar and pestle until the fennel is coarsely ground.

Arrange the fatback pieces, skin-side up with their longest sides closest to you, on a work surface or cutting board. Using a sharp knife, score the skin with shallow cuts, going across the length of the pieces. Do this at intervals the size of the tip of your little finger. Take care not to cut through to the fat. Using a clean tea towel, pat the skin until it's fully dry, then rub the fennel salt over the skin and into the scores. Let it stand, loosely covered, for 1 hour.

Preheat your oven to 450°F / 230°C, and move the rack to the bottom third.

Using a new clean towel, pat the skin dry again, then cut the fatback into strips, using scored cuts as a guide. Arrange the strips close together in a large, shallow baking dish and slowly pour ¾ cup / 174 milliliters of water into the baking dish, taking care not to let it cover the skin or to splash on top.

Roast the fatback in the oven for 30 to 40 minutes, skin-side up, allowing the water to evaporate. When the strips are golden brown, blistered, puffed up, and crisp, they are done. If not, keep baking, checking every 5 minutes for doneness.

Using a slotted spoon, transfer the pieces to layers of brown paper to drain, then discard the fat remaining in the pan.

NOEL'S WAY

- Spread brown bread with peanut butter and crumble on the pork cracklings.
- Put them in a resealable plastic bag and toss with any spice mixture from Chapter 9.

OVEN-DRIED JERKY: THE SIMPLE STORY

Humans have been drying meat into jerky as a way to preserve it for as long as we've been killing animals for food. Once a necessity, it's now become an art. No longer thought of as overprocessed junk food eaten only by truck drivers who can't stop for meals or by working-class laborers on the go, jerky is enjoying an artisanal status. Making jerky at home is anything but difficult, but these few tips will help you to success.

1. **Choose your cut:** I recommend lean beef, such as the eye of the round, flank steak, and top round. Already low in fat, these take less time to dry.

2. **Cut the fat:** Fat is responsible for the meat's turning rancid. To get started, slice your meat into ultra-thin strips, using a very sharp knife. If you're slicing it at home, freeze the meat first. For a fee, your local butcher may oblige and hand a roast back to you already sliced. As you are preparing the slices to dry, cut off as much fat as you can.

3. **Marinate for flavor:** Once sliced, refrigerate your meat for a solid day, allowing it to float in a marinade. I like to use resealable plastic bags, but any tightly sealed container in which the meat can be fully submerged is fine. A basic marinade of olive oil and white vinegar, with salt and pepper added, will get you started but there are lots more interesting options, such as:

   Rapeseed or canola oil, cider vinegar, and salt
   Soy sauce, sesame oil, white pepper, and scallions
   Rapeseed oil, white vinegar, cayenne pepper, and brown sugar
   Guinness, honey, and garlic
   Worcestershire sauce, lime juice, and habañero peppers
   Pineapple juice, sesame oil, fresh ginger, and soy sauce
   Red wine, liquid smoke, and red pepper flakes

4. **Salt and rub it:** After your meat marinates, drain it and lay it on wire racks to dry for 30 minutes before salting it well and coating it in dry seasonings for extra flavor, such as:

Garam masala

Dried oregano, garlic salt, paprika, and chili powder

Salt and lemon pepper (see Lemon Pepper, page 241)

Chili powder, ground cinnamon, and onion salt

Dried basil and red chile flakes

5. **Dry it completely:** As you arrange the strips of meat on wire racks or slotted broiling trays, leave enough room between the pieces to allow air to flow. Preheat your oven to at least 180°F / 80°C. You don't want to raise the temperature higher, as it will cook the meat instead of drying it. Lower temperatures, however, are unsafe and encourage quick spoilage because they won't kill already-present bacteria. If you have an electric dehydrator, you can follow the manufacturer's directions and safely dry your jerky using that.

6. **Hide and watch:** Making jerky is not a quick process. Because temperatures, humidity levels, and slice thickness will vary, there can be no set time for the process to complete. Usually, the process takes 2 to 6 hours.

7. **Store it:** Store the jerky in airtight containers. The less air that gets in, the longer it will last. You can use mason jars, resealable plastic bags, or lidded plastic containers. For long-term storage, I recommend double-sealing: wrapping jerky in plastic and storing in a lidded container. Keep jerky in the refrigerator or freezer until you're ready to eat it.

POTTED PRAWNS

THE KEY FLAVORING IN THIS RECIPE is the mace. It's the lacy outer layer of the nutmeg, a unique spice that has a warm flavor vaguely reminiscent of allspice, and it's the distinctive seasoning in traditional potted prawns. Those who grew up eating them would be sorely disappointed at its absence. I like to serve these the classic way, with toast points on which to spread the savory butter and stack the tender prawns. Garnish with radishes, watercress, and a slice of lemon.

MAKES
4 SERVINGS

---

1 pound / 450 grams small Atlantic prawns, peeled and deveined

8 tablespoons (1 stick) / 120 grams unsalted butter

2 tablespoons anchovy paste

¼ teaspoon freshly grated mace

Pinch of freshly grated nutmeg

Grated zest of ½ lemon

½ teaspoon cayenne pepper

In a stockpot, bring 1 quart / 950 milliliters of seawater to a boil (this is the traditional way, if you can get your hands easily on seawater) or, for inland cooks, boil 1 quart / 950 milliliters of water combined with 2 tablespoons of sea salt. Prepare a bowl of ice water and set aside.

Add the prawns to the boiling water, cover the pot, and bring back to a rapid boil for no more than 3 to 4 minutes. Test by cutting them open: The prawns are done when their flesh has lost its glossy appearance and they are opaque in the center. When they are fully cooked, plunge the prawns into the cold water to stop the cooking process, and let them cool completely. Drain the prawns.

In a medium saucepan, melt the butter, anchovy paste, mace, nutmeg, lemon zest, and cayenne. Add the prawns and heat gently for no more than 3 minutes. Divide the coated prawns among 4 ramekins and let them cool in the refrigerator for an hour, reserving the butter in the pan.

Once the prawns have cooled completely, rewarm the butter in the pan and divide the butter evenly among the ramekins to cover the prawns, then cover and refrigerate for at least 2 days to allow the flavors to blend. Potted prawns will keep tightly covered in the refrigerator for up to a week. Let stand at room temperature for 1 hour before serving.

POTTED SALMON

POTTED SALMON IS A BRILLIANT TREAT to tuck into your hamper for an early summer picnic. Chill the ramekins until the butter topping is firm, and wrap them carefully. By the time you're ready to spread your blanket or rug, they'll be the perfect temperature for forking directly onto rounds of freshly sliced Traditional Irish Soda Bread (page 84). Bring lemons and a paring knife along with a pepper mill to add the final touches before serving with crisp salad vegetables and cool white wine.

MAKES
4 SERVINGS

8 tablespoons (1 stick) / 120 grams unsalted butter,
plus more as needed

1 pound / 450 grams (1-inch / 2.5-centimeter-thick)
boneless salmon fillet, skin on

1 tablespoon olive oil

1 tablespoon jarred capers, packed in liquid brine

2 tablespoons finely chopped fennel fronds,
plus extra fronds for garnish

¼ teaspoon freshly ground white pepper

¼ teaspoon sea salt

Preheat the oven to 300°F / 150°C.

In a small saucepan over low heat, melt the butter slowly. Spoon off any white foam that rises to the surface, leaving clarified butter in the pan (any white solids will fall to the bottom). Let cool on the countertop. Brush 4 ramekins with some of the butter, reserving the rest.

Put the salmon in a 1-quart / 950-milliliter baking dish and drizzle with the olive oil. Pour over the salmon the capers in brine, fennel, white pepper, and sea salt, and half of the remaining clarified butter (reserving the rest), and add 2 tablespoons of water. Cover the dish tightly with foil. Cook for 15 to 20 minutes, until the salmon is completely cooked through and flakes easily with a fork. (If it is not flaking easily, depending on the thickness of your fillet, cover it again and cook for another 10 to 15 minutes.) Leave the oven on.

Allow the salmon to cool slightly. Remove the skin and discard it.

Recipe continues

Flake the fish with a fork, keeping an eye out so you can discard any tiny pinbones you may find, even in "boneless" fillet. Spoon the salmon into the 4 prepared ramekins, pressing the surface flat with the back of a spoon. Divide the remaining clarified butter among the ramekins, leaving any white butter solids in the bottom of the saucepan. Stand the ramekins in a large baking dish (such as a 9 x 13-inch / 23 x 33-centimeter baking dish). Pour boiling water into the dish so that it comes halfway up the sides of the ramekins and bake them in the oven for 10 minutes.

Let cool on the countertop to room temperature and then serve or store the ramekins in the refrigerator, tightly covered, for up to a week.

WHAT IS "POTTED" ANYTHING, ANYWAY?

Potting food is a clever way of preserving it by cloaking it in an airtight seal of fat, effectively keeping oxygen and any harmful microorganisms out. According to food historian Bee Wilson, potted food is a descendant of savory pies. She calls the top crust "medieval cling film." With potted food, that top crust's preserving action is replaced by a layer of fat or butter. Meg Dods, author of the 1826 *Housewife's Manual,* claimed that game "to be sent to distant places" would keep for a month if potted correctly. Potting is used largely to preserve animal products. Common potted delicacies included whole pigeons floating in claret, spiced cheese bits, and ground meat and vegetables.

Mealy, tan-colored canned meats have given potted food a bad name since the dawning of factory processing. Many diners have been put off the idea of it by deviled ham, potted crab, and salmon spread that are hardly distinguishable from one another. Potting fresh foods, when done correctly, is a wonderful alternative preparation method when you've an abundance of something tasty or rare. Potted foods are a great luncheon offering, and a wonderful conversation piece.

POTTED HAM

LIGHT AND FRESH IN FLAVOR, this dish is just the thing to serve as a starter for a summer luncheon of consommé and a green entrée salad, such as a Caesar or a Niçoise. I like to offer a slightly chilled ramekin of potted ham in the middle of a serving plate, flanked by triangles of pumpernickel toast and slices of cold, boiled potatoes, garnished with a spoonful of pungent prepared horseradish.

MAKES
6 SERVINGS

---

8 tablespoons (1 stick) / 120 grams unsalted butter

1 pound / 450 grams lean cooked ham

1 tablespoon chopped fresh parsley

½ tablespoon chopped fresh dill

¼ tablespoon ground cloves

½ teaspoon mustard seeds, yellow and brown mixed

1 tablespoon cider vinegar

½ teaspoon coarse sea salt

Gently melt the butter in a small saucepan. Remove it from the heat and let it rest for 5 minutes. Using a slotted spoon, skim off the white foam from the top and discard it, and slowly pour the clear yellow fat from the melted butter into a small bowl, leaving any white solids behind in the pot. Using a chef's knife, chop and shred the ham as finely as possible into thin, stringy strips. Once you think you've chopped it finely enough, chop it again for another few minutes. You want it to be nearly like ground beef.

In a large mixing bowl, combine two-thirds of the clarified butter with the ham, parsley, dill, cloves, mustard seeds, vinegar, and sea salt.

Divide among 6 small ramekins. Press down and flatten the surface with the back of a spoon or your fingers, then spoon or pour the remaining one-third of the clarified butter over the ham mixture.

Refrigerate for at least 2 days to allow the flavors to blend. It will keep tightly covered in the refrigerator for up to a week. Let stand at room temperature for 2 hours before serving.

POTTED CHICKEN

HAPPILY, THE NEED FOR POTTING AS A PRESERVATION METHOD is a thing of the past, but, consequently, a lot of potted proteins disappeared off tables as refrigeration became widespread. Potted chicken, however, survived past its surge of Victorian popularity and remained a constant well into the 1930s and '40s as a spread for teatime sandwiches. This version has less butter than some of the classic versions, making it a little more friendly for everyday eating. I like it as a snack, spread on Rye Crackers (page 260) or Whole Flax Crackers (page 266).

MAKES
8 SERVINGS

1 (3½-pound / 1.6-kilogram) whole chicken
(look for a broiler or a fryer)

¼ teaspoon ground cloves

¼ teaspoon ground allspice

¼ teaspoon salt

¼ teaspoon freshly ground black pepper

3 medium-size shallots

4 slices streaky bacon

4 tablespoons (½ stick) / 60 grams butter,
chilled and cut into 8 pieces

Recipe continues

Preheat the oven to 350°F / 180°C.

Place the chicken in a lidded stockpot, cover it with water, and bring it to a boil over high heat. Once it boils, lower the heat to a very gentle simmer and cook the chicken for 60 to 75 minutes, or until fully cooked, so that the meat easily separates from the bone.

Transfer the chicken to a plate to cool and reserve 1¼ cups/ 300 milliliters of the chicken stock, allowing it to cool (I like to reserve any leftover stock to make soup, so I recommend refrigerating or freezing what's left over right away).

Allow the chicken to cool and remove all the meat, discarding the bones and skin. Chop the chicken coarsely and toss the meat with the cloves, allspice, salt, and pepper. Add the chopped shallots and stir.

Transfer the mixture to a food processor and add the reserved chicken stock. Process for about 1 minute, until the mixture is finely chopped but with some remaining small chunks of chicken and shallots, stopping before it reaches a creamy paste.

Dice the bacon strips into small pieces. Butter 8 ramekins and divide about two-thirds of the diced bacon between the ramekins. Divide all of the chicken mixture among the ramekins and level off the top of each with the back of a large spoon. Place a cube of butter on top of each ramekin, and divide the last third of the diced bacon, sprinkling across the tops the ramekins.

Stand the ramekins in 1 large or 2 medium baking dishes, so that they fit loosely with some space in between. Fill the dishes with hot water to reach halfway up the sides of the ramekins. Bake for 30 minutes, or until the tops are golden brown and the edges begin to pull away from the sides of the ramekins.

Once they're done, run a knife around the edges of the cups and allow them to cool. Once cooled, press down the tops with the back of a spoon to tamp down the mixture, compressing it gently. I store mine on a cold, marble slab in the pantry for up to 3 days, tightly covered with foil or plastic wrap, or you can store them in the refrigerator for up to a week.

PEPPERCORN-TOPPED POTTED BEEF

GREEN PEPPERCORNS ARE THE UNRIPE BERRIES of the pepper plant; you already know them dried as common black peppercorns. The green berries are highly perishable, so when they're not freeze-dried, they're often packed in brine to preserve. Fresher and milder than black peppercorns, they still bring a bit of texture and some heat to otherwise mild potted beef, along with a slight salty and tart flavor from the brine. Brined green peppercorns are usually easy to find in gourmet markets and Asian specialty stores. If you can't get your hands on any, soak dried green peppercorns in a solution of equal parts of warm meat stock and white vinegar. The berries will soften and plump, which heightens their peppery tang.

Potted beef is delicious spread onto crisp rye toast as a snack. To make an elegant starter, serve it with cucumber spears that have been drizzled with rice vinegar and sprinkled with sea salt and white pepper.

MAKES
4 SERVINGS

8 tablespoons / 120 grams unsalted butter

½ teaspoon freshly grated nutmeg

½ teaspoon ground ginger

½ teaspoon salt

¼ teaspoon cayenne pepper

2 garlic cloves, peeled and minced

½ teaspoon freshly ground black pepper

12 ounces / 340 grams braising steak fillets,
fat and sinew removed

PEPPERCORN TOPPING

2 tablespoons / 30 grams unsalted butter

4 teaspoons green peppercorns in brine, drained

Preheat the oven to 300°F / 150°C.

Put the butter in a small saucepan and sprinkle in the nutmeg, ginger, salt, cayenne, and garlic cloves. Sprinkle on the black pepper and warm over a low heat. Allow the butter to melt slowly, stirring occasionally.

Cut the beef into 4 or 5 large chunks and place them in a small 1-quart / 950-milliliter baking dish with a lid. Pour the melted butter mixture over the beef.

Place the baking dish on a baking sheet and cover it with a tightly fitting piece of foil or the lid. Bake for 1½ hours, remove the dish from the oven, and turn the beef pieces over. Cover the baking dish again tightly and bake for an additional hour, until the beef is very tender.

Test for doneness by pressing a fork against a piece of beef. If it shreds easily, it's done. If not, cover the dish tightly again and return it to the oven for another 30 minutes. Test again, and when done, uncover and allow it to cool on the countertop for 30 minutes.

Using a fork, shred the beef and mix with the butter, garlic, and pan juices until the mixture is like a coarse pâté. Transfer to a small glass or ceramic bowl and smooth the surface.

For the peppercorn topping, melt the butter slowly in a small saucepan over low heat. Spoon off any white foam that rises to the surface, leaving clarified butter in the pan. Carefully spoon the clarified butter onto the potted beef, leaving the white sediment from the butter at the bottom of the pan. Scatter the peppercorns over the top of the butter layer. I store mine on a cold, marble slab in the pantry for up to 3 days, or you can store them in the refrigerator for up to a week.

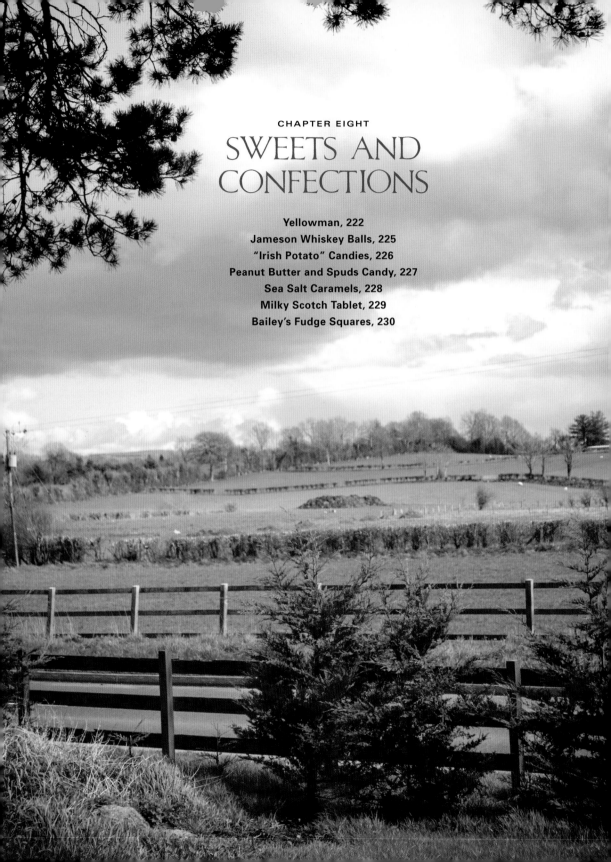

CHAPTER EIGHT

SWEETS AND CONFECTIONS

THE SWEET LIFE

D addy's mother, Mary, lived in our house until 1975, and she welcomed us kids into her room for jolly visits. She'd pull out a green cookie jar and share what was on offer: boiled sweets, toffees, curly wurlys, fruit pastilles, fruit tella, and yellowman. I've still a sweet tooth, and, to this day, I'll accept just about any sweet someone pushes into my hand. And when I eat it, I close my eyes and remember Gran's company as being just as sweet.

YELLOWMAN

AS CHILDREN, MY BROTHERS, SISTER, AND I were always taken to the Ould Lammas Fair in Bally-castle, a fair held every August without interruption for more than three centuries. The word *lammas* means "loaf mass" and refers to the custom of placing on the church altar loaves of bread baked from the first harvest grains. The many joys of the day included seeing all our friends and neighbors in their Sunday best, being bought a bal-loon to tie to our wrists, and, of course, partaking at the most popular stalls at the fair: the yellowman vendors.

We children would crunch through the pale yellow, toffeelike sponge candy, too eager to let it melt in our mouth as the grown-ups did.

This candy is traditionally eaten on its own, but I often break it up with a mortar and pestle to use as an ice-cream topping, or to stir into custard to add a pleasantly crunchy texture.

MAKES
6 TO 8 SERVINGS

1 tablespoon unsalted butter, plus more for buttering pan

1 cup / 180 grams light brown sugar, packed

1 tablespoon corn syrup or golden syrup

1 teaspoon white vinegar

2 teaspoons baking soda

Butter a large loaf pan and set it aside. Have ready a bowl of cold water.

Melt the tablespoon of butter in a heavy pan over medium-high heat. Add the brown sugar, corn syrup, vinegar, and 1 tablespoon of water and bring to a boil swirling the pan, but without stirring, taking care as the mixture begins to caramelize: It will be very hot. Cook for 10 to 15 minutes, until the mixture is amber in color. If you have a candy thermometer, you'll know it's done when the temperature reaches 250°F / 120°C, or you can test it using the hardball test.

To test the Yellowman, carefully spoon out a mound of the mixture and drop it into the bowl of cold water. It's ready if the mixture turns into a crisp and brittle ball. When it passes the hardball test, remove the pan from the heat and add the baking soda, working quickly and stirring with a long spoon. You'll find that it will foam and froth. Pour it into the pre-pared pan and allow it to cool. When the Yellowman is cool (about 30 minutes), cover the loaf pan with a double layer of plastic wrap and hit it with the back of a spoon until the candy breaks into bite-size bites. Keep the candy covered, and store at room temperature in a cool, dry place for up to a year.

JAMESON WHISKEY BALLS

THE TWO SECRETS TO THESE RICH, MOUTH-MELTING, warm-flavored candies are these: good whiskey and good butter. Use Kerrygold, if you can lay hands on it; it's now widely available in American supermarkets.

MAKES
30 TO 40 BALLS

½ cup / 120 grams good-quality unsalted butter,
at room temperature

4 cups / 400 grams confectioners' sugar

4 to 5 tablespoons Jameson Irish whiskey

6 ounces / 170 grams semisweet chocolate

30 to 40 whole pecan halves for garnish

Using an electric mixer, beat the butter and sugar until smooth, about 5 minutes. Add the whiskey and mix until incorporated. Refrigerate the mixture for 1 hour. Form the mixture into 1-inch balls and place on waxed paper. Refrigerate until firm. Transfer the candies to a resealable plastic freezer bag and freeze for several hours or overnight. (Reserve the lined pan for the next step.)

Stick a toothpick through the center of each whiskey ball. Melt the chocolate in a small bowl in the microwave or a double boiler, stirring and heating until smooth. Working quickly, dip the whiskey ball centers into the chocolate, one at a time. Tap the toothpick against the side of the bowl to shake off any excess chocolate. Set the coated whiskey ball on the lined baking sheet. Use another toothpick to push the whiskey ball gently from the dipping toothpick, and cover the hole with a pecan half. When all whiskey balls have been dipped, allow them to rest until set. (To speed the process, the pan of whiskey balls can be placed in the refrigerator.) When set, transfer the candies to a holiday tin or other storage container, and store in a cool, dark place or in the refrigerator.

"IRISH POTATO" CANDIES

THE NAME OF THESE CANDIES IS MISLEADING. I'll admit that they're not Irish, and that they don't feature potato as an ingredient. But they are hilarious! I can't think of anyone who's not charmed by them. Resembling tiny, dusty potatoes, these sweet divinity-like candies taste as good as they look. Many regions and candy makers claim to have invented them, but there doesn't seem to be a definitive answer to stop the arguments. I know these are bought and sent widely in the United States for St. Paddy's. Here's my recipe so you can make them yourself.

MAKES ABOUT
2 POUNDS CANDY

---

4 tablespoons (½ stick) / 60 grams unsalted butter, at room temperature

4 ounces / 110 grams cream cheese,
at room temperature (not low-fat or whipped)

4 cups / 400 grams confectioners' sugar, plus more for coating hands

1 teaspoon vanilla extract

7 ounces / 200 grams dried unsweetened coconut flakes

2 tablespoons ground cinnamon

½ cup / 75 grams toasted walnut pieces

Cream together the butter and cream cheese in a medium mixing bowl, using an electric mixer, until light and fluffy, about 10 minutes. Beat in the sugar and vanilla. Stir in the coconut flakes with a spatula.

Put the cinnamon into a small bowl. Coat your dry hands with confectioners' sugar. Take 2 teaspoon–size pieces of the dough and form them into irregular potato shapes. Drop the potatoes into the cinnamon and roll to coat. Place them on a baking sheet and set them aside while you work. When all the potatoes have been formed and dipped in the cinnamon, press small pieces of toasted walnuts randomly into the sides of each ball to form the potato's eyes. Refrigerate for several hours until firm before serving, and store tightly covered in the refrigerator for up to 2 weeks.

PEANUT BUTTER AND SPUDS CANDY

"LIFE'S TOO SHORT NOT TO BE IRISH," they say. To show that I'm Irish through and through, I'm going to share my recipe that combines my favorite Irish thing, the potato, with enough sugar to make my sweet tooth sing. An unlikely pairing, maybe. But here's a case of the sum being even better than its parts.

MAKES ABOUT
1 POUND CANDY

1 large floury potato

4 cups / 400 grams confectioners' sugar, plus more for rolling

½ cup / 125 grams crunchy peanut butter

Peel and cube the potato. Cover the potato with cold water in a medium saucepan and bring it to a boil. Cook until the potato is fork-tender, then drain the potato through a colander and place the cubes in a large bowl. Mash them with a potato masher until fluffy.

Sift the sugar into the potatoes a little at a time, stirring to mix, and don't panic when the potato gets watery. Keep adding the sugar until the mixture starts to look like dough. Lay out parchment paper and sprinkle it with confectioners' sugar. Roll out the dough with a rolling pin until it's thinner than a piecrust but not falling apart. Warm the peanut butter in the microwave for 10 seconds at a time until it's smooth but not runny, checking after each increment. Spread over the dough. Roll up from the long side like a jelly roll and put in the refrigerator for 2 hours, until firm. Slice into small pieces. Store tightly covered in a cool, dark place or in the refrigerator.

SEA SALT CARAMELS

THE SEA IS A BIG PART OF EVERY IRISH PERSON'S LIFE: It's never too far from wherever we are. The taste of sea salt is natural to us from childhood on. Our family used to take holiday trips to the shore, and we'd be treated with a sweet on most days. This salty, buttery candy is everything good from my childhood, distilled into a sweet.

MAKES ABOUT
1 POUND CARAMELS

Vegetable oil, for brushing

2 cups / 480 milliliters heavy whipping cream

4 tablespoons (½ stick) / 60 grams unsalted butter,
cut into small cubes

1 teaspoon sea salt, plus more for sprinkling

4 tablespoons honey

1 cup / 200 grams granulated sugar

½ teaspoon vanilla extract

Line an 8-inch / 20-centimeter square baking pan with parchment paper and brush it lightly with vegetable oil.

In a medium saucepan over low heat, melt the cream, butter, and the teaspoon of salt together. Once the butter has melted, remove the pan from the heat and set it aside.

Combine the honey, sugar, and 4 tablespoons of water in a heavy-bottomed saucepan and stir well. Over high heat, bring to a rapid boil, and continue to boil the mixture until it turns a golden brown color, about 10 minutes, stirring occasionally. Remove from the heat.

Pour the butter mixture into the sugar mixture, working slowly and stirring constantly. Be careful that the mixture doesn't boil over.

Have a candy thermometer handy. Return the pan to the heat and cook for 10 minutes, or until the caramel reaches 250°F / 120°C and turns a light amber color, or until it passes the hardball test. To test the caramel, carefully drop a teaspoon of the mixture into a bowl of cold water. It's ready if the mixture turns into a crisp and brittle ball. Remove the pan from the heat, then add the vanilla and stir well.

Pour the mixture into the prepared pan. Place the pan on a cooling rack and allow it to cool. Once it's fully cooled, refrigerate it, covered, for at least 4 hours.

Lift the block of candy onto a cutting board by lifting with the parchment paper. Cut the pieces into uniform cubes and sprinkle with sea salt.

Store in an airtight container for up to 2 weeks, or freeze for up to 1 year.

MILKY SCOTCH TABLET

THIS CANDY IS KNOWN AS SCOTTISH, but we're happy to claim it as traditional since we're but a stone's throw from there. It's a comforting treat that is as basic as mother's milk. Creamy and sweet, this candy calls to me. I've usually eaten more than I should before I realize it, lulled in by the welcoming smoothness.

MAKES ABOUT
1 POUND CANDY

---

1 pound / 450 grams granulated sugar

¼ cup / 50 grams dark brown sugar, packed

2 tablespoons golden syrup, or either 1 tablespoon each maple syrup and honey,
or 4 teaspoons light corn syrup plus 2 teaspoons molasses

½ cup / 120 milliliters sweetened condensed milk

2 tablespoons unsalted butter

1½ teaspoons vanilla extract

Line an 8-inch / 20-centimeter square baking pan with parchment.

Combine the granulated sugar, brown sugar, golden syrup, sweetened condensed milk, butter, and vanilla in a large saucepan and bring to a fierce, rolling boil over high heat, and allow it to boil for 5 minutes, stirring constantly with a circular motion.

Lower the temperature to medium-high, but keep the mixture boiling. Do not lower the heat to a mere simmer as the intention here is to boil off the liquid. Continue to stir in a circular motion, while boiling for about 20 minutes; eventually the mixture will turn a dark caramel color and about double its original thickness.

Remove the pan from the heat and beat with an electric mixer for 3 to 5 minutes, until it thickens to the consistency of brownie batter or a stiff custard and sticks to the sides of the pan. Don't overmix, as it will get tough.

Pour the mixture into the prepared pan and smooth the top with a spatula dipped in cold water.

Allow it to set for 30 minutes, then score it into squares so it will separate when fully set. Once set, cut into squares and store it covered in the refrigerator.

BAILEY'S FUDGE SQUARES

BAILEY'S IRISH CREAM AND FUDGE. This is so rich and satisfying, you will want nothing else but a cup of strong, milky tea to wash it all down.

MAKES
2 DOZEN PIECES

1¼ pounds / 600 grams dark chocolate

6 ounces / 175 grams white chocolate

4 tablespoons (½ stick) / 60 grams unsalted butter

3 cups / 350 grams confectioners' sugar

1 cup / 250 milliliters Irish cream liqueur

2½ cups / 350 grams chopped almonds or walnuts

TOPPING

6 ounces / 175 grams dark chocolate

½ cup / 100 grams chopped white chocolate

¼ cup / 60 milliliters Irish cream liqueur

2 tablespoons unsalted butter

Butter an 8-inch / 20-centimeter square baking pan.

In the top half of a double boiler, melt the dark chocolate, white chocolate, and butter until combined and melted through. Stir in the sugar and Irish cream until the mixture is smooth. Stir in the nuts. Place the mixture in the prepared pan and lay a sheet of plastic wrap over the top. Press and smooth the top down.

For the topping, melt the dark chocolate and white chocolate in the top half of a double boiler until melted. Remove from the heat, and with a fork, beat in the Irish cream and butter until smooth. Spread the topping over the cooled fudge, using a knife. To get the smoothest top, place plastic wrap over the top and smooth it lightly with your fingertips. Refrigerate until firm, 1 to 2 hours at least. Store in an airtight container in a cool, dark place, or this fudge can be easily frozen in resealable plastic bags.

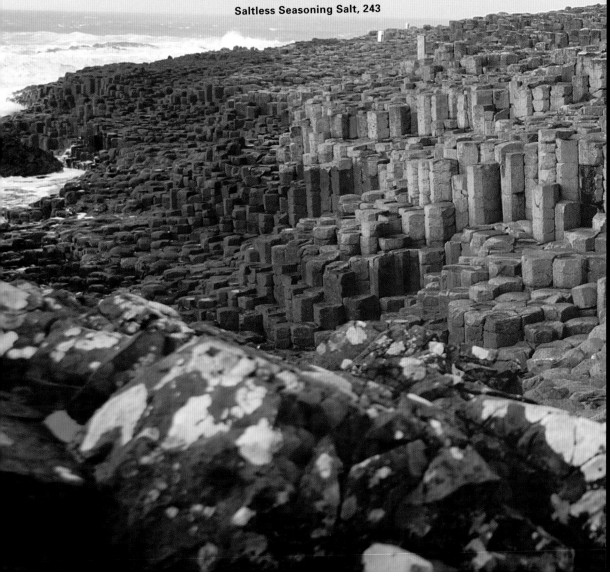

CHAPTER NINE

SPICE BLENDS AND RUBS

PLEASE YOURSELF
AND YOU'LL PLEASE OTHERS

I n cooking, there are some principles that are the same the world over. You spice your meat before you cook it. That's how it is with every people, and in every cuisine. You don't need to overcomplicate it. Flavor things how you like them, and how you think they'll be pleasing to your guests.

Making wholesome, tasty food for yourself or to offer to others needn't cause stress, if the reward is in the creation as well as the consumption. I teach people to slow down and consider what they're cooking, what they're eating, and where it came from.

When you experiment, you're putting your stamp on it. I can't think of a better way to honor guests at your table than by showing them who you are and that you want to make them happy.

MY FAVORITE
GARAM MASALA

THE FOOD OF INDIA IS AS VARIED AS the country's terrain, religions, and regional dress. There is a great presence of Indian immigrants in Northern Ireland, making them the third-largest minority ethnic group in Northern Ireland. Their positive influence on Irish cuisine cannot be denied.

Masala is a spice mixture common in India and other South Asian countries, such as Pakistan and Bangladesh. Spices added to the mixture are rich, bitter, or hot in flavor. *Garam* means "hot" and *masala* is a mix of spices. It can change the personality of the basic foods in the recipe when used in stewing meats and vegetables or sprinkled on top of already cooked foods. A meal spiced with fragrant and piquant garam masala is the very opposite of a comforting roast dinner.

MAKES
½ CUP / 50 GRAMS GARAM MASALA

¼ cup / 20 grams coriander seeds

1 tablespoon cumin seeds

1 tablespoon black peppercorns

1½ tablespoons black cumin seeds

5 black cardamom pods (for about ¾ teaspoon seeds)

¾ teaspoon ground cloves

¾ teaspoon ground cinnamon

¾ teaspoon crushed bay leaves

1½ teaspoons ground ginger

Heat a heavy skillet on a medium flame and gently roast the coriander seeds, cumin seeds, black peppercorns, black cumin seeds, black cardamom (leave the cardamom in its pods till later), cloves, cinnamon, and bay leaves, stirring until all of the spices turn a few shades darker. Do not be tempted to speed up the process by turning up the heat, as the spices will burn on the outside and remain raw on the inside. When the spices are roasted, turn off the heat and allow them to cool in the pan.

Once cooled, remove the cardamom seeds from their pods and mix them back in with all the other roasted spices. Stir in the ginger. Grind them all together into a fine powder in a clean, dry coffee grinder. Store in an airtight container in a cool, dark place for up to a year.

SPICY SEA SALT BLEND

THIS BLEND, LIKE OTHERS IN THE BOOK, can be sprinkled or dusted on nearly any savory food, depending on what you fancy. I love this one on simple potato wedges. Leave the skins on floury potatoes, cut them lengthwise into eights, toss with olive oil, and sprinkle with this salt mixture. Bake until crisp on the outside and fluffy on the inside. The salt melts in your mouth and the spices turn ordinary potatoes into something sublime. I'll bet you don't reach for the ketchup.

**MAKES ABOUT
6 TABLESPOONS SALT BLEND**

¼ cup / 50 grams sea salt (in flakes, if you can find it)

4 teaspoons granulated sugar

1 teaspoon paprika

½ teaspoon turmeric

½ teaspoon onion powder

½ teaspoon garlic powder

½ teaspoon cornstarch

Shake together all the ingredients in an airtight container
and store in a cool, dry place for up to a year.

HERBES DE PROVENCE

THE VERY SCENT OF THIS TRADITIONAL BLEND turns any dish into a trip to a French country bistro. This classic mixture isn't as hard to find at the supermarket as it once was, but if you make your own herb mixture you can adjust the flavors to suit your own taste, at a fraction of the cost. It makes lovely gifts when funneled into pretty jars.

MAKES ABOUT
1 CUP / 40 GRAMS HERBES DE PROVENCE

2 tablespoons dried thyme

2 tablespoons ground rosemary

2 tablespoons dried summer savory

2 tablespoons dried food-grade lavender

2 tablespoons dried marjoram

2 tablespoons dried basil

2 tablespoons dried sage

2 tablespoons dried oregano

Shake together all the ingredients in an airtight container
and store in a cool, dry place for up to a year.

LAVENDER PEPPER

MANY OF US ARE PARTIAL TO THE SOFT, pleasing fragrance of lavender, and it's prized in most cultures as a scent in soaps, potpourri, and powders. My mother steeped lavender in boiling water to sprinkle the laundry before ironing it. It's more surprising as a flavoring, but well worth knowing about. I was always partial to the little lavender pastilles my gran would pull from a tin in her night table drawer and gift me with when I popped into her room for a visit.

Often found in French dishes, lavender has a floral, herbal overtone that lends itself to both sweet and savory dishes. I advise using it sparingly as its strong and pervasive flavor insists on taking center stage.

For a whiff of something different, try this unique, handcrafted blend on seared ahi tuna, lightly grilled breasts of chicken, veal cutlets, and buttery boiled lobster.

MAKES ABOUT
1 CUP / 60 GRAMS

¼ cup / 20 grams black peppercorns

2 tablespoons white peppercorns

2 tablespoons dried garlic powder

1 tablespoon dried onion powder

1 tablespoon dried food-grade lavender

1 tablespoon fennel seeds

5 tablespoons sea salt crystals

Shake together all the ingredients in an airtight container and store in a cool, dry place for up to a year. To use, put the mixture into a pepper mill or crush it with a mortar and pestle.

LEMON PEPPER

JUST THE THOUGHT OF FRESH LEMON PEPPER makes my mouth water. Even the memory of the heat of the coarse-ground black pepper and the dry tang of the lemon zest makes my nose tingle and my eyes glisten. The memory is great, and the real thing is better. I sprinkle this liberally on light, flaky fish for grilling, and on roast fowl. On a bowl of just-tender buttered broccoli, it becomes a meal, savory and satisfying.

MAKES ABOUT
¼ CUP / 30 GRAMS LEMON PEPPER

---

3 lemons

2 tablespoons crushed peppercorns

2 tablespoons kosher salt

Preheat the oven to 200°F / 90°C. Line a baking sheet with parchment paper.

Zest all the lemons with a Microplane zester and set the grated zest aside. Grind the peppercorns coarsely with either a pepper mill, a food processor, or a mortar and pestle. Mix the lemon zest and crushed peppercorns together in a bowl, then spread out the mixture on the prepared baking sheet and bake until the zest is completely dried, about 45 minutes to an hour. Transfer to a spice grinder, food processor, or a mortar, and grind until well mixed and finer in texture. Transfer the mixture to a medium mixing bowl, add the salt, and stir. Store in an airtight container for up to a month.

JAMAICAN JERK RUB

I LEARNED ABOUT JAMAICAN JERK during my time in California. The dry-cooked, spice-dusted method of cooking goat and chicken was just catching on, and it looks like it's here to stay. Here's a blend I created myself: It's salty-sweet with a kick. Bake thin slices of potato tossed with oil and jerk rub, or sprinkle it on roasted nuts. Or stir it into beef gravy and turn comfort food into a special offering.

MAKES ABOUT
½ CUP / 40 GRAMS

---

2 tablespoons granulated sugar

1 tablespoon dark brown sugar

1 tablespoon dried onion flakes

1 tablespoon dried thyme

1 tablespoon ground allspice

1½ tablespoons freshly ground black pepper

1 teaspoon chili powder

1 teaspoon salt

½ teaspoon cayenne pepper

½ teaspoon ground nutmeg

½ teaspoon dry mustard

¼ teaspoon ground cloves

Shake together all the ingredients in an airtight container
and store in a cool, dry place for up to 6 months.

SALTLESS
SEASONING SALT

THERE'S A TIME TO LADLE ON THE SALT and a time to leave it out. When guests with special diets come to call, it's no longer a sad affair with a naked chicken breast and unadorned steamed veg. This tangy spice makes even sensible food feel like a festival.

MAKES ABOUT
⅓ CUP / 25 GRAMS SEASONING SPICE

1 tablespoon dry mustard

1½ teaspoons garlic powder

1 tablespoon onion powder

1 tablespoon freshly ground white pepper

1½ teaspoons crushed basil leaves

1½ teaspoons turmeric

1½ teaspoons ground dried thyme

1½ teaspoons paprika

Shake together all the ingredients in an airtight container
and store in a cool, dry place for up to 6 months.

NOEL'S WAY

• Stir into mashed root vegetables with a few tablespoons of olive oil.

• Use on fish or clam chowder. They're naturally salty enough,
and these flavors complement seafood.

• Shake broccoli and cauliflower florets in a bag with olive oil
and this mixture, then roast for a healthful starter.

CHAPTER TEN

BISCUITS, COOKIES, BARS, AND CRACKERS

SWEET

SAVORY

ON THAT
YOU CAN DEPEND

G rowing up on the small, working dairy farm, handed down to us by my dad's people, I learned about what a person can rely on. A strong, stone house. Our own two hands. Family.

Regardless of the soil and the weather, we always had a stock of milk, butter, and eggs. There's a lot you can make from those three holy ingredients. There was never a shortage of homemade sweets at Rock Cottage, and their delicious goodness fueled and cheered us as we all pitched in to milk, cook, clean, mend, and look after my brothers John and Owen.

And doling out the sweets, along with the orders and the hugs, was my mum. Solid, reliable, and nurturing. As sure as eggs is eggs.

THE ROCK'S
SHORTBREAD

AT THE RISK OF SOUNDING PROUD, I'm going to tell you that this is my best recipe. No one could ever compete against it, and I challenge anyone in Scotland to do better. It was handed down to me by the kitchen artists and wizards before me. I love it straight as it is . . . buttery and rich. But you can gild the lily if you like, with any flavoring that strikes your fancy.

MAKES ABOUT
3 DOZEN PIECES

3½ cups / 450 grams all-purpose flour

1½ cups / 230 grams cornmeal

1 pound (4 sticks) 450 grams unsalted butter,
at room temperature

1¼ cups / 230 grams granulated sugar

Preheat the oven to 350°F / 175°C. Place all the ingredients in a mixing bowl and stir with a spoon until they have come together. Roll out and cut into rounds or fingers.

Transfer to a baking sheet lined with parchment paper, and chill for 20 minutes. Transfer to your hot oven, and bake for 15 to 20 minutes until pale golden. Let cool on a cooling rack and serve at room temperature, or store in an airtight container for up to 2 weeks.

SUGAR-DUSTED LEMON TEA BISCUITS

DAINTY AND LIGHT, THESE ARE JUST THE THING to lay out on a doily for a proper afternoon tea. The tart lemon is a foil for the tea, and you'll have no need for sugar in your cup, owing to the light sweetness.

MAKES
4 TO 5 DOZEN BISCUITS

3¼ cups / 390 grams all-purpose flour,
plus more for dusting

½ teaspoon baking soda

Pinch of salt

12 tablespoons (1½ sticks) / 180 grams unsalted butter,
at room temperature

1¼ cups / 230 grams granulated sugar,
plus more for sprinkling

½ teaspoon lemon extract

1 tablespoon freshly squeezed lemon juice

2 large eggs

Confectioners' sugar, for dusting

Preheat the oven to 375°F / 190°C. Grease 2 baking sheets and set aside.

In a large mixing bowl, sift together the dry ingredients and set them aside.

Using an electric mixer on high speed, cream together the butter, sugar, lemon extract, and lemon juice, about 10 minutes. Beat in the eggs, then gradually add the flour mixture, mixing to make a soft, smooth dough.

Turn out the dough onto a lightly floured surface, and roll it out to about ⅛-inch / 3-millimeters thick. Cut into 2-inch / 5-centimeter squares and place 1-inch / 2.5-centimeters apart on the prepared baking sheets. Sprinkle with granulated sugar. Reroll the scraps.

Bake for 10 to 12 minutes, or until golden brown. Transfer to a cooling rack to cool completely, and serve at room temperature or store in an airtight container for up to 2 weeks.

IRISH LACE BISCUITS

PEOPLE EAT WITH THEIR EYES FIRST. These delicate biscuits could not look prettier on a plate and are a traditional teatime snack. Proud bakers differ as to whether you should roll them into tubes or leave them flat. Either way, they melt in your mouth and are the perfect complement to Ireland's favorite hot beverage.

MAKES ABOUT
3 DOZEN BISCUITS

---

12 ounces (3 sticks) / 360 grams unsalted butter,
at room temperature

2¾ cups / 495 grams light brown sugar

2 tablespoons all-purpose flour

2 tablespoons milk

2 tablespoons vanilla extract

1¼ cups / 110 grams old-fashioned rolled oats

Preheat the oven to 350°F / 175°C. Grease 2 baking sheets with vegetable oil or line with parchment paper, then set in the oven while it is heating up.

Using an electric mixer on high speed, cream the butter and brown sugar together until smooth. Beat in the flour, milk, and vanilla. Fold in the oats. Place teaspoonfuls of dough 3-inches / 7.5-centimeters apart on the hot pans. Bake for 10 to 12 minutes, keeping a close eye on them so you can remove them from the oven as soon as they are fully spread and turn light golden brown.

When the cookies are done, let them cool on the pans for 1 minute, or until they are just firm enough to be moved with a metal spatula. (If you like them rolled into tubes, turn the cookies upside down on the pans and, working quickly with your hands, roll them into cylinders on the pans. (If the cookies become too firm to roll, return them to the oven for a few seconds and allow them to soften.) Transfer the cookies to a cooling rack and let them cool completely, then serve at room temperature or store in an airtight container for up to a month.

CHERRY CHEWS

MY AUNT ROSE GOT THE RECIPE FOR THESE TRAYBAKES from a schoolmistress she roomed with during World War II. Her daughter, my cousin Mary, perfected it, and we eagerly awaited her arrival at every celebration, knowing she'd be carrying a tin of these rich, sweet bars. With a melt-in-your-mouth chocolate base and a chewy cherry topping, they straddle the fence between candy and cookie. As children, we all loved them with milk chocolate, but I find I now prefer them with dark chocolate.

MAKES
16 SERVINGS

---

2 (6-ounce / 175-gram) bars milk or dark chocolate

1 cup / 120 grams self-rising flour

¼ cup / 30 grams all-purpose flour

1 cup / 100 grams confectioners' sugar

8 tablespoons / 120 grams unsalted butter, melted

¾ cup / 150 grams granulated sugar

½ teaspoon baking powder

2 large eggs, lightly beaten

½ cup / 45 grams dry unsweetened, shredded coconut

½ cup / 100 grams chopped candied cherries

Preheat the oven to 350°F / 175°C. Line an 8-inch/ 20-centimeter square baking pan with parchment paper, leaving an overhang of 1 inch / 2.5 centimeters on either side. Break the chocolate into the pan and set it in the oven for 3 to 4 minutes to melt.

Remove the pan from the oven and spread the chocolate evenly across the bottom, using a rubber spatula. Let the baking dish cool on the countertop so the chocolate hardens.

Meanwhile, sift the flours and confectioners' sugar into a medium mixing bowl. Add the butter, and cream the ingredients together with an electric mixer on low speed, until well combined, 3 to 5 minutes. Press the mixture over the chocolate in the baking dish.

Using the same mixing bowl, stirring with a fork, combine the granulated sugar, baking powder, eggs, coconut, and cherries, then spread the mixture over the previous layer.

Bake for 35 minutes, or until golden brown on top. Cool in the refrigerator for 30 minutes to set the chocolate. Then leave the baking pan at room temperature for 30 minutes before using the parchment overhang to lift the cake onto a cutting board. Trim it into 16 bars, using a knife dipped in hot water between each cut. Serve immediately, or allow the bars to cool completely, then store in an airtight tin for up to 2 weeks.

GRAHAM CRACKERS

FRIENDS ARE OFTEN SHOCKED TO HEAR graham crackers can be anything that doesn't come wrapped in cellophane and boxed up in orderly stacks. Old-fashioned and satisfying, these crackers have just the slightest amount of sweetness. I roll mine out thickly, so they're hearty and substantial for dipping in milk or tea.

MAKES ABOUT
2 DOZEN CRACKERS, DEPENDING ON SIZE

½ cup / 60 grams all-purpose flour

2 cups / 240 grams whole wheat flour, plus more for dusting

¼ cup / 50 grams granulated sugar

½ teaspoon salt

½ teaspoon baking soda

1 teaspoon baking powder

½ teaspoon ground cinnamon

8 tablespoons (1 stick) / 120 grams cold unsalted butter,
cut into small pieces

2 tablespoons honey

1 tablespoon molasses

Combine the flours, sugar, salt, baking soda, baking powder, and cinnamon in a large bowl. Cut in the butter until the texture is dry and crumbly. (You can also do this in a food processor; just blend the butter in short bursts.)

In a small bowl, mix the honey, molasses, and ¼ cup / 60 milliliters of water. Toss this with the dry ingredients until well blended. Scrape the sides of the bowl and form the dough into a ball. Wrap in plastic wrap and chill for at least an hour.

Preheat the oven to 350°F / 175°C. Roll the dough out on a countertop or on waxed paper, sprinkled with whole wheat flour. Use a pastry scraper or an index card as a guide to cut the dough into small rectangles. Poke each rectangle with a fork, then place them on an ungreased baking sheet. Bake for about 15 minutes, or until lightly browned and crispy. Once baked, allow them to cool on the pan before serving, or transfer to an airtight container. These can store for up to 1 month.

GINGER SNAPS

THESE COOKIES FEATURE EYE-POPPING fresh ginger and deep, spicy cloves: not for the faint of heart. I eat these by the handful for elevenses. Try crumbling them into the bottom of a pie pan and layering on vanilla custard and whipped cream, for a decadent treat that balances smooth and crunchy textures in a magic way.

MAKES
3 DOZEN GINGER SNAPS

1 cup / 200 grams granulated sugar, plus more for coating dough

1 medium-size egg

¼ teaspoon salt

12 tablespoons (1½ sticks) / 180 grams unsalted butter, at room temperature

2 cups / 240 grams all-purpose flour

½ teaspoon baking soda

2 teaspoons peeled and grated fresh ginger

1 teaspoon ground ginger

1 teaspoon ground cloves

1 teaspoon ground cinnamon

Preheat the oven to 350°F / 175°C. Using an electric mixer on high speed, cream together the sugar, egg, salt, and butter. In a separate mixing bowl, combine the flour, baking soda, ginger, and spices. Add the dry mixture to the wet mixture a little at a time and make sure it's evenly mixed, taking care not to overwork it.

Prepare baking sheets by lining them with parchment paper. Fill a small bowl with granulated sugar.

Using your hands, roll the dough into balls about the size of a large grape, then roll the balls in the sugar and place them on the prepared baking sheets. Bake for 6 to 8 minutes, or until browned.

Transfer the ginger snaps to a cooling rack, and let cool slightly before serving, or allow them to cool completely and store in an airtight container for up to a month.

EVERYDAY CRACKERS

I GET A LOT OF PRAISE WHEN I LAY OUT HOMEMADE CRACKERS. People just don't think to make them at home, but the artisanal texture and original shapes take people's breath away. Guests swear they've been transported back to a simpler time. The funny thing is, even a beginner can ace this recipe.

If you've got more crackers than you can finish as a snack, they make excellent crumb toppings for casseroles or even baked chicken. Bash them up in a plastic bag to get fine crumbs.

MAKES ABOUT
2 DOZEN CRACKERS

---

2 cups / 240 grams all-purpose flour

¼ teaspoon salt

2 tablespoons unsalted butter, at room temperature

1 cup / 240 milliliters milk

Preheat the oven to 300°F / 150°C. Add the salt to the flour, and, in a mixing bowl or food processor, cut in the butter until the mixture looks like fine breadcrumbs. Slowly mix in enough milk to form a soft, but not sticky dough (Be aware that you may not use all the milk). Divide the dough into 2 or 3 portions and roll out one at a time, until paper-thin. You can do this on a lightly floured work surface, or directly on large, ungreased baking sheets. Using a sharp knife or pizza roller, cut the dough into crackers. Prick each 2 or 3 times with a fork and transfer carefully to the baking sheet if you rolled out the dough on a work surface. Bake for 15 to 20 minutes, until lightly browned and crisp. Allow to cool completely on the pan, then serve at room temperature, or store in an airtight container for up to a week.

TRADITIONAL IRISH CREAM CRACKERS

A TRUE IRISH ORIGINAL, THE CREAM CRACKER is flat and square with distinctive air pockets and a mild, savory flavor. Despite the name, this traditional treat does not contain any cream. Rather, the name refers to the creaming process involved in making the sponge batter that's the basis of the cracker.

When you bite a cream cracker a few flakes may fall, but these crackers won't crumble into bits like some other appetizer crackers, so they're ideal as a vehicle for delicious starter treats. Pair these basic crackers with Dubliner or other Irish cheeses, or potted meat (see Chapter 7). I like to layer on simple cream cheese with smoked haddock or salmon and a sprig of dill. Simple, crisp, and light, they're substantial enough to support a topping, but simple enough not to steal the show.

MAKES ABOUT
2 DOZEN CRACKERS, DEPENDING ON THICKNESS

2 teaspoons active dry yeast

⅔ cup / 160 milliliters warm, but not hot, water

1½ cups / 200 grams all-purpose flour,
plus more as needed

½ teaspoon salt

½ teaspoon baking soda

2 tablespoons melted unsalted butter for brushing,
plus more for buttering bowl

Kosher salt, for sprinkling

In a small bowl, sprinkle the yeast over the warm water; stir to dissolve and let stand for 5 minutes. In a large bowl, mix the flour, salt, and baking soda. Add the yeast mixture and stir it vigorously with a wooden spoon. If the dough is sticky, add sprinkles of flour until a soft dough forms. Knead the dough until it is soft and has an elastic consistency, about 5 minutes. Add sprinkles of flour to control the stickiness, as needed.

Drop the dough into a buttered bowl, cover with plastic wrap, and place in the refrigerator to rest for at least 1 hour and up to 18 hours (the longer, the better.)

Arrange the rack in the middle of the oven and preheat to 425°F / 215°C. Line a baking sheet with parchment paper.

On a floured surface, roll the dough into an 18 x 6-inch / 45 x 15-centimeter rectangle no thicker than ⅛ inch / 3 millimeters. Fold the dough from the short ends as if folding a business letter, brushing off the excess flour, to make 3 layers, for extra-flaky crackers. Roll out the dough again until it's about ½-inch / 1.3-centimeters thick. Prick the dough all over with the tines of a fork. Using a pizza wheel or fluted pastry cutter pushed along the edge of a ruler or a straight edge, evenly cut the dough into individual crackers.

Place the crackers close together on the prepared baking sheet. Sprinkle lightly with the kosher salt from 12 inches / 40 centimeters above the crackers, to distribute it evenly. Bake until lightly browned and crisp, 15 to 20 minutes, depending on the thickness of the crackers. Check the crackers several times during the baking period to make certain those on the outer edge of the baking sheet are not getting too brown. If so, switch the ones on the outside with those in the middle. Remove from the oven and brush the crackers with the melted butter. Let cool on a cooling rack and serve at room temperature, or transfer to an airtight container and store it in a cool, dark place for up to a month.

PARMESAN-GARLIC CRACKERS

HEARTY AND THICK, THESE CRACKERS HAVE A HEFT TO THEM. They resemble a cookie in texture, making them ideal for supporting substantial toppings. I like to make my own version of bruschetta with these crackers. Dice up fresh summer tomatoes, crush garlic, chop basil, and mix them together. Layer it on the crackers and top with coarse salt.

MAKES ABOUT
4 DOZEN CRACKERS

8 tablespoons (1 stick) / 113 grams unsalted butter,
at room temperature

1 cup / 80 grams grated Parmesan cheese

1¼ cups / 150 grams all-purpose flour, plus more for dusting

½ teaspoon garlic salt

½ teaspoon garlic powder

1 teaspoon chopped fresh thyme leaves

½ teaspoon freshly ground black pepper

Place the butter in the bowl of an electric mixer fitted with a paddle attachment and beat until creamy. Add the Parmesan, flour, garlic salt and powder, thyme, and pepper and mix until just combined.

Dump the dough on a lightly floured board and roll into a 13-inch / 32-centimeter-long log. Wrap the log in plastic wrap and place in the freezer for 30 minutes to firm up.

Preheat the oven to 350°F / 175°C. Cut the log crosswise into ¼- to ½-inch / 6- to 13-millimeter slices. Place the slices on a baking sheet lined with parchment paper, and bake for 22 minutes, or until golden brown. They will spread a little, but not much. Transfer them to a cooling rack to cool completely, and serve at room temperature, or store in an airtight container in a cool, dark place for up to a month.

CHEDDAR CRACKERS

I LOVE TO OFFER THESE TANGY AND HEARTY NIBBLIES with wine before dinner, alongside a bowl of nuts. The salt is a lovely counterpoint to a smooth wine, and tweaks the appetite for the big meal to come.

MAKES ABOUT
4 DOZEN CRACKERS

---

2 cups / 240 grams all-purpose flour

1 teaspoon salt

¼ teaspoon freshly ground white pepper

¼ teaspoon dry mustard

12 tablespoons (1½ sticks) / 180 grams very cold unsalted butter

½ cup / 113 grams shredded Irish Cheddar cheese
(such as Dubliner)

6 tablespoons cold water, or as needed

In a medium bowl, stir together the flour, salt, white pepper, and mustard. Cut in the butter with a fork until the mixture resembles coarse crumbs. Stir in the Cheddar cheese. Stir in the cold water 1 tablespoon at a time, until the dough is able to hold together. Press the mixture into a ball, wrap with plastic wrap, and refrigerate for at least 30 minutes. Preheat the oven to 350°F / 175°C. Line baking sheets with parchment paper. On a lightly floured surface, roll out the dough to a 16 x 12-inch / 40 x 30-centimeter rectangle about ⅛-inch / 3-millimeters thick. Using a shot glass with a floured rim, cut out small round pieces (don't forget to reflour your glass as you go, to prevent sticking). Place the dough about 1-inch / 2.5-centimeter apart on the prepared baking sheets. Bake for 10 to 12 minutes, or until golden and crispy. Reroll the scraps. Transfer to a cooling rack to cool completely, then store in an airtight container in a cool, dark place for up to 2 weeks.

RYE CRACKERS

RYE IS AN OVERLOOKED GRAIN, IN MY OPINION. I love it for its hint of sour flavor, and its vinegary tang. These crackers taste lovely with dilled tuna salad, egg salad with cracked peppercorns, and with sharp Cheddar stacked with sliced red onion.

MAKES
2 DOZEN CRACKERS

2 cups / 480 milliliters buttermilk

½ cup / 100 grams granulated sugar

8 tablespoons / 120 grams unsalted butter, melted

1 teaspoon salt

1 scant teaspoon baking soda

4 to 5 cups / 410 to 510 grams coarse rye flour,
plus more for dusting

Caraway seeds, for sprinkling

Preheat the oven to 425°F / 220°C.

Mix the buttermilk, sugar, butter, salt, and baking soda with 4 cups of the rye flour to make a stiff dough, adding more flour as needed. Roll the dough into a ball and cut into quarters. Roll each quarter into a 2-inch / 6-centimeter log and cut each log into 6 pieces. Sprinkle rye flour liberally on the countertop, then roll out each slice into a circle as thinly as you can—about 6 inches / 15 centimeters in diameter and ⅛-inch / 3-millimeters thick.

Transfer each slice carefully to a baking sheet and sprinkle very lightly with caraway seeds, pressing them in gently with your fingertips. Bake for about 15 minutes, until lightly browned. The crackers will be best if you let them brown slightly, but they can quickly become too brown. Watch carefully until you get the timing right for your oven—the browning is hard to see as the rye dough is already brown. Transfer to a cooling rack to cool completely, then store in an airtight container.

SPICED OAT CRACKERS

THERE'S LITTLE MORE BASIC THAN IRISH OATS, and these sweet but savory crackers illustrate everything good about them. They're wholesome, hearty, nutritious, and tasty, and I make these to use for a light breakfast offering or a midnight snack.

MAKES ABOUT
3 DOZEN CRACKERS

1½ cups / 135 grams old-fashioned rolled oats

1 cup / 120 grams whole wheat flour

½ teaspoon salt

1 tablespoon granulated sugar

1 teaspoon ground cinnamon

5 tablespoons olive oil

Preheat the oven to 350°F / 175°C. Line a baking sheet with parchment paper.

Place the oats into a blender or the work bowl of a food processor and pulse several times to grind them into a coarse flour. Stir the oat flour together with the whole wheat flour, salt, sugar, and cinnamon in a bowl. Pour in ½ cup / 120 milliliters of water and the olive oil and mix to form a soft dough. Place the dough on the prepared baking sheet and roll out ⅛-inch / 3-millimeters thick. Using a knife, partially slice through the dough into your desired shapes.

Bake until just barely brown, 10 to 15 minutes. Watch carefully, as they burn easily. Allow to cool completely on the baking sheet before breaking along the score lines into individual crackers. Serve at room temperature, or store in an airtight container for up to a month.

BLUE CHEESE AND PECAN CRACKERS

CASHEL BLUE IS AN EXAMPLE OF ONE OF IRELAND'S many fine cheeses. Fragrant and sharp, baked into crackers, it's a great accompaniment to fruity white wines and full-bodied reds.

MAKES ABOUT
2½ DOZEN CRACKERS

---

8 tablespoons (1 stick) / 120 grams unsalted butter, at room temperature

8 ounces / 230 grams blue cheese, such as Cashel Blue,
crumbled, at room temperature

1½ cups / 180 grams all-purpose flour, plus more for dusting

2 teaspoons kosher salt

1 teaspoon freshly ground black pepper

2 medium-size eggs, beaten

½ cup / 75 grams roughly chopped pecans

In the bowl of an electric mixer fitted with the paddle attachment, cream the butter and blue cheese together on high speed for 1 minute, or until smooth. With the mixer on low speed, add the flour, salt, and pepper and mix until it's in large crumbles, about 1 minute. Add 1 tablespoon of water and mix until combined. Dump the dough onto a floured board, press it into a ball, and roll it into a 12-inch / 30-centimeter-long log. Brush the log completely with the egg wash. Spread the pecans in a square on a cutting board and roll the log back and forth in the pecans, pressing lightly, distributing them evenly on the outside of the log. Wrap in plastic wrap and refrigerate for at least 30 minutes or for up to 4 days.

Meanwhile, preheat the oven to 350°F / 175°C. Line a baking sheet with parchment paper.

With a sharp knife, cut the log into slices ⅜-inch / 9-millimeters thick and place them on the prepared pan. Bake for 22 minutes, until very lightly browned. Rotate the pan once during baking. Transfer to a cooling rack, and let cool completely. Serve at room temperature, or store in an airtight container in a cool, dark place for up to a month.

SAVORY IRISH OATCAKES

THIS ANCIENT FOOD WAS A STAPLE when little else was cultivated in the north of Ireland. Mixed with fat and water, this essential bread was baked on rocks, and later on tin plates over open fires to sustain travelers and soldiers. In more modern times, this plain cake grew tastier with the addition of a bit of salt and sugar. We modern Irish like our oatcakes with butter, cheese, or honey. Wholly Irish, steeped in history, these will comfort and fill the belly.

MAKES ABOUT
1 DOZEN OATCAKES

2 cups / 240 grams old-fashioned rolled oats

½ cup / 60 grams whole wheat flour,
plus more for dusting

2 tablespoons unsalted butter, melted

2 tablespoons honey

½ teaspoon fine salt

½ teaspoon baking powder

2 large egg whites

Raw or turbinado sugar or coarse salt, for sprinkling

Preheat the oven to 325°F / 160°C. Line a large baking sheet with parchment paper and set aside.

Put the oats into a food processor and pulse several times to grind them into a coarse flour. Place the oat flour in a large bowl with the flour, butter, honey, fine salt, baking powder, and egg whites and stir just until combined. Turn out the dough onto a floured surface and roll out into a ¼-inch / 6-millimeter-thick rectangle. Using a round cookie cutter, cut the dough into 2½-inch / 6-centimeter circles and transfer to the prepared baking sheet. Sprinkle the tops with raw sugar or coarse salt and bake until deep golden brown and firm, 20 to 25 minutes. Transfer to a cooling rack and let cool completely before serving at room temperature, or store in an airtight container for up to 2 weeks.

WHOLE FLAX CRACKERS

THE DARK WHOLE FLAXSEEDS DOTTING THESE crispy crackers add color, texture, and decidedly nutty flavor. What's more, flaxseeds offer omega-3 fatty acids, excellent for the health. But I think these simply taste wonderful, whether good for me or not.

MAKES ABOUT
1 DOZEN CRACKERS

---

1 cup / 120 grams whole flaxseeds

2 tablespoons soy sauce

¼ teaspoon garlic powder

¼ teaspoon curry powder

Salt and pepper

Place the flaxseeds in a medium bowl with 1 cup / 240 milliliters of water and mix. Let sit for 1½ hours. Expect the mixture to thicken. Even once it thickens, this will be thinner than some cracker doughs, but with patience and care, it'll crisp up nicely.

Preheat the oven to 300°F / 150°C. Line a rimmed baking sheet with parchment paper.

Mix the soy sauce, garlic powder, curry powder, and salt and pepper to taste into the flaxseed mixture. Pour onto the prepared baking sheet, and with a spatula, spread into a large rectangle about ⅛-inch thick. Bake for 40 minutes, then check for firmness. If it's firm, flip the whole cracker and continue baking for another 40 minutes or so. If not, keep baking in 5-minute increments. The exact cooking time can be difficult to judge, so just keep checking in until the whole thing is crispy but not burned.

When the cracker is crisp and browned, allow it to cool on the pan, then cut or break it into bite-size squares. Serve at room temperature, or store in an airtight container.

CHAPTER ELEVEN

DRY MIXES

WELL STOCKED
AND READY

I love storing quick mixes. Grabbing one from the cupboard means I can serve something delicious and wholesome at a moment's notice. When I have guests, my goal is to enjoy their company. When possible, I involve them in the meal's preparation. There's something so congenial about standing around in the kitchen, mixing and chopping elbow to elbow, but the work should be brief, and the relaxation and conversation lingering. Ready-made mixes let me serve a treat at a moment's notice, or to present a personal gift when I'm invited to celebrate a surprise joyful occasion.

Growing up on a farm, I learned that planning ahead and doing work in big batches is a smart way to conduct life. You can't plan for the future if you don't understand the history, I always say. Making mixes in advance, to me, is like saving for a rainy day. I work when I've the time and inclination, and enjoy the fruits later at my leisure. There's not a day goes by when I don't recall practical lessons I learned as a child in Toomebridge. Canning jams, drying beef, and premixing delicious breads give me a sense of security and pride of accomplishment.

CINNAMON-SUGAR QUICK BREAD MIX

THE SMELL OF CINNAMON LINKS ME to my mother. At the first whiff, I'm transported back to her small, cozy kitchen, waiting impatiently for her flaky, oozing apple dumplings to come out of the oven. Spicy and sweet, the aroma of this simple quick bread conjures up that warm, comfortable feeling for me.

The housework my mum did may seem like simple work, as the world never praises loudly enough the woman who keeps the house and family. My mother's legacy will be that she looked after her children and reared a good family. It's fitting that she's burstingly proud of her children. She likes to tell people that "her children will never have to look over their shoulders." I take great pride in living up to her standard in that regard, as well as in turning out such warming, delicious treats as this quick bread that'll please anyone who sits at my table.

MAKES
ONE 9 x 5-INCH / 23 x 13-CENTIMETER LOAF

Zest of 1 large lemon

1½ cups / 180 grams all-purpose flour

1¼ cups / 250 grams granulated sugar

¾ teaspoon salt

¾ teaspoon baking powder

1½ teaspoons ground cinnamon

1 whole vanilla bean

Spread out the zest in a single layer on a baking sheet lined with parchment paper. Bake at 250°F / 130°C until crispy and golden, 20 to 30 minutes. The goal is to dry the zest out, so that it will store.

In a large mixing bowl, sift the flour, sugar, salt, baking powder, cinnamon, and dried lemon zest together and spoon into a large, wide-mouth jar or large resealable plastic bag. Add the vanilla bean. Store in a cool dry place until ready to use, for up to 6 months.

To bake the bread: Preheat the oven to 350°F / 175°C and remove the vanilla bean from the mix. (Don't waste the precious bean! Reuse it. Rinse it off, and lay it on a tea towel to dry. Once dried, use it to make vanilla sugar [see page 152].) Put the dry mix into a large mixing bowl, make a well in the center, and add ¾ cup / 180 milliliters of milk, ⅔ cup / 160 milliliters of vegetable oil, 1 large beaten egg, and 1 teaspoon of vanilla extract. Beat for 2 minutes. Pour into a buttered 9 x 5-inch / 23 x 13-centimeter loaf pan.

Bake for 1 hour, or until a toothpick comes out clean. Let it cool slightly and then remove from the pan.

To make the glaze, combine 1 cup / 100 grams of sifted confectioners' sugar, 2 tablespoons of heavy whipping cream, and 1 teaspoon of ground cinnamon in a mixing bowl and beat until pourable. Add up to 1 more tablespoon of cream, if needed.

To assemble and serve the bread once it's baked, run a butter knife around the edges of the pan and turn out the bread onto a cooling rack. Place a plate under the rack, pour the glaze over the warm bread, and sprinkle it with additional ground cinnamon. Once the glaze is set, slice and serve warm, or store in an airtight container in a cool, dry place or in the refrigerator for up to 3 days.

LEMON–POPPY SEED BREAD MIX

EARLY IN MY CAREER, I HAD THE GOOD FORTUNE to work at Roscoff as a commis chef for Paul Rankin, arguably one of Northern Ireland's finest chefs. I asked him what he thought of my food, and he bluntly and helpfully said, "You should make your food simpler."

I was just heading to America, so I wrote the sentiment in my journal and took it with me to Chez Panisse. Paul had told me that it would be there that I'd learn the essence of what he meant. It turns out Paul's advice was excellent, and I later wrote in my journal, "Every dish will be a winner with the philosophy of simplicity."

Simple needn't be bland or boring, and this bread is an excellent example. I love this easy-to-make, home-style bread for its earthy poppy seeds and tart lemon zest.

MAKES
ONE 9 x 5-INCH / 23 x 13-CENTIMETER LOAF

Zest of 1 large lemon

1½ cups / 180 grams all-purpose flour

1¼ cups / 250 grams granulated sugar

¾ teaspoon salt

¾ teaspoon baking powder

1 tablespoon poppy seeds

Recipe continues

Spread out the zest in a single layer on a baking sheet lined with parchment. Bake at 250°F / 130°C until crispy and golden, 20 to 30 minutes. The goal is to dry the zest out, so that it will store.

In a large mixing bowl, sift together the flour, sugar, salt, and baking powder, then stir in the poppy seeds and lemon zest, using a fork, until they're evenly distributed, and spoon into a large, wide-mouth jar or large resealable plastic bag. Store in a cool, dry place until ready to use, for up to 6 months.

To bake the bread: Preheat the oven to 350°F / 175°C. Butter and flour a 9 x 5-inch / 23 x 13-centimeter loaf pan.

Combine the dry mix with 1 lightly beaten large egg, ⅔ cup / 160 milliliters of rapeseed or canola oil, ¾ cup / 180 milliliters of milk, ¼ teaspoon of almond extract, and 1 teaspoon of vanilla extract. Beat them together for 2 minutes, using an electric mixer.

Bake in the prepared pan for about 1 hour, or until a skewer inserted into the middle comes out clean.

To make the glaze, whisk together 1 cup / 100 grams of sifted confectioners' sugar, the juice of 1 lemon, 1 tablespoon of melted butter, and ¼ teaspoon of vanilla extract in a mixing bowl. Beat with an electric mixer until smooth. Pour the glaze over the hot bread. Serve warm, or store in an airtight container in a cool, dry place or in the refrigerator for up to 5 days.

NOEL'S WAY

• Crumble the bread into dessert glasses, top with Lemon Curd (page 29), and shave on dark chocolate.

• Toast slices and spread with soft, sweet cheese and apricot preserves.

• Top a slice with raspberry sorbet and drizzle on Chocolate Syrup (page 157).

OATMEAL–CHOCOLATE CHIP LOAF MIX

THIS HEARTY, SATISFYING LOAF MAY AS WELL BE A GIANT COOKIE. The butter, sugar, and egg smell will leave your kitchen smelling like love. The twist is the tang in the buttermilk. It provides a counterpoint to the sweetness, so adults will love this treat as much as the kids do.

MAKES
ONE 9 x 5-INCH / 23 x 13-CENTIMETER LOAF

1⅓ cups / 160 grams all-purpose flour

⅔ cup / 60 grams quick-cooking or rolled oats

⅓ cup / 65 grams granulated sugar

⅓ cup / 60 grams light brown sugar, packed

1½ teaspoons baking powder

¾ teaspoon baking soda

½ teaspoon ground cinnamon

½ teaspoon salt

⅓ cup / 50 grams chopped walnuts

⅓ cup / 60 grams chocolate chips

Whisk all the dry ingredients together, then stir in the walnuts and chocolate chips. Spoon into a large, wide-mouth jar or large resealable plastic bag. Store in a cool, dry place until ready to use, for up to 6 months.

To make the bread: Preheat the oven to 350°F / 175°C and grease and flour a 9 x 5-inch / 23 x 13-centimeter loaf pan.

Put the dry mix into a large bowl. In a separate bowl, whisk together 1 beaten large egg, 3 tablespoons of melted butter, and 1 cup / 240 milliliters of buttermilk. Make a well in the dry ingredients and pour in the wet mixture a little at a time, stirring just until combined; the batter will be lumpy.

Bake for 40 to 45 minutes, or until a skewer inserted into the middle comes out clean. Allow the loaf to cool in the pan before cutting and serving, or store in an airtight container in a cool, dry place or in the refrigerator for up to 3 days.

DATE AND WALNUT SCONE MIX

FARM LIFE TAUGHT US TO EXPLOIT THE BOUNTY OF NATURE. Plucking blackberries from their canes and gathering apples that have fallen from trees was light work. Gathering English walnuts was another thing altogether. Picking them up was easy enough, but freeing them from their hard outer husks was no small task. We'd take turns with a hammer, cracking them on the stone pathway. There were more than a few little fingers sacrificed to this task! When we tired of the hard labor, we'd line the driveway with them and wait for car tires to do the work, cracking them open on the gravel.

The best thing about hard work is that it pays off in the end. The fruit we picked and the sweet meat we gleaned from nuts were handed over to our mum, who turned them into such goodies as Blackberry and Lime Jam (page 21), St. Stephen's Day Chutney (page 285), and this Date and Walnut Scone Mix. Whether they were eaten right away or stored for leaner times, we took pride in our work when we enjoyed the sweet results.

MAKES
8 SCONES

Zest of 1 small lemon

2 cups / 240 grams all-purpose flour

½ cup / 100 grams vanilla sugar (see page 152)

¼ cup / 25 grams nonfat dry milk powder

2 teaspoons baking powder

¼ teaspoon salt

⅓ cup / 80 grams vegetable shortening

5 ounces / 150 grams pitted and chopped dried dates

½ cup / 75 grams chopped walnuts

Recipe continues

Spread out the zest in a single layer on a baking sheet lined with parchment. Bake at 250°F / 130°C until crispy and golden, about 20 to 30 minutes. The goal is to dry the zest out, so that it will store.

In a large mixing bowl, lightly stir together the flour, sugar, milk, baking powder, lemon zest, and salt. Cut in the shortening using a pastry cutter or 2 butter knives until the mixture resembles coarse crumbs. Stir in the dates and walnuts. Store in a large glass jar or resealable plastic bag in a cool, dry place for up to 2 months.

To make the scones: Preheat the oven to 400°F / 200°C.

Place the mix in a large mixing bowl. Make a well in the center and add 1 lightly beaten large egg and ¼ cup / 60 milliliters of water. Mix just until blended and still a little lumpy. Turn out the dough onto a lightly floured surface and knead lightly for 10 or 12 seconds, just until smooth. Pat into a ½-inch / 1.3-centimeter-thick circle. Cut into 8 wedges and transfer to an ungreased baking sheet. Brush with a little milk. Bake for 12 to 15 minutes, or until golden. Transfer to a cooling rack to cool slightly, and serve warm, or allow it to cool, and store in an airtight container in a cool, dry place or in the refrigerator for up to 3 days.

EASY CINNAMON-RAISIN SCONE MIX

THIS IS A LOVELY FIRST-TIME-OUT-OF-THE-GATE RECIPE for beginning bakers. It is the best kind of food gift, because anyone can master making it well.

MAKES ABOUT
16 SCONES (TWO BATCHES OF 8 SCONES EACH)

5 cups / 600 grams all-purpose flour

¾ cup / 150 grams granulated sugar

1 cup / 100 grams nonfat dry milk powder

1 tablespoon baking powder

2 teaspoons ground cinnamon

1½ teaspoons salt

¾ cup / 180 grams vegetable shortening

10.5 ounces / 300 grams raisins

In a large bowl, combine the flour, sugar, milk powder, baking powder, cinnamon, and salt. Cut in the shortening until the mixture resembles coarse crumbs. Add the raisins. Spoon into a large, wide-mouth jar or large resealable plastic bag. Store in a cool, dry place until ready to use, for up to 6 months.

To make a batch of 8 scones: Preheat the oven to 400°F / 200°C. Grease a baking sheet.

In a large bowl, combine 4 cups of the mix, 1 lightly beaten medium-size egg, and ½ cup / 120 milliliters of milk or water and stir with a fork until moistened. Turn onto a lightly floured surface and knead five or six times. Transfer to the prepared baking sheet and pat into a 9-inch / 23-centimeter circle. Cut into 8 wedges (do not separate) and sprinkle the tops with raw or turbinado sugar. Bake for 20 to 25 minutes, or until golden brown. Serve warm, or allow to cool and store in an airtight container in a cool, dry place or in the refrigerator for up to 3 days.

CHAPTER TWELVE
HOLIDAY GOODIES

OUR IRISH CHRISTMAS

I can hardly explain the breathless excitement and joy that surrounded Rock Cottage at Christmas when I was little. In the time leading up to the holiday, the house was bursting at the seams with all manner of family, friends, and neighbors stopping by to leave tasty dishes or to join us for the ones my mum and granny would create, such as fluffy buns with icing and glassy cherries on top. Aunt Greta showed up with glorious hedgehog cakes and float-away sponge with buttercream and her own strawberry jam, and taught her daughter Mary to carry on the tradition.

During that time, my sister, Ita, and I would bundle up against the damp winter's chill and sit at the end of our drive with our dog, Nip, counting cars to pass the time as we waited for company. Our parents taught us that the guests were the most important part of the celebration and showed us from an early age how to look after them. We kids all used real elbow grease to make the house spotless, and our cleaning was powered by heart, not machines. In our house, the table was nicely set, the brass was polished to gleaming, and everyone was welcomed at the curb.

My mother would start the Christmas cake preparations at the end of November and got along with baking all the biscuits, cookies, and breads to store in the pantry. I remember the smell of the fruit soaking in spirits overnight, signaling that the cake was coming, and my brothers and sister and I would come home from school to look at it, with a stern warning not to touch it. My mother would wrap it meticulously in waxed paper and seal it airtight, unveiling it from time to time—oh, the aroma of the spices was so tempting—so we could poke it with skewers and baste it in brandy.

The night before Christmas, my mother would start the turkey, which we always

got from Eileen Barry's farm up the road. We'd get huge birds (one year it was a 32-pounder, standing in the barnyard) and she and her son would deliver it and help us hang it in the pantry with a bag around its head. I'd help Mum take the neck off and stuff it. She'd have a batch of bread made for the stuffing, and I'd cut crusts off the loaves and grate them finely to fry up with good butter, onions, celery, and fresh parsley. I have to admit that we'd take turns going into the pantry and stealing slices of that roasted bird lying on the marble slab . . . we couldn't help ourselves. The delicious smell drove us to it. That night, we'd go to midnight Mass as a family, and come home to Daddy's favorite meal for the occasion: traditional Irish stew, which was mostly just fork-tender beef in a gleaming, aromatic onion gravy with maybe a carrot or two, and we sopped it up with soda farls baked on the stove top.

For the big dinner, we'd start with vegetable soup and, if it wasn't too cold, melon. There would be a ham dotted with cloves and smeared with English mustard.

And, of course, the long-awaited turkey. Rounding out the feast were tureens of crunchy Brussels sprouts, boiled carrots and potatoes, soda bread, treacle bread, and wheaten bread with huge hunks of butter. For dessert, those who didn't take Christmas cake would be treated to a lemon jelly beaten with evaporated milk and served with ice cream or homemade custard, and, of course, handheld mincemeat pies.

Everyone wore paper crowns and hats, and we'd pop crackers, out of which would fall small prizes or coins. To this day, I cannot for the life of me picture where we all sat. We must have been shoulder to shoulder, bumping elbows and eating off one another's forks! What I do remember, though, was the warmth. Like my daddy always said, "It's not money that makes a man rich," and our Christmas feasts truly brought that sentiment to life.

Warm Holiday Feelings

In Ireland, we slow down and savor holidays in a way that some modern countries no longer do. You'd be hard-pressed to find even a pharmacy open on Christmas Day in Ireland, let alone a supermarket or hardware store. In some countries, people dutifully report to work the day after Christmas, but, in Ireland, no one's expected back for days, or even the week. On December 26, everyone who's mobile is expected to take a bracing walk, stroll, or hike, and the tradition is to take along sandwiches concocted of the leftover meats from the feast, dressed with cheery condiments, such as my St. Stephen's Day Chutney (page 285), and accompanied by slabs of cakes, such as my Cranberry–White Chocolate Loaf (page 300).

Easing up the pace, resting, and celebrating with special foods are the hallmarks of Christmas, and all holidays, where I'm from. Friends, families, and feasts. Life doesn't get sweeter than that.

APPLE CIDER OR SPICED WINE
MULLING BLEND

THIS SIMPLE BLEND TAKES MINUTES TO ASSEMBLE. The results, though, are spectacular. Mulling with these fruits and spices fills the house with an aroma promising good things to come. It's like a holiday in a mug.

MAKES ENOUGH FOR
ONE 750-MILLILITER BOTTLE OF WINE

Zest of 1 lemon

Zest of 1 lime

½ cup / 100 grams granulated sugar

½ cup / 100 grams dried cranberries

6 whole cloves

1 cinnamon stick

1 whole nutmeg

2 star anise

4 cardamom pods

Shake together all the ingredients in an airtight container and store in a cool, dry place for up to a year.

To use, just add it to a bottle of wine (I suggest unoaked reds) and warm over low heat for as long as you'd like to let it stand. Alternatively, farm-fresh cider may be mixed in equal parts with French chardonnay; or, for nondrinkers, substitute a blend of half cranberry juice and half grape juice, then mull as if wine.

ST. STEPHEN'S DAY CHUTNEY

ST. STEPHEN'S DAY, OR WREN DAY, is celebrated in Ireland on December 26. Traditionally, children or young men dress in straw outfits or old clothes and paint their faces. An old custom involved literally going out to the fields and hunting for a wren that was said to have betrayed St. Stephen himself. Today, parties go door to door singing, or from pub to pub playing instruments, hoping for treats or a few coins in return.

For some families, the wren hunt turned into a fox hunt, or, barring that, a very cold picnic. People enjoy Christmas dinner leftovers while all bundled up. Sometimes, they're repurposed into a stew or a savory pie filling, served hot. In my corner of Ireland, they were made into sandwiches, and nothing suits a sandwich better than chutney. I like to give this relish for Christmas presents, hoping it may appear alongside a Stephen's Day feast.

MAKES
2 CUPS / 480 MILLILITERS CHUTNEY

½ cup / 75 grams chopped almonds

½ cup / 80 grams chopped pitted dates

¼ cup / 50 grams chopped apricots

2 ounces / 50 grams raisins

2 large tart apples, peeled and finely chopped

2 teaspoons ground cinnamon

¼ teaspoon ground cloves

2 to 3 tablespoons red wine

2 teaspoons honey

Place the almonds in a food processor fitted with the chopping blade. Pulse until ground coarsely. Add the dates, apricots, raisins, apples, cinnamon, and cloves and pulse 4 to 6 times, until mixed. Scrape into a bowl and mix in just enough red wine to make a pasty consistency so the mixture sticks together (you may need more or less than a few tablespoons). Stir in the honey. Serve immediately, or ladle into clean jars with tight-fitting lids and store in the refrigerator for up to 5 days.

CRANBERRY AND FIG CHUTNEY

THE MOST APPEALING THING ABOUT CHUTNEYS, to me, is the sheer symphony of flavors it's possible to combine into one humble, easy-to-execute food. While I love the following recipe for its balance, I give you full permission to color outside the lines with other flavors. Chutneys keep for ages because of the preserving quality of the vinegar, and they'll dress up any simple dish with an exotic flair. I like this one with roast fowl or sautéed pork chops, or even alongside a simple, homey dish, such as cheese on toast. I'll wager guests at your table will ask for the recipe. Keep a few extra jars on hand, so you can send those guests off with not only a recipe, but a beribboned jar of your very own for inspiration.

MAKES ABOUT
3½ CUPS / 700 MILLILITERS CHUTNEY

---

2 tablespoons vegetable oil

1 medium-size yellow onion, chopped

4 ripe figs, cut into wedges

1 mild chile pepper (like banana or poblano), seeded and chopped

⅓ cup / 65 grams granulated sugar

⅓ cup / 70 milliliters red wine vinegar

1 teaspoon ground cinnamon

1 tablespoon ground cloves

1 cup / 120 grams fresh cranberries,
blanched in boiling water for 1 minute

Sea salt

Freshly ground black pepper

In a large, heavy-bottomed, nonreactive saucepan, heat the oil over medium heat. Cook the onion until it has softened and is beginning to become transparent, stirring often. Add the fig wedges and chopped chile pepper, and stir well. Add the sugar, vinegar, cinnamon, and cloves, and bring to a boil over high heat. Add the cranberries and lower the heat, then simmer for 20 to 25 minutes, or until the fig wedges and cranberries are soft enough to smash easily with a fork. Season to taste with sea salt and freshly ground pepper.

Ladle into hot, sterilized jars (see page 17), leaving a ½-inch / 1.3-centimeter headspace, and seal using the hot water bath (see page 43) for 5 minutes. This should keep for up to 6 months in a cool, dark place, if properly sealed.

GRANNY'S CHRISTMAS MINCEMEAT

AS A RULE, YOU WON'T FIND A SCRAP OF MEAT in today's fruit- and nut-based version of mincemeat, which is more of a dessert than a savory dish. The roots of this highly spiced dish can be traced to the eleventh century, and the return of the Crusaders to Britain from the Holy Land. Historical recipes used vinegars and wines to preserve the meat, along with Middle Eastern spices such as cinnamon, nutmeg, and cloves.

Christian associations were layered onto the food, and soon the exotic spice trio was linked to the three Magi, the oblong piecrusts into which the mince was baked was said to represent the cradle of the Christ child, and it became the custom to eat one handheld pie on each of the twelve days of Christmas.

Each season, I make vats of the delicious mixture to make pies, to mix into Holiday Flapjacks (page 294), to stuff baked apples, and to warm and spoon onto vanilla ice cream.

MAKES ABOUT
1 QUART / 1 LITER OF MINCEMEAT (ENOUGH FOR TWO 9-INCH / 23-CENTIMETER PIES
OR ABOUT A DOZEN SMALL HANDHELD PIES)

---

2 medium-size tart green apples, peeled, cored, and minced

8 tablespoons / 113 grams unsalted butter, cut into cubes and
frozen hard (you can substitute suet, if you prefer)

6 ounces / 175 grams sultanas

4 ounces / 110 grams raisins

6 ounces / 175 grams dried cranberries

2 ounces / 55 grams candied fruit peel, finely chopped

1 cup / 175 grams light brown sugar, loosely packed

Zest and juice of 1 lemon

Zest and juice of 1 lime

Zest and juice of 1 orange

¼ cup / 25 grams walnuts or pecans,
coarsely chopped

¼ teaspoon ground cloves

¼ teaspoon ground cinnamon

½ teaspoon ground nutmeg

2 tablespoons brandy

2 tablespoons Jameson Irish whiskey

In a very large mixing bowl, combine all the ingredients, except the brandy and whiskey, and mix lightly. Cover and let sit overnight. The next day, preheat the oven to 225°F / 100°C. Transfer the mixture to a Dutch oven, cover, and bake for 2½ to 3 hours, stirring occasionally, until all the butter has melted and the solid ingredients have begun to soften and meld. Allow the mixture to cool in the Dutch oven. Once completely cool, stir in the brandy and whiskey and spoon into hot, sterilized jars (see page 17). Use immediately as a dessert topping or Holiday Flapjacks ingredient (see page 294), or to spoon into your own home-made or store-bought piecrusts or tart shells. To store, seal tightly and refrigerate for up to 2 months.

CHRISTMAS SPICED BEEF

TODAY IN IRELAND, SPICED BEEF IS A HOLIDAY DISH, likely for two reasons: Many poor families enjoyed meat only on special occasions, and this dish in particular has a preparation time of almost two weeks. Before refrigeration, the large amounts of salt, and the salt-peter, also known as sodium nitrate, were employed to preserve meat. In Ireland, you'll find saltpeter at the pharmacy. Elsewhere, specialty stores carry it to cater to hobbyists who smoke and cure meat at home. The saltpeter isn't strictly necessary. Some people enjoy the characteristic cured flavor it brings, along with the distinctive pink color. If you can't find it, leave it out.

Fragrant Christmas spices and sugar were eventually added to the curing process in celebration of the season. Every family seems to have its own version. In the south of Ireland, particularly in Cork, where the beef export trade dates back for centuries, most butchers who prepare and sell holiday spiced beef keep sealed lips regarding their special proprietary spice blends.

To serve, slice thinly and lay out on a Christmas buffet with crackers, gherkins, chutney, and cheeses or thinly sliced party bread for festive sandwiches.

MAKES
15 TO 20 SMALL SERVINGS

---

5 pounds / 2.26 kilograms beef rump roast
(you can also use sirloin or round roast)

¼ cup / 45 grams dark brown sugar, packed

2 tablespoons ground allspice

2 teaspoons saltpeter (optional)

½ cup / 125 grams coarse kosher salt

DAY ONE:

Rub the beef all over with the brown sugar and place it in a glass
or ceramic dish just large enough to hold it. Cover with plastic wrap
and refrigerate it overnight.

DAY TWO:

Combine the allspice and saltpeter (if using) and rub them over
the sugared beef. Re-cover and refrigerate overnight.

DAY THREE:

Rub the spiced and sugared beef with salt. Re-cover and refrigerate for 7 days.

DAY TEN:

Put the beef into a large stockpot and cover it by at least 2 inches / 5 centimeters of cold
water. Bring it to a boil, lower the heat, and simmer gently over low heat for 2 hours.

Transfer the beef to a large casserole dish and cover it with a large sheet of plastic wrap so
that the wrap hangs loosely off the sides, rather than sealing the top tightly. Lay on top a
plate that's slightly larger than the beef roast, and stack several heavy cans of beans on top
to really press down on the meat. Refrigerate it for 2 days. This will compress it in a manner
similar to making pastrami.

After 2 days, slice the beef very thinly as you serve it. Because of the salt and spices, this
beef can last a week wrapped loosely in a clean towel and stored in a cool, dry, dark place,
but most people store it in the refrigerator.

BEST SHROVE TUESDAY PANCAKES

THESE AREN'T TRADITIONAL FLUFFY PANCAKES stacked high and robed in maple syrup, as the Americans do it. These are thin and delicate like crêpes. On Pancake Day, pancakes are traditionally sprinkled with sugar and a healthy squeeze of lemon. Little children quickly learn to roll them into a tube, and the tasty treats are eaten without cutlery as fast as they're released from the skillet.

MAKES ABOUT
12 PANCAKES

1¾ cups / 230 grams all-purpose flour

Pinch of salt

2 medium-size eggs

2 teaspoons unsalted butter, melted

2½ cups / 540 milliliters milk

Sift the flour into a large mixing bowl and add the salt. In a small bowl, beat the eggs lightly. Make a well in the center of the dry ingredients with your hand and add the eggs a little bit at a time, beating well until the batter is smooth.

Add the melted butter and half of the milk to the batter and mix well. Add the rest of the milk and mix just until it is incorporated.

Allow the batter to rest for about 10 minutes while lightly buttering an 8-inch / 20-centimeter, heavy-bottomed skillet and setting it over high heat. Using a ladle, pour in the batter to coat the pan thinly, then cook the pancake until it's set and just becoming golden.

Flip the pancake over with a spatula (we flipped them in the air as children, but it's a risky proposition) and cook on the other side for a scant 30 seconds. Remove the pancake from the pan and serve immediately. Repeat with the rest of the batter.

PANCAKE DAY

Shrove Tuesday—also known as Pancake Day—is the day before Ash Wednesday, marking the start of Lent. During the religious observance of Lent, abstinence from luxury is often practiced as an opportunity to repent for sins and for self-reflection. In fact *shrove* is the past tense of *shrive,* an Old English word meaning "to obtain absolution from wrongs."

In olden days, pancake recipes enabled housewives to use up any stocks of milk, butter, sugar, and eggs, all of which were forbidden during the stark abstinence of Lent. The night before the start of the Lenten fast is a time when many still engage in making and eating great stacks of pancakes. Eating till you burst is allowed and encouraged. As schoolchildren, we devoted Ash Wednesday mornings to boasting tales of our pancake-eating accomplishments.

In an old traditional Irish practice, wedding during Lent was forbidden, so matchmakers hurried to find suitable spouses for single folk in the weeks leading up to Ash Wednesday. In the "unfortunate" households still "burdened" with unmarried daughters, the poor spinsters (regardless of their age) were encouraged to toss the first cake in the air, as a ritual to bring luck. The link between the girls' pancake-making prowess and ability to flip them golden and whole was analyzed as a predictor for the next year's chances of marrying.

HOLIDAY FLAPJACKS

THERE'S EVERYTHING TO LOVE ABOUT TRADITIONAL IRISH FLAPJACK: It's simple to make, filling and comforting, chewy and gooey, and even a bit healthy for you. Not to be confused with pancakes, our flapjack is basically an oat bar, bound together by butter and sugar, with flavorings added in.

During the Christmas time, I like this version, flavored with mincemeat and fragrant with the spices of the season.

MAKES
8 TO 12 PIECES

½ cup / 90 grams dark brown sugar, packed

8 tablespoons / 113 grams unsalted butter

1 tablespoon honey

¼ teaspoon table salt

2⅔ cups / 240 grams old-fashioned rolled oats

¾ cup / 150 grams Granny's Christmas Mincemeat (page 288),
or store-bought

2 tablespoons brandy

Preheat the oven to 350°F / 180°C and line an 8-inch / 20-centimeter square baking pan with parchment paper or buttered foil, allowing the parchment or foil to overhang the edges by 2 inches / 5 centimeters on either side.

In a large saucepan over medium heat, melt the brown sugar, butter, honey, and salt together. Remove the pan from the heat and add the oats, mincemeat, and brandy. Stir until evenly mixed and turn the mixture into the prepared pan. Bake for 25 to 30 minutes, until slightly puffed and golden on top.

Let cool completely in the pan, then use the overhanging parchment or foil to lift the flapjack out of the pan and onto a cutting board. Slice into 16 pieces, then cut each square into a triangle for 32 small flapjacks. Store in an airtight container for up to a week. These also freeze well in resealable plastic bags for up to a month.

BRANDY BALLS

A CROSS BETWEEN COOKIES AND CANDY, these are a favorite among the old folks I know, and are becoming popular in a resurgence of "everything old is new again" with my younger friends. These are just the right amount of festive for the holidays, and they're easy to make.

MAKES ABOUT
50 BALLS

---

1 (6-ounce / 170-gram) can evaporated milk

⅔ cup / 150 grams chocolate chips

1 pound / 450 grams packaged almond biscotti, crushed very finely

½ cup / 120 milliliters brandy or rum

10 ounces / 280 grams chopped walnuts (about 2 cups)

1¼ cups / 120 grams confectioners' sugar, for coating

In the microwave or in a metal bowl set over a pan of simmering water, melt the evaporated milk and chocolate chips together, stirring frequently until smooth.

Remove the mixture from the heat and stir in the crushed cookies and brandy until well blended. With wet hands, roll the mixture into 1-inch / 2.5-centimeter balls, then roll the balls in chopped walnuts, then in the confectioners' sugar. Store, covered, in the refrigerator.

NOT-FOR-LENT FUDGE

MANY PEOPLE IN IRELAND GIVE UP ALCOHOL FOR LENT, but some of us try, now and then, to give up sugar. So I can't precisely call this a Lenten dish, as it's full of indulgence for sugar lovers, but it's a fabulous treat to make on Pancake Tuesday, if you can't manage to use up those last bits of butter and cream in the traditional way.

MAKES
2 DOZEN PIECES

2 cups / 200 grams confectioners' sugar

5 tablespoons light cream

6 tablespoons / 85 grams unsalted butter

2 cups / 75 grams mini marshmallows

1¼ cups / 250 grams bittersweet chocolate chips

¼ teaspoon vanilla extract

3 tablespoons unsweetened cocoa powder

Line an 8-inch / 20-centimeter square pan with parchment paper, allowing the parchment to overhang the sides by 2 inches / 5 centimeters, and set it aside. In a heavy saucepan over medium heat, combine the confectioners' sugar, cream, and butter. Mix well and stir constantly until the sugar dissolves and the mixture begins to boil, about 10 minutes. Lower the heat to medium-low and continue to cook for 5 minutes, stirring constantly.

Remove from the heat and add the marshmallows, chocolate chips, vanilla, and cocoa powder. Beat by hand for 1 minute, and pour the mixture into the prepared pan. Chill thoroughly in the refrigerator until firm, before cutting into squares. Refrigerate in an airtight container.

GINGERBREAD
COOKIE MIX

GINGERBREAD IS THE VERY SYMBOL OF HOLIDAY GATHERINGS, served with rich cups of hot chocolate and topped with whipped cream. Dead easy to make, it's a sure crowd-pleaser. Give the mix as a gift or make several batches to store in your pantry to pull out when surprise guests pop by to carol or deliver presents and good wishes.

MAKES ABOUT
4 DOZEN COOKIES

3½ cups / 420 grams all-purpose flour,
plus more for dusting

1 cup / 180 grams dark brown sugar, packed

2 teaspoons ground ginger

1 teaspoon ground cloves

1 teaspoon ground cinnamon

1 teaspoon ground allspice

1 teaspoon baking powder

1 teaspoon baking soda

Whisk all the ingredients together and spoon into a large, wide-mouth jar or large resealable plastic bag. Store until ready to use, up to 6 months.

To make the cookies: Preheat the oven to 350°F / 175°C. Lightly grease a baking sheet.

Empty the contents of the jar into a large mixing bowl and stir well. Mix in ½ cup / 113 grams of room-temperature butter, ¾ cup / 180 milliliters of molasses, and 1 beaten egg. The dough will be very stiff, so use your hands to mix it. Cover and refrigerate for 45 minutes.

Roll the dough into a ¼-inch / 6-millimeter-thick rectangle on a lightly floured surface. Cut into shapes with a cookie cutter. Place the cookies about 2-inches / 5-centimeters apart on the prepared baking sheet.

Bake for 10 to 12 minutes, then transfer to a cooling rack to cool completely. Store in an airtight container.

MOTHERING SUNDAY

In Ireland, the fourth Sunday in Lent marks the celebration of Mothering Sunday, a day during which families gather and reunite for fellowship and a relaxation of Lenten vows amidst the austerity of the forty-day period. Most Catholic families spend the early part of the day at Mass, during which the congregants "clip the church": joining hands and surrounding the building to symbolize embracing it.

In days gone by, domestic workers and children in service to wealthy families were given the day off and sent home to spend time with their families: a rare and treasured event as long working hours and infrequent days off generally prevented the gathering of all the kin in working-class households. During the Victorian era, the honorable thing for employers to do was to provide either the ingredients or the money to buy the ingredients for a light fruitcake topped with eleven marzipan balls to represent Jesus's apostles, minus Judas.

On the way home, children would gather wildflowers to adorn the church, or, later, to present to their mother, and the more religious practice shifted to a secular day of giving gifts to one's mother, as on Mother's Day.

Today, families eat Simnel Cakes throughout the Lenten season leading up to Easter, and, for some, it's the annual centerpiece to a festive Easter dinner.

CRANBERRY–WHITE CHOCOLATE LOAF MIX

THIS EASY-TO-MAKE LOAF IS PERFECT for the holidays. Unusual and festive, it's just different enough to stand out from ordinary loaf cakes, but hearty and wholesome enough to be comforting.

MAKES
ONE 9 x 5-INCH / 23 x 13-CENTIMETER LOAF

1½ cups / 180 grams all-purpose flour

1 teaspoon baking powder

½ teaspoon salt

1 cup / 200 grams granulated sugar

½ teaspoon ground cinnamon

¼ teaspoon ground nutmeg

¼ teaspoon ground ginger

2.5 ounces / 75 grams dried cranberries

½ cup / 80 grams white chocolate chips

½ cup / 75 grams chopped pecans

Sift together the flour, baking powder, and salt and then spoon into a large, wide-mouth jar. (You can use a large resealable plastic bag, but you won't get the colorful layering effect.) Tap the jar gently on the countertop to settle the flour. Combine the sugar, cinnamon, nutmeg, and ginger in a bowl and pour over the flour in the jar. Continue the layers with the dried cranberries, then the white chocolate chips, and finally the pecans. Put the lid on the jar and decorate as desired. Store until ready to use, up to 6 months.

To make the bread: Preheat the oven to 350°F / 175°C and grease and flour a 9 x 5-inch / 23 x 13-centimeter loaf pan.

Pour all the dry ingredient from the jar into a large mixing bowl and stir well. Make a well in the center and crack in 2 eggs, beating lightly. Add ½ cup / 120 milliliters of sour cream and 4 tablespoons / 60 grams of melted butter. Stir in the dry ingredients just until incorporated; the batter will be lumpy. Spoon into the prepared loaf pan and bake for 45 to 50 minutes, or until a tester comes out clean. Let cool slightly in the pan before turning out onto a cooling rack to cool completely. In a small bowl or cup, whisk together ¼ cup / 25 grams of confectioners' sugar and 2 teaspoons of milk and drizzle the glaze over the top.

SIMNEL CAKE

WHEN I WAS SIXTEEN, I REMEMBER LOOKING in the window of The Rendezvous in Balleymena, County Antrim. I'd drool over row after row of neatly decorated Simnel Cakes. When I was eighteen, owners Sally and Davey Harper did me the kindness of hiring me as extra help at this popular patisserie and coffee shop. They started me chopping veg for soups, and doing easy tasks such as whipping cream and spreading jam between cake layers. Weekends and evenings leading up to the end of Lent, I'd take the bus in to help fill the mad rush of orders from local families. To this day, I can make as pretty a Simnel Cake as you can imagine, and I owe it to their patient training.

MAKES
1 LARGE CAKE

About 48 ounces / 1.25 kilograms marzipan (see page 309)

¾ cup / 180 grams unsalted butter at room temperature,
plus more for buttering pan

2 cups / 250 grams all-purpose flour

Pinch of salt

1 teaspoon ground nutmeg

1 teaspoon ground cinnamon

9 ounces / 250 grams dried currants

9 ounces / 250 grams sultanas

4 ounces / 110 grams mixed peel

1⅔ cups / 170 grams granulated sugar

3 large eggs

1 large egg yolk

⅔ cup / 180 milliliters milk

Prepare the marzipan (see page 309) and roll it out into 2 sheets, each slightly bigger than a 9-inch / 23-centimeter round cake pan. Trim the sheets and use the trimmings to roll 11 small balls (about 1 inch / 2.5 centimeters in diameter) from the remaining paste (these symbolize Jesus's apostles, minus Judas). Refrigerate the sheets and balls.

Preheat the oven to 350°F / 175°C. Butter a 9-inch / 23-centimeter round cake pan and line the bottom with parchment paper. As the baking period is long (1 to 1½ hours), prevent the cake from drying out by wrapping a double thickness of brown paper around the pan and securing it with twine, forming a tube (see The McMeel Family Irish Christmas Cake, page 305).

In a large mixing bowl, sift together the flour, salt, nutmeg, and cinnamon, then gently stir in the currants, sultanas, and peel, using a fork. In a separate large mixing bowl, using an electric mixer on high speed, cream together the butter and sugar until the mixture is light and fluffy and pale yellow in color, about 5 minutes.

Beat in the eggs, one at a time, until the mixture is fluffy. Stir in the flour mixture, a little at a time. If the mixture is too thick and sticky, thin it out with a drop of milk. Pour half of the mixture into the prepared pan and cover it with one sheet of almond paste. Cover that with the remaining cake batter. Smack the cake pan firmly on the countertop, to settle the batter. Bake on the middle rack of the oven for 1 to 1½ hours, or until a metal skewer inserted in the middle of the cake comes out clean. Remove the cake from the oven, and while the cake is still hot, cover it with a piece of parchment, then place a heavy pan on top to level the surface. After about half an hour, turn out the cake onto a cooling rack, peel off the parchment, and cool completely.

Cover the top of the cake with the second round of almond paste. Place the 11 balls of paste evenly around the top of the cake. Beat the egg yolk and brush it onto the top of the cake. Very lightly brown the cake under the broiler until the almond paste turns light golden brown, before transferring the cake to a countertop and leaving it to cool.

HOW TO SET A CHRISTMAS CAKE
OR PUDDING ALIGHT

Ferrying a flaming dessert to an eager table of merrymakers takes a bit of care, but the result is well worth it: You can expect cheers and gasps, especially when blazed as an antidote to the long, dark evenings of winter. This technique is commonly used for a traditional Christmas pudding, but feel free to light up any sturdy, heavy dessert—such as pound cake or fruitcake—that would benefit from absorbing some warming spirits.

Once your dessert is plated on a heatproof platter with no paper decorations on it, warm a small cup of brandy, whiskey, or other spirit in a small saucepan over direct heat (make sure the handle is heatproof, and that you're holding it with a pot holder), and, as soon as the liquid is hot, ask someone to set light to it. Holding the dessert in your weaker hand, and the flaming saucepan in your stronger hand, put the bottom of the saucepan on top of the pudding or dessert and rest it there. Do not pour it out yet!

Walk carefully to the table, and, once you've the attention of all present (and guests' hair and clothing are well clear!), slowly pour the fiery spirits over the dessert, taking care to drizzle it down the sides, and watch it flame. Feel free to bask in the glow of your masterpiece for a moment or two. When the flames and hurrahs come to an end, serve the pudding with Honeyed Whiskey Butter (page 34), or a nice rum sauce.

THE MCMEEL FAMILY
IRISH CHRISTMAS CAKE

THERE ARE COUNTLESS PERSONAL RECIPES for Irish Christmas Cake, all with tiny variations on the theme. If you asked an Irishman to describe Christmas Cake, he'd paint a picture of what his gran and mum laid out: an extra handful of nuts here, dried cranberries substituted for sultanas there, frosted or naked. Here's the version that fills my head with visions of festive paper crowns, loud crackers, gaily wrapped presents, and family crammed in around the farm table.

Christmas cakes are always rich, spicy, toothsome cakes stuffed to bursting with nuts and fruit, which are traditionally baked at least eight weeks before the holiday and then "fed" brandy, whiskey, or other spirits as the Advent calendar windows are peeled back in preparation for the feast day.

The final pastry will often have both marzipan and white icing or royal icing. Or, you can refer to my instructions for setting your dessert ablaze (see page 304), then glazing it with sweet, fragrant butter sauce (see Honeyed Whiskey Butter, page 34).

A word to the wise: This one is not a "whiz it in a mixer, bake, and serve" cake, and it's even more labor intensive if you plan to frost it or wrap it in sheets of marzipan. It is a big project, but it's worth the trouble, and no Irish Christmas would feel festive without one, and the sighs of pleasure it evokes.

You can buy mixed spice in a bottle, but I think it's more fun to fashion your own. My mixed spice is made from nearly equal amounts of baking spices: ground allspice, ginger, cinnamon, cloves, and nutmeg. You need only use those that strike your fancy.

Some people (especially children) don't like candied peel. If it doesn't appeal, leaving it out won't ruin the recipe, nor will adding in any dried fruit that you prefer, such as dried cranberries or chopped dried apricots.

MAKES
16 TO 20 SERVINGS

12 ounces / 340 grams sultanas

8 ounces / 225 grams raisins

12 ounces / 340 grams dried currants

4 ounces / 115 grams glacé cherries, halved

2 ounces / 55 grams mixed candied peel, chopped

½ teaspoon mixed ground spice (see recipe headnote)

Ingredients continue

¾ teaspoon vanilla extract

Grated zest and juice of 1 orange

½ large tart apple, peeled, cored, and chopped finely

1 heaping cup / 140 grams slivered almonds, toasted

1 tablespoon honey

¼ cup / 60 grams Irish whiskey, plus more for basting

20 ounces (2½ sticks) / 300 grams unsalted butter, at room temperature,
plus more for buttering pan

1½ cups / 270 grams dark brown sugar, packed

5 large eggs

2½ cups / 300 grams all-purpose flour

¾ teaspoon salt

DAY ONE:

The day before you start your baking, combine the sultanas, raisins, currants, glacé cherries, candied peel, mixed spice, vanilla, orange zest and juice, apple, almonds, honey, and whiskey in a large bowl and mix lightly, then cover and allow the mixture to blend overnight.

DAY TWO:

The next day, just before you intend to bake, line the bottom and sides of a 9-inch / 23-centimeter round cake pan carefully with parchment paper (don't use waxed paper) coated with butter. Allow the paper tower up a little over the top of the pan, making the pan's walls just a little taller.

Next, lay down 3 layers of brown paper or grocery sacks, in the shape of a long rectangle about 3 times as long as your pan, as if you were going to wrap a present. Wrap this paper around the outside of the pan and tie it securely in place with kitchen twine, making the pan's walls about 3 times their height. The whole effect is like a paper tube into which you can look down to see the batter in the pan.

Now, cut another piece of parchment, about the size of the cake pan, fold it in half, then cut a square about the size of the pan. Using kitchen shears, cut a 1½-inch / 3-centimeter-wide cross in the middle of the paper. (When the paper is folded in half, it is easiest to cut out a T shape, which will look like a cross when it's unfolded.)

Recipe continues

Preheat the oven to 300°F / 150°C.

Using an electric mixer on high speed, cream together the butter and brown sugar for about 10 minutes, until smooth and dark yellow. Beat the eggs in a small bowl, then add them a bit at a time, beating thoroughly between each addition to prevent curdling.

In a separate bowl, sift the flour and salt together, then fold lightly into the wet mixture, using a spatula. Add the soaked fruit that was set aside and mix lightly.

A little at a time, scoop the mixture—which should be stiff and slightly sticky—into the lined cake pan, smoothing with a rubber spatula dipped in water as you work. Make sure the batter is higher at the edges of the pan than at the middle. Without pressing it into the batter, place the square of paper with the cross-shape cut in it loosely on top.

Bake the cake on the middle rack for 3½ hours. As with a pot of rice, it's tempting to sneak a peek to check on the progress, but don't: Resist the urge to open the oven door.

After the time elapses, remove the cake from the oven to test it by inserting a metal skewer or butter knife into the middle of the cake: if it emerges dry, the cake is done: if not, put it back in the oven for another 30 minutes. It can take up to 4 hours, or even more. Check the cake every 30 minutes or so, until the skewer or knife comes out clean. When the cake is done, set the whole pan on a cooling rack to cool overnight, covered loosely with a clean tea towel.

DAY THREE:

Remove the cake from the pan by gently passing a butter knife between the cake pan and the lining paper, then slowly and carefully lift out the cake, peeling off the paper. Turn the cake upside down and pierce it eight times with a large fork. Pour a teaspoon of whiskey into each hole and let the overflow soak into the cake in its own time. Repeat this feeding process every 10 days or so until Christmas Day, shooting to "feed" about 5 times. This cake keeps for a very long time (no surprise, with all that liquor!) if it is carefully wrapped. In between feedings, wrap the cake tightly in brown paper or grocery sacks, and tape it shut. Then wrap the paper-covered cake in foil and put the whole thing into an airtight tin or plastic cake keeper, if you have one. If not, the foil should do nicely, if tightly wrapped. Each time you feed the cake, rewrap the cake meticulously.

The day before serving (or if you plan to cover with marzipan and icing, one week before serving):

Some eat this cake as is, or with a simple sprinkle of confectioners' sugar. My family liked ours buttered or set alight and finished with Honeyed Whiskey Butter (page 34). Traditionally, it's finished with royal icing covering a layer of marzipan. If you choose to go this

Recipe continues

HOW TO MAKE MARZIPAN

This recipe yields a large batch of marzipan, but, for my money, it's better to have too much than to be caught short. Depending on how you roll out and drape this paste for covering a cake, you may find yourself with leftovers. No worries! I like to roll it into balls and roll them in cocoa powder to make a kind of truffle, or dip them in melted chocolate, then let them dry to make rich candies. Or you can use leftovers for decorations. Use food coloring to dye the paste, then sculpt it like molding clay to make charming and edible shapes or animals for your cake.

For this recipe, feel free to substitute almond meal cup for cup for the ground almonds, but the texture will be slightly less substantial. I prefer to grind my own but, for ease, the choice is yours.

MAKES ABOUT
48 OUNCES / 1.25 KILOGRAMS MARZIPAN

7 cups / 900 grams whole blanched almonds

8 cups / 1 kilogram confectioners' sugar

4 large egg whites

1 teaspoon vanilla extract

2 teaspoons freshly squeezed lemon juice

Working in batches, grind the almonds in a food processor for 3 to 5 minutes. After about a minute or so, the mixture will look crumbly. Grind until the crumbs become a fine powder. After this stage, continue to grind for another minute until it just begins to clump but before it turns into butter; watch it carefully.

Pour all of the ground almonds back into the bowl of the food processor, and add the confectioners' sugar and process until blended, about 1 minute. Add the egg whites, vanilla, and lemon juice and process until you have a smooth, stiff paste, pulsing as you go.

Turn out the dough onto a clean surface dusted with confectioners' sugar and knead until smooth. Roll the paste into a log and chill for 1 hour.

Using a rolling pin, roll the paste flat until you have a sheet of marzipan large enough to wrap your cake or, if you are using the marzipan as molding clay for decorations, take a small amount into your hand at a time, roll it into a ball, and sculpt from there.

To color the marzipan, make sure you're wearing rubber gloves, or you'll dye your hands. Pinch off the amount of almond paste you want to use as "clay," and massage in food coloring a scant drop at a time. Work slowly, and in small batches, adding more color as you go to achieve the desired shade.

route, start the marzipan at least a week before the big dinner, and the icing a day or two before, because they take some time and effort. Then, the decorations are up to your family! You can pipe icing onto the cake, writing a Christmas message or your family's surname; you can color the marzipan to make leaves, holly berries, and yule logs; or you can use family heirloom Santa, reindeer, or Holy Cross ornaments and push them gently into the icing.

ICING AND DECORATING A CHRISTMAS CAKE

For many Irish families, a snowy white Christmas cake, wrapped in marzipan, covered in royal icing, and decorated is the centerpiece of the entire festive gathering.

48 ounces / 1.25 kilograms marzipan (see page 309)

¼ cup / 80 grams apricot, raspberry, or strawberry jam

ROYAL ICING

3¼ cups / 325 grams confectioners' sugar, sifted

2 large egg whites

2 teaspoons freshly squeezed lemon juice

To get started, place your baked and "fed" cake on a cooling rack set over a rimmed baking sheet. As you ice the cake, the excess will roll down the sides of the cake and drip onto the sheet. This keeps your serving platter clean and clear, with the added benefit of capturing excess frosting for future use.

Roll out a layer of marzipan larger than the top and sides of your cake and set it aside.

The first layer will be a jam layer: Warm and brush it over the sides and top in a thin layer.

Lay the marzipan sheet over the cake, using your hands to smooth it on, starting at the center and working your way around and down the sides, gently pressing out any air bubbles. Using a butter knife, cut away the excess at the bottom of the cake. Cover the cake with a clean tea towel and dry it on the counter for 1 week. This layer helps preserve the cake: Wrapping it keeps it moist.

For the royal icing, use an electric mixer to beat the egg whites until they're stiff but not dry

Recipe continues

and they form glossy peaks, 5 to 7 minutes. Add the confectioners' sugar and lemon juice and beat for about 1 minute longer. To test, plunge a spoon to the bottom of the bowl and pull it straight upward and out. The icing should form a little peak that holds its shape for about 15 seconds, before "melting." If the icing is too stiff, add another egg white. If it is too runny, add more sugar. Use immediately, or store in an airtight container in the refrigerator for up to 3 days.

When you are ready to ice the cake, uncover the cake on the cooling rack. Spoon a generous dollop in the center of the cake (over the marzipan layer) and use a palette knife or offset spatula to smooth it, working from the center and down the sides in long, slow, clean strokes.

While the icing is still soft, decorate your cake as you like, using shapes that you color and form out of the leftover marzipan, silver dragées or sugar pearls, candied fruit, shelled nuts, or even inedible items such as well-washed pinecones, holiday ornaments, or ribbon.

Set the cake aside for at least 1 day, and for up to 3 days, to allow the icing to harden. Before serving, transfer it to an attractive serving platter. If not serving within 3 days, store the cake in a cake tin or plastic cake keeper to prevent it from drying out.

INDEX

Note: Page references in *italics* indicate recipe photographs.